AF361572

FINDING FRANCIS

FINDING FRANCIS

ONE FAMILY'S JOURNEY
FROM SLAVERY TO FREEDOM

ELIZABETH J. WEST

Published by the University of South Carolina Press
Columbia, South Carolina 29208

www.uscpress.com

Manufactured in the United States of America

31 30 29 28 27 26 25 24 23 22
10 9 8 7 6 5 4 3 2 1

Library of Congress Cataloging-in-Publication Data
can be found at http://catalog.loc.gov/.

ISBN 978-1-64336-357-8 (hardcover)
ISBN 978-1-64336-358-5 (paperback)
ISBN 978-1-64336-359-2 (ebook)

To the Descendants of Noah who knew we
needed the remembrances.

To my brother, Edgar Johnson, and my great
Uncle Bonnie, who recently passed.

Contents

Acknowledgments   ix

Introduction   1

CHAPTER 1
Francis in Georgia: Kinship and Family
Formation in the Black Antebellum South   23

CHAPTER 2
Neshoba to Noxubee: Pre-Civil War to Reconstruction   58

CHAPTER 3
Post-Reconstruction and a New Century: Anxious and
Audacious Times (1870s–1910)   85

CHAPTER 4
Hillman: A Man's Story Bookended by Women   119

Coda: Reflections on Methodology   136

Appendix   153
Notes   159
Bibliography   175
Index   185

Acknowledgments

The completion of what evolved into this narrative of a remarkable matriarch and her family was made possible through institutional and individual support, generosity, and encouragement almost too expansive to recall. But if I am to stay true to the lesson I learned in the process of writing this book, it is imperative to remember, and when that happens through the spirit of Ujima, the memory belongs to more than a single person. I start with deep gratitude to the institutions and the persons behind the scenes who helped my research along the way. At Georgia State University (GSU) this work was supported through the commitment of annual English department graduate research assistantships, a 2021 departmental summer research grant, and a spring 2022 College of Arts & Sciences semester research grant. It was through a collaboration with Brennan Collins, director of GSU's Project Mapping Lab, and Joshua Jackson, an incredibly committed and enthusiastic graduate research assistant, that mapping Francis's location in Harris County was successfully undertaken. This mapping journey consisted of several semesters with undergraduate researchers joining the project as a way to introduce them to and build their archival research skills and experience in the digital humanities. In particular I note that Courtney Flowers, Chance Kendrick, Abubuker Mohammad, Andrea Merritt (also a GSU Mellon HIP mentee), Lance Ridley, and John Washington were not only exceptional researchers but also reminders that the real challenge of teaching is to help students find pathways to tap into their innate creativity, curiosity, and intellectual power. I especially thank my Mellon HIP mentee and research assistant, Safiya Miller, whose keen gift at sleuthing brought us to some key discoveries along the way, and to graduate research assistant, Mike Saye, for his work on the South Carolina side of the search.

Beyond the support of my home institution, I am grateful to the Johannes Gütenberg University Obama Institute for a summer research fellowship in 2019. This award allowed me the focused time to draft what became sections in chapters 1 and 2 of the final book version. In 2018 through an invitation from Professor Kameelah Martin to participate in the College of Charleston's Ancestries of Enslavement series, I was afforded not only the opportunity to present and entertain feedback on aspects of my work but also to explore their library's South Carolina archives. The responsiveness, patience, and enthusiastic help of specialists at the Georgia Archives, Mississippi Department of Archives and History, Noxubee County Courthouse, Macon (MS) Library, and special collections division of the College of Charleston Library were of great help, often at times when I thought I was staring down a dead end. Through the outreach of the Asylum Hill Project, under the leadership of Dr. Ralph Didlake and Lida Gibson, I discovered the history of the Mississippi Insane Asylum and its connection to the story of Francis Sistrunk's last surviving son in 1920.

I owe Lida Gibson huge thanks for pointing me to the 1895 publication on Hillman's ownership of the land that marked the earlier nineteenth-century signing of the Dancing Rabbit Creek Treaty between the US government and the Choctaw Indians. Dr. Patricia Colomo worked with me in search of a fuller account of Heinrich Sistrunk's captivity in Cuba. Colomo's search in the Spanish archives brought to greater clarity the tenuous circumstances of Sistrunk's two years in Cuba and how that might have influenced the new world vision that he would establish for himself and his antebellum descendants. Ms. Jeanette Parks took time out on a Saturday morning in early spring 2022 to meet me and share her knowledge of Brushfork Missionary Baptist Church and to have the church's old records pulled for my review. The assistance of Mr. James Bridges of Noxubee County was varied and priceless. I came to think of him as the griot who showed me Noxubee. He was my guide to numerous sites during my visits and researching the court records. During the period when the pandemic severely limited travel, he was especially helpful in locating and sending records.

I am grateful for colleagues and friends who read chapter drafts and listened to ideas that were key to the rewriting, revising, and editing process, as reading is the bread and butter of our profession. Drs. Tanya Washington, Tiffany King, and Ian Afflerbach read versions of different chapters and provided much-needed input during key moments in the writing process.

I greatly appreciate the contributions of resources and talent from family and friends. Candace West was an indispensable research companion and photographer during the trips to Noxubee. Arrangement and zoom depiction of the Noxubee County map was set by Jose Navarro. James Cistrunk and Kenneth Brown Sr. generously shared photographs of Cistrunks that are among images included in the book. Talecia Cistrunk created a concept collage that served as the foundation for presentation of the female images on the book cover.

Numerous descendants of Noah Cistrunk have journeyed with me along the way in researching and writing this story. Until his death in March 2022, Bunnie Cistrunk, the last living child of Noah Cistrunk, not only shared the oral accounts of family that he remembered but also consented to take DNA tests that helped confirm questions of paternal lineage to Francis Sistrunk's son, Shadrick. Cistrunk descendants Johnnie Pearl Smiley, Martha Brown, Helen C. Harrington, and Noah Cistrunk have shared family stories and accounts that not only expanded my knowledge of the Cistrunk family but also served on some occasions as correctives to information that was not wholly accurate.

Writing this story has been a journey itself, and I have been fortunate to have had the long list of collaborations and resources that made it possible. Along the way I have been contacted by a few white Sistrunk descendants. Several of these communications provided fruitful bits of information and leads to resources. I was pleased to have had these conversations. They reminded me that many among us are working to more fully piece together history and approach it in a way that we can face the good and not so good and arm ourselves with new histories that might help us shape a better tomorrow.

INTRODUCTION

Through my mother's paternal lineage, I am sixth generation in the line of descent from Francis Sistrunk, matriarch of the post–Civil War Cistrunks of Noxubee County, Mississippi.[1] I did not begin this work in search of Francis. I couldn't have: she did not exist in my knowledge bank of familial history. I had never heard her name invoked in any oral or written family accounts before I began what was my initial goal to simply compile stories of Noah Cistrunk, my family's ancestral patriarch. Born in 1882, Noah's memory lives through the descendants who gather biennially for the Noah Cistrunk reunion to honor his legacy and their connection to his line of descent. He was my mother's paternal grandfather; however, it seems that my mother and most of her nine siblings had little to no firsthand memory of Noah. While they did not grow up knowing their grandfather, as adults they would embrace the larger family's homage to Noah as the early patriarch. In turn I grew up accepting and reciting the designation of Noah as the earliest known ancestor of our Cistrunk genealogical line. This changed, however, a few years before the death of my aunt Dr. Annie J. Cistrunk (1929–2005). Among her many skills Annie was a linguist, and this informed her inclination to order and preserve information, especially in written form. During the 1990s she gathered the oral history of the Carl Cistrunk-Anna Denson lineage, committed it to a typewritten genealogical sketch, and distributed copies to family members. The document revealed that while the family's prevailing narration of descent started with Noah, family knowledge went back at least one generation before him. Annie's outline identified Noah's parents as Shadrick and Susan Cistrunk. Though not specified in her sketch, it struck me that given Noah's year of birth, his parents had likely been enslaved. I was intrigued and curious, but another ten years passed before I returned to my aunt's sketch and in earnest set out in search of these nineteenth-century forebearers. I was excited at the possibility that I might learn more about them than just their names.

I began my search with a review of census records, finding them enumerated as a family in the 1880 Census. The record showed Shadrick, Susan, and their family, and, to my surprise, it also listed Shadrick's mother, Francis. On the record in the household of her son Shadrick, Francis replaced both Noah and Shadrick as the oldest named ancestral figure in my family's Cistrunk lineage. This name, which I had not heard previously uttered among family members, became quickly emblazoned into my mind. I had to know more about her, this matriarch who had held her family together in pre- and post-emancipation Mississippi. At this early stage I was simply looking for information on these ancestral figures, hoping that this would bring me to a deeper and clearer understanding of my family and its history. As my rumblings through the archives and my family's own historical records intensified, I began to feel as if I had been transported to the nineteenth-century world of Francis and her children. The more I learned, the deeper and richer my family's history became. Their story also took me back to the history of Mississippi, the state of my birth, and grounded me more firmly on my place and identity as southern and Black.

As I unlocked the story of Francis and family and their daring effort to claim their place in the land where they had been enslaved, I gained insight into some of the curiosities and mysteries of my family that I had carried since childhood. Most perplexing to me as a child was the unshakeable dignity that was so deeply rooted in my mother and her siblings. With their move in the 1940s from their rural birthplace in Jasper County, MS, they had themselves barely escaped the snares of the Mississippi sharecropping system. In my childhood mind they seemed to navigate the world with an assuredness and optimism that didn't quite connect to such humble beginnings. They were demanding, their expectations were high, and they were deaf to excuses. There was pressure. I often felt that they were out to prove something, to right something, to rectify something, and their children were charged to carry out the mission. In striking contrast, I found them more openly compassionate to those outside their immediate households. They were my models, sheroes, and heroes, though they were not the icons in the history books I encountered in the classroom. Despite the repeated requirements to engage these figures under the premise of educational readings, the people in these books were not real or heroic to me. Their striking contrasts to the principles of community, generosity, and love that anchored my family's teachings relegated them in my mind as part of a project called democracy that had no immediate imprint in my experience of America or the South. I had clear sheroes and heroes, and they were the extraordinary everyday people in my own world. From my mother and aunts who were teachers, church leaders, seamstresses, community organizers, gardeners, fisherwomen, and caretakers, to my father and uncles whose skills ranged from hunting, carpentry, electrical wiring and repairs, carpet laying, plumbing, and appliance and auto repairs, I grew up with the impression that I lived in a self-sufficient family and community. I saw the adults in these spaces working collectively in the interest of the whole. The examples of parenting and socialization exemplified by my family elders came to mind in my discoveries of the emancipated Cistrunks of Noxubee County and their first-generation freeborn Black children.

The sketchy narrative of my grandfather Carl Cistrunk was a mystery that was made clearer for me as well through the search for Francis. While my mother and most of her nine siblings were customarily silent about their father, occasionally I found that some would share fond memories of him. In general, though, there was a silence that was born out of his departure from the family. Much of what I learned of him was through the stories that my aunts would share here and there. He and my grandmother, Anna Cistrunk had ten children, and after more than twenty years of marriage, he left some time in the early 1940s before all the children were adults. I'm not sure that I saw my grandfather before my first year in college when I took an excursion from Jackson to Pascagoula to meet him. I had gotten his address from one of my aunts, and under the pretense of a spring break trip with friends, I went in search of him. He was not at home that early afternoon when I arrived, but a neighbor directed me to his favorite lodge hangout that was in walking distance. I loved his neighborhood. It was a Black working-class community filled with small wooden houses that were probably built around the 1940s and 1950s. Most of the houses did not appear to have more than two bedrooms, but they all had front porches. Front porches in the Black communities of my childhood were landing pads where you were welcomed to stop, come sit, and enjoy the company of others while you take life in. There were not many people out because it was a workday, but those who were nodded their heads and greeted me in that Black southern way that lets you know you are good in that place.

I had no memory of how my grandfather looked, but when I walked in and saw a dark-skinned man at the bar having a drink, I approached and asked if he was Carl Cistrunk. After he confirmed that he was, I told him I was his granddaughter, child of his daughter Wessie. I was 17 years old at the time, but I accepted his offer for a drink. We sat at the bar and talked, and it was as if we had talked all our lives. I don't recall the details, only that I liked him and that though I did not understand why, I could forgive him for leaving my grandmother and their children. My grandmother had been deceased more than a decade when I visited my grandfather. I was told by my aunts that though he had left the family, my grandmother never allowed them to speak ill of him. Perhaps that was the memory that drove me to find him. Something in the story seemed complicated beyond my comprehension, but I wanted to know and to understand. I left there late that afternoon, headed for nearby Biloxi and the gulf beach with my friends, with no more clarity on the story of my grandfather and grandmother than when I found him sitting at the bar hours earlier. But my head and my heart felt better about him. Within two years of our meeting, my grandfather would become gravely ill and though he lived several years after with both legs amputated to save his life, I would never learn from him what I had wanted to hear. My conversations with him never made clear to me how a good, decent man could leave a wife and children, especially a woman like my grandmother, who I remembered as loving, kind, and witty.

I had not anticipated at the start of my search for either Noah or his descendants, that the journey would lead me to some clarity on my grandfather. It is particularly in the search for details of the Noxubee County Cistrunks in the first two decades of the twentieth century, decades after my grandfather's death in 1979, that I gained an understanding of the agony he both suffered and imposed on his family. From accounts that I had heard of his strengths and attributes, Carl was a proud, smart, hardworking man. In both official records and oral family accounts, it is clear that he had been mentored and groomed by men of that same ilk. They wanted things for their families; they wanted to pave a path of hope for their children and their community. But the story of my grandfather reminded me that the pride factor can operate to both good and ill fortunes. By 1920, 20-year-old Carl had witnessed his father, Noah, his grandfather Shadrick, and granduncle Hillman lose their land and their livelihood. Carl left Noxubee County by 1920, and with that departure he left behind his childhood memories of Black industry and economic autonomy that had been exemplified through the men in his family. It was a departure from a world of promise that he would not experience again in that form. Today, I understand the loss he must have felt at such a young age and how that feeling of loss intensified as the years and decades passed. It would become clear to him that he could not deliver himself and his family out of the nightmarish cycle of sharecropping. If he could not shake the great loss of his young manhood, the disappointment could only swell and fester as time passed.

It is ironic that behind this line of patriarchs—Carl, Noah, and Shadrick—was a woman and matriarch, Francis, whose central place in our family's history was for the most part unspoken, unknown, and at the precipice of being forgotten. It felt particularly alarming when I realized that Cistrunk elders who were familiar with her name and place in the family's genealogy were not passing on her name. Information surfaced only after I began asking that they share memories of what they had been told. Finding Francis reminded me of the necessity to record, research, and tell the stories of early Black women's contributions to Black families and histories, especially in a society where outside their communities, Black women and mothers are often derided and dismissed. The everyday life of Francis Sistrunk illustrates the problem with simplistic and vilifying references to the "single Black mother" as the source of familial and social challenges in Black communities. What *Finding Francis* sheds light on is the legacy of extraordinary resilience and determination that everyday Black women and mothers planted into their families and communities. *Francis* further illustrates how Black people's uncompensated labor and bodies built the wealth of the American South and the ethos of prosperity for poor as well as wealthy whites. The story of Francis and her children that unfolds in the chapters to follow brings the interiority of their lives to the forefront, giving voice to their humanity in a depth that Black southerners are rarely granted in histories of the nation that continue to dominate American classroom and public discourses.

African American voices have been silenced or disregarded in official historical accounts of this country from its inception, and this practice is more evident in the dearth of scholarship focusing on the lives of everyday Black people, particularly those in the early American South. A biohistoriography by design, *Francis* is at its core a narrative project inspired by the need to tell these stories. While we are early in building a body of narratives that tell the everyday stories of Black people through their lens, there are recent narrative histories that provide compelling blueprints for this work. In texts such as Saidiya Hartman's *Wayward Lives* (2019), Tiya Miles's *All That She Carried* (2021), Lawrence Jackson's *My Father's Name* (2012), and Isabel Wilkerson's *The Warmth of Other Suns* (2010), we see how this kind of narrative historical scholarship breaks us out of the opaque and muffled representations of Black life that have been scripted for centuries. Wilkerson's text is probably most noted for its exhaustive coverage of the Great Migration, the decades of the Black exodus out of the American South, beginning around World War I. In her focus on three main characters, Wilkerson personalizes what is too often represented in numbers rather than human experiences. Jackson's work originates from a more personal search for his grandfather's Virginia home. The archival trail takes Jackson back into the nineteenth century as he traces the arc from his ancestors' Civil War location and experiences to his twenty-first century quest to fill in the empty spaces of his family's story. Wilkerson and Jackson demonstrate the importance of returning to conventional archives to reread for the wealth of information they can offer, even when these sources ignore the presence and relevance of Black people. It is in the works of Miles and Hartman, however, that I found a greater resonance with my hopes for *Francis*. In *All That She Carried* and *Wayward Lives,* the authors' historiographical accounts engage conventional archives, but where those sources lead to dead ends, Miles and Hartman draw connections to Black cultural resources/artifacts and epistemologies to speculate and narrate more cohesive and comprehensive stories. In Miles's work, the seed sack that the enslaved mother, Rose, gives to her young daughter, Ashley, exemplifies "a persistent Black matriline, a continuation of radical vision that should have been impossible, given the logic and enforcement of American enslavement."[2] The symbolic nature of the sack calls to mind a commonplace, yet intangible, artifact Francis bestowed on her descendants. In the deliberate naming of her children (born in the mid-1800s), Francis created a marker to connect them to their lineages and histories. This artifact would prove central to the story of Francis and her children that I have been able to reconstruct.

It was in *Wayward Lives* that I found an especially resonant model for the counternarrative that I wanted to tell. While I do not follow Hartman's bold fusion of narrator voice with narrative subjects, I do, however, acknowledge, like Hartman, that the story I narrate is told from within the circle.[3] I am perhaps a bit deeper in the circle than Hartman in *Wayward Lives,* for my connection to *Francis* is a familial one. Without question or reservation, this inside perspective, or internal archival proximity, informs the narrative that unfolds, at times perhaps blending third- and first-person perspectives into a singular narrative voice. The result, however, is the radical or counternarration that undergirds this telling of a story of the American South through the voice of a Black woman of the South.

Ironically, Francis Sistrunk was not among the names and generations recorded in Annie Cistrunk's sketch. The maternal line, the Densons, pointed to a formerly enslaved matriarch, "Grandma Louise," who my mother and most of her siblings had known during their childhood. She was their great-grandmother and had lived to give a firsthand account of slavery to three generations of descendants. In contrast to Francis, the added element to Louise's story was a photograph of Louise in my aunt's possession since the time of my grandmother's death. This photograph and the story of Grandma Louise that I had heard since childhood compelled me to begin a search to fill out a fuller narrative of her life and the family history. Although I had direct oral accounts of Louise, I had sparse information on my mother's paternal side because until I attended the Cistrunk reunion in 2012, I had very little contact with that side of my family. After that reunion I began to look more closely at the Cistrunk lineage, and a few years later after reaching an impasse in the Denson line, I decided to pause that search and see how fortune would play out on the paternal side. This led me back to my aunt's one-page genealogical sketch that listed Shadrick and Susan as the earliest Cistrunk ancestors. She listed no birth or death dates for them or for Noah, and she did not list the parents of either Shadrick or Susan. Her record of the Cistrunks was scant but would nevertheless lead me to Francis Sistrunk and the broader and deeper story of the South that her life and legacy bring to light.

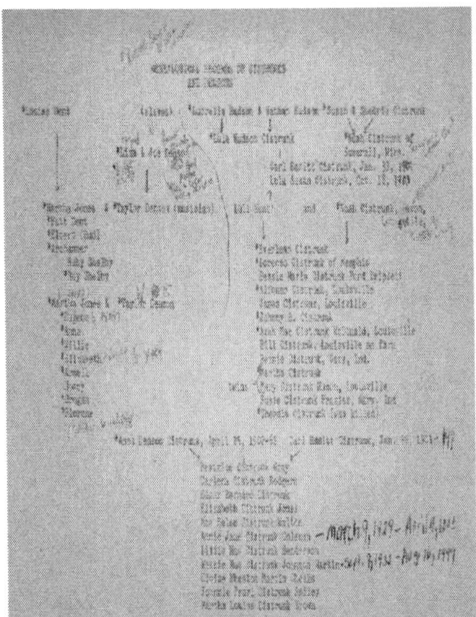

Annie J. Cistrunk
Genealogical Chart, 1990s

On the sketch drawn up by Annie Cistrunk, the paternal line was traced back to Shadrick (b. ca. 1847) and Susan Cistrunk (b. ca. 1852), the parents of Noah Cistrunk (1882–1937). Annie never met Shadrick, Susan, or Noah, but through oral history she knew them as the parent and grandparents of her father, Carl Cistrunk (1901–1979). Annie Cistrunk's accounts of her family's Cistrunk lineage came in large part from Noah's sister, Sophie (Francis) Cistrunk Marsh (1882–1967),[4] who though she had no children felt compelled later in life to pass on the names of her parents to her brother's descendants. Sophie conveyed to Annie what she knew, and the names Susan and Shadrick were added in the family record that Annie set to writing. Transcription of the oral account marks the first stage of sampling in what began as my attempt to trace the history of Carl Cistrunk's line of descent. Noah is the known familial entity among his twentieth-century children and their descendants who since his death in 1937 have maintained formal and informal family reunions to remember and honor their patriarch Noah and his second wife, Luella (1883–1989). Until I assumed the task that Annie Cistrunk had begun, family remembrances were rooted in Noah, Luella, and their lives in Louisville (Winston County), MS. While I had heard oral stories of ancestors that had entered Mississippi from Virginia, little else of family history beyond Mississippi was conveyed in the circle of stories and people that I encountered. Through government records such as census reports, birth and death certificates, and military draft records I found that the history of the

Sophie (Francis) Cistrunk Marsh (1882–1967); granddaughter of Francis Sistrunk, image ca. 1950s

Noah Cistrunk lineage in Mississippi was not a long one, that in fact, Noah and his sister Lula represented the first generation of native-born Mississippi Cistrunks from their family line.

In 2012 when I began what was the initial task of merely constructing a genealogical timeline and summary of my family's Cistrunk–Denson line of descent, I had never heard of an ancestor named Francis. At that time, my sense of my family's history was limited to their origins in Louisville, MS, the place I assumed was my grandfather's place of birth and that of his father. The oral account of the family's Cistrunk lineage that I regularly heard from my mother and her sisters usually started with their father, Carl Cistrunk, and his departure as a young man from the larger household of his father, stepmother, and a rapid addition of siblings. Perhaps the limited account of the family's lineage was due to Carl's early separation from his family. Carl's mother, Lula, died when he was a toddler and his sister, Lula, an infant. A widower with two young children, their father, Noah, would remarry by 1903, and he and his new wife, Luella, would begin a marriage of thirty-three years and the birth of fourteen children.

Carl is reported to have left the household during his teen years, and his departure may not have been under the most agreeable of circumstances. I

Cistrunk reunion,
Louisville, MS, 1980

grew up hearing the story from my mother and her sister Elizabeth that Carl had told them he had not been happy in the household of his father and stepmother. Whether or not his grievances were reminiscent of the common disagreements between teenagers and parents, Carl separated from his family and eventually moved from Winston County to nearby Jasper County, where he began a new life. By 1920 Carl and Anna Denson married and began to establish their family in Montrose, MS. He shared some accounts of his childhood with some of his children; however, in general he did not impart to them the story of his parents or foreparents. It was only after Carl and Anna separated that Carl's siblings in Louisville located and established contact with Anna and Carl's ten children. Until his death in March 2022, Carl's brother, Bunnie Cistrunk, regularly shared the story of their sister, Arah Cistrunk McDonald, who sometime in the early 1940s spearheaded the reunion of Carl's family with their Cistrunk relatives in Louisville. According to Bunnie, Arah was concerned about the dispersion of some of her siblings and their families. Noah Cistrunk had fathered 14 children who had lived into adulthood in the early 1940s, but some, like Carl, had taken off for other places. Several would leave the state altogether, as Bunnie eventually did. Arah feared that the family would get splintered and as time passed would break off communication totally. She made it her mission to reconnect with the households that had gone silent. Carl's was one of those. Arah made contact with Carl's first wife Anna and arranged the trip for the Louisville relatives to travel to Jasper County, MS, to reestablish family bonds with Carl's family. This reconnection

Cistrunk reunion, Atlanta, GA, 2012

of family would open up to Carl's children a more expanded history of their Cistrunk lineage. The kinship connection has been maintained for more than eighty years, most notably through the biennial Noah Cistrunk family reunions where many Cistrunk descendants from Carl's line and those of his Louisville siblings gather to remember and celebrate family.

Through recollections and stories passed down from Carl Cistrunk's surrogate/stepmother Luella Hunt Cistrunk Lynch, and his Aunt Sophie (Francis) Cistrunk Marsh, Cistrunk descendants heard these stories and in their own households as well as gatherings such as family reunions, they continued to pass on oral accounts of the family. It appears that in the 1990s when Annie Cistrunk drafted her family chart, she was by then depending on oral stories that she had heard and remembered over the years from a number of Cistrunk family members from several generations. Her grandmother Luella and great aunt Sophie would have been her oldest living sources, and again, both had kept the story of Francis in the family's written and oral accounts. She would also likely have heard of Francis and her children from her own father, Carl, who had been raised in the kinship circle of Francis's four adult children. Annie noted Francis's son Shadrick and his wife Susan as the earliest known Cistrunks, but none of her records listed Francis or offered an account of the family's pre-Mississippi history.

The first generations of freeborn Cistrunks recorded key family milestones like many of this era. It was common practice to maintain genealogy and lineage records in family Bibles, where often written documents related to family events, business affairs, and history were also stored. Unfortunately, those who recognized that written documents offered a second means to preserve family history could not control misfortunes such as home fires or the discarding of documents after deaths in the family. In such cases, which were not uncommon before the modern era of fire prevention and greater awareness of archival preservation, written family records dating from post emancipation into the early twentieth century were lost. This seems to be the case for the story of Francis Sistrunk and her children. According to descendant Helen Cistrunk Harrington (Noah and Luella's granddaughter) it was in Luella Cistrunk's Bible that the name Francis Sistrunk and that of her children were recorded. With the destruction of the Bible in a home fire, the survival of Francis's story and that of her children has rested in the oral accounts passed along by descendants.

The Noah Cistrunk Family National Organization (NCFNO) is anchored in the lineage of Noah (b. 1882), his first wife, Lula Hudson (b. 1884), and second wife, Luella Hunt (b. 1883). Informally, the organization dates back to the 1940s when Noah's children and their families would gather annually in Louisville, Mississippi to reaffirm their family ties, and to honor God and ancestors. The Cistrunks were maintaining a practice that had become culturally institutionalized in the Black South as decades of the Great Migration fueled migrations from the rural South. Families remained committed to this pilgrimage, even as populations left and spread out across the country. In the case of Noah Cistrunk's family line, this ritual and lineage group was formalized in writing sometime in the late 1990s or early 2000s. By 2000 Annie Cistrunk had begun to expand her original genealogical sketch into more detailed relationship charts of descendancies from the lineages of Noah Cistrunk and his son Carl. She also began to compile and distribute family directories for Cistrunk descendants. In 2012 the organization's by-laws were amended to form a national committee to create a liaison among regional and state groups. Until his death in March 2022 at age 94, Bunnie Cistrunk, Noah Cistrunk's last surviving son, was recognized as the lifetime national chairman of the organization. During the biennial reunion of NCFNO, when the family engages in the ceremonial calling of ancestral names and recently deceased family members, those memorialized and remembered date from Noah and his line of descendants. A representative from each line of descent lights a candle for and calls the name of their first-generation ancestor born from the union of either Noah and Lula or Noah and Luella. This ritual is then followed by a spontaneous

Cistrunk reunion, Louisville, MS, 2014

Cistrunk reunion, Louisville, MS, 2014

calling of ancestral names. The NCFNO has no established ritual that acknowledges Noah's foreparents, named or unnamed. Therefore, Noah's father, Shadrick, and Shadrick's mother, Francis, are not called and are not central to the family's story as it is passed down through the organization. It is not clear why preservation of the stories of Francis and her children waned among Noah Cistrunk's descendants, but from the latter decades of the twentieth century to today, these first-generation freed Cistrunks were at risk of obscurity in the family's collective memory. Though the organization has no formal platform for remembering and memorializing these ancestors, they have not been altogether forgotten or unremembered. It appears that as often in life, the key is that you have to know what and whom to ask. This became apparent to me as I began to search for information on Shadrick Cistrunk. After encountering this name for the first time through Annie Cistrunk's family sketch, I rather quickly found him in census records.[5] More astounding than the discovery of Shadrick in conventional records, where African Americans are generally considered absent or undiscoverable, was what I initially surmised as my "discovery" of Francis. Because I had not heard older family members speak of Shadrick or Francis, I concluded that no one had maintained their story in Cistrunk history. However, as I eventually circled back and spoke individually with older family members I learned that the story of Francis had in fact survived in the memories of at least two living descendants. Helen Cistrunk Harrington and her sibling Noah Cistrunk (grandchildren of Noah) recalled that throughout their grandmother Luella's life, she regularly shared the story of Francis and her children. Helen grew up spending considerable time with her grandmother Luella, listening intensely to the stories she told of deceased family members. Luella shared stories of her husband, Noah Cistrunk, and his ancestors, and she welcomed viewings of the family Bible in which she had recorded Noah's family line, going back to his grandmother Francis. Helen emphasized also the similar commitment of Noah's sister, Sophie, who passed along accounts of the family's history that included the names of her parents, Shadrick and Susan, and Shadrick's mother, Francis. Luella lived until 1989 and Sophie until 1967, and both were born into the first post–emancipation freeborn generation of African Americans in Noxubee County. Their parents had been enslaved and they came to know the stories of enslavement through firsthand accounts. While they passed these stories on directly to generations that followed, at the dawn of the twenty-first century few family members were alive who remembered these stories.

Noah's grandchildren, Noah and Helen, are unable to tie the names to specific stories, yet they know the names Francis and Shadrick, and they emphasize that Luella Cistrunk had been their source. It is worth noting that the family matriarchs were the central source for the surviving memories of these first-generation freed Cistrunks. Noah Cistrunk's wife Luella and his sister, Sophie, represent the legacy of Black women who kept family histories—especially those of the women—alive by speaking the names of those in the past. In particular for Noah Cistrunk's descendants, the name Francis survives because her female descendants spoke her name and passed it on. It is further noteworthy that while Luella was a Cistrunk by marriage, she nonetheless passed along the stories of both her own family line, the Hunts of Noxubee County, and that of her husband's, the Cistrunks. Similarly, while Sophie had no children that lived into adulthood, she was determined to keep alive the story of her foreparents, particularly that of her grandmother, Francis. Luella and Sophie exemplify the nature of kinship in African American culture—a relationship network that forms familial bonds beyond the tight circle of parents and children and strictly biological lineage. Core family relations cover generations—direct and indirect, biological, and surrogate. And these bonds are respected and honored as full family—not "extended" as they tend to be classified out of the white-originating ethos of the nuclear family. When Luella Hunt married Noah, she assumed the role of archivist for Noah's ancestral narrative as well as that of the Hunts, her own biological line. Although Carl was not her biological child, his children and their children were raised to know her as grandmother and great-grandmother. Similarly, although Sophie was childless for most of her adult life, she was the family griot and central matriarchal figure in the Cistrunk line of her brother, Noah. During the years she lived in the household of her in-law grandniece, Anna Cistrunk, Sophie shared the names and stories of her parents and her father's mother, Francis.

As exemplified in the account of how the Cistrunk family history survived, to more fully explore narratives of extraordinary everyday Black life, we must acknowledge the reality of a Black family ethos and experience that operates outside western myths of the nuclear family. *Francis* reveals the complex history of Black family formations and structures that were shaped by the practices and paradigms of American slaving. Her story reveals how Black people had to navigate around white-constructed paradigms that attempted to deny Black humanity while also creating and maintaining legacies to sustain themselves and future generations. The story of Francis's enslavement is linked to an antebellum enslaver of Swiss German lineage whose immigrant patriarch, Heinrich Süsstrunk, arrived in Charleston, SC, in 1746. Though a captive himself before being rescued and delivered to Charleston's port, Heinrich would lay the foundation for future generations of Sistrunk enslavers. In less than two decades on South Carolina soil Heinrich began to fashion himself out of the mold of prosperity outlined by the British Colony that would claim his allegiance. By the time of his death in 1762 he had settled into the anglicized version of his name, Henry Sistrunk, claimed land bounties for which he was eligible, and though not operating a plantation was in legal possession of enslaved people. There is glaring irony of Heinrich's initiation into the new world in 1743 as a captive in Cuba and his later position as enslaver of a young girl and infant by the time of his death. This would prove the origin of generations of Sistrunk enslavers in the US South that persisted until the fall of the Confederacy. The story of the post–Civil War Black Noxubee Cistrunks unveils the legacy that shaped the ethos of enslavement that would be passed down from Heinrich to his great grandson, Jacob Sistrunk Jr.

As evident in the three genealogical works published on the descendants of Heinrich Süsstrunk, the eighteenth-century immigrant forefather of white Sistrunk lines that spread across the antebellum South, Blacks were present and as well documented in the records on Heinrich and his antebellum descendants.[6] These genealogical records have not been examined with the intention of acknowledging the enslaved, however. Instead, they are woven into the seamless thread of white illusions of the present Black body and the absent Black human. Without the infusion of Francis's voice or the voices of her immediate descendants, reliance on conventional records, documents, and scholarly histories silences her story and subjects it to a white hegemonic interpretation that persists in scholarly and public discourses on the Black family. This is not to suggest that we must discard or ignore conventional sources but rather that we must examine them through methodologies and interpretations that unveil the lives of the enslaved and their descendants as more than property or controlled entities.

If the 1840 Census paints an accurate picture, Francis was at that time the lone slave of Jacob II. She may have come into his possession through an auction block or similar interstate sale. Even if this were the case, given the proximity of Jacob II's land to that of his father and the likelihood that Jacob I (Sr.) loaned or shared his enslaved laborers with his son, Francis was probably part of the larger community of those enslaved on Jacob I's plantation. Jacob II held Francis and her children from the 1830s to 1850s in Georgia and then in Mississippi until the end of the Civil War. During and after enslavement, Francis remained unmarried. By western conventions, she is a social outlier— an unmarried mother assuming the role of household head. American society has been shaped out of the concept that family constitutes a unit originating in marriage, consisting of father, mother, and children, with the father as head and women and children subject to his rule. For Blacks in America, the concept and structure of family did not originate in or develop from this simplistic and limiting vision. While America's 1960s feminist movement is often lauded as the twentieth-century movement that pushed the needle toward gender equality, Black women in this century had already been challenging and rejecting white imposed gender and familial norms. In her 1949 article entitled "An End to the Neglect of the Problems of the Negro Woman!" Claudia Jones summarizes and praises the Black woman for her central role in Black survival: "From the days of the slave traders down to the present, the Negro woman has had the responsibility of caring for the needs of the family."[7] Understanding that the nuclear family paradigm rests in the trope of the male head of household assuming authority from his position as economic source for the family unit, she points out that the model is in general unrealistic for Blacks. She explains that Black women's role as co-source for household income "is primarily a result of low-scale earnings of Negro men," and is a phenomenon that has persisted since emancipation.[8] Decades after Jones's articulation of how the slaving economy informed the prominent roles of Black women in Black family structures, historian Deborah Gray White echoes and expands on this read. White explains that Black society was not a historical anomaly: "In almost all societies where men consistently dominate women, their control is based on male ownership and distribution of property and/or control of certain culturally valued subsistence goods."[9] Given the general lack of shared property and a racialized culture that denied enslaved husbands the means to provide essential resources for their family, enslaved men were unable to apply key leverage to assert their power over their wives.[10] The history of Black matriarchy does not represent a cultural ill, but is rather an outcome of an enslaving institution that prohibited Black families from establishing household operations that mirrored the white nuclear family.[11] While Francis's status as unmarried throughout her life was not uncommon for Black enslaved women, that she is reported as widowed in the household of her son Shadrick in the 1880 Census, hints at the increasing pressure Blacks felt in the post-emancipation era to perform the nuclear paradigm.

Positing a contrasting read of what would emerge into an institutionalized denigration of the "single Black mother," Jones reminds us in her 1949 article that everyday Black folks did not initiate or advance this trope. From the earliest captives delivered to the Americas, Africans and their African American descendants relayed to their posterity a history of African origins and ways of knowing that countered white-originating accounts. Jones's insistence that African traditions informed African American family formation demonstrates that challenges to white-centric history making are not merely recent reactionary "rewritings" of established history but have been integral to Black cultural memory—that is, history.[12] In 1949 America was eight decades beyond emancipation, but many Black communities knew firsthand or secondhand someone who had been enslaved, and these stories were conveyed to new generations. In my own family, my mother and her siblings as children had heard accounts of their parents' familial and community narratives of enslavement and had known older family members or neighbors who had been enslaved. These stories and ancestral names and images were then passed to my generation with many continuing the pass to newer generations. Jones's historical assertion in 1949 is rooted in a narrative tradition that informs my twenty-first-century telling of my own family and community story. In Black communities, the validity of these stories and figures are not questioned: They represent generational accounts that originate at locations of early Black experiences in enslavement. Recalling the evolution of African American language, it is clear that generations of early Africans and African Americans maintained stories of Africa that originated from the African-born enslaved: "At any one time prior to 1830, it is possible that from two-thirds to three-fourths of all African-born slaves either could not or did not speak recognizable English or French. This means they were either speaking their native languages to one another or a version of English/French so Africanized as to be unintelligible to whites, or both."[13] This dynamic or "tinkering" with language was a form of power that allowed the enslaved to "maintain distance, distinctiveness, and some sense of ownership."[14] This distance in language provided African Americans a means to construct distances between their private interior selves and the outer selves that they often had to maintain for their own safety and that of their families and communities.

Among the extensive histories and biographies of the antebellum and post–Civil War South, the predominance of these works rest in traditions of white western historiography. This tradition tells us whose voices count as authoritative and reliable, what persons are worthy of recognition and reverence, what texts, documents, or records constitute credible sources, and from this tradition scholars then follow a template of interpretation and narration. Western/white history has a long-standing skepticism of biography—except those biographies of people deemed important or prominent and authored by presumed credible biographers. Hence, for example, historians are willing to accept as credible and sound those accounts written by "founding fathers" or patriots. Out of this tradition historians will even build their work on the accounts of proven disreputable or questionable figures. US history has been grounded in the accounts of those who arrived and displaced the Indigenous nations and people of the land, with little to no accounts from the voices of those displaced and subjugated. Southern history has been anchored in biographical accounts of its Confederate leaders; and the history of slavery has been grounded in the accounts of the enslavers. The story of America's founding, its fight against the tyranny of the British, rests in the accounts of patriot slaveholders such as George Washington, Thomas Jefferson, James Madison, and James Monroe. We continue to encounter new biographies of these figures while we are told that biography is an unreliable resource for narrating history. In classrooms throughout US institutions, students are told and readily assert that biography is not history. The established exception to this rule, however, tells us that the biographies of important and prominent figures can be taken as reliable historical resources that expand our understanding of periods and events of the past.

Through the lens of western history, we are told that those who were silenced, nameless, or common do not offer the large scope of history that the big players can provide—they only understood the world within the limited space of their existences. In the case of the enslaved then, there are few records penned by them, and though we have slave narratives, they are comparatively few in number when we consider the available narratives of the enslavers. In general, slave narratives written by the enslaved or formerly enslaved, have been treated as supplemental readings for history. It is this long-standing practice that Lisa Lindsey and John Sweet call into question in the introduction to their collection, *Biography and the Black Atlantic.* They argue that biography, including the biography of the enslaved—oral as well as written—fills in pieces of the historical puzzle that have long been missing: "By attaching names and faces to broad processes such as slaving, enslavement, identity formation, empire-building, migration, and emancipation, biography can illuminate the meanings of these large, impersonal forces for individuals."[15]

Narratives passed down by descendants of those enslaved in the United States have for the most part gone untapped as a source for understanding Black experience in the country or the country's history at large. In recent times, however, the escalating interest of Blacks in their genealogical histories has opened up innovative and creative possibilities for scholars studying the people and the world of US slavery and its aftermath. These approaches to and perspectives of history will test the scholarly framework "that pervades the study of 'slavery' as if it were a structure controlling people's lives rather than an ideological construction of the masters."[16] It is this historically limited and formulaic account of Blacks in the Americas, including the US South, that leave us circling back always to a look at those enslaved and their descendants as entities always acted upon and making their way through history only as the fallout or debris from the chiseled story of European new-world settlement. It is out of the prism of recent scholarship revealing the necessity of working beyond conventional historical and academic practices/methods that I envisioned this biohistoriographical study of a Black southern family extending across geographical and time boundaries. With its focus on an ordinary enslaved woman and her family, *Francis* rests in the everyday experiences of enslaved people in the antebellum and postwar South, people who, as author Ibram X Kendi reminds us, are no less important than the reverential figures that survive in public consciousness. In his 2019 essay in *The Atlantic* reflecting on the 400th-year anniversary of the first Africans delivered to Virginia as slaves, Kendi underscores this point through the example of Angela, one of those first arrivals of Africans into Virginia who would also be "one of the first known Africans in British North America."[17] Regarding Angela and her importance as representative of the larger story of African American history and experience, Kendi writes, "In recapping African American history, someone like Angela is indispensable. She is not the famed slave-revolt leader, the daring runaway, the author of an antislavery screed, the maker of an enduring cultural product, the anointed Black leader, the Phillis, Sojourner, Mary, Malcolm, or Maya. There is history in regular African Americans behind the scenes surviving the regularity of racist policies, ideas, abuse, and violence for 400 years. Angela is the woman of today who works in a low-wage health-care gig, moving from crisis to crisis and joy to joy, all the while raising her hopes for a better day, or not."[18]

Individual and collective biographies of everyday African Americans can broaden our understanding of the intricacies of enslavement from the perspectives of those enslaved. These narratives can tell us more about the ways in which the enslaved both endured and resisted slavery and how they forged ideals and practices that shaped foundations of community and family. Their perspectives make clearer that while enslavement was a system, there were people integral to the machinery of that system. The system was created and controlled by white people who actively enslaved and/or supported laws and practices that sanctioned abuses and violations of Black people. This centuries-long infraction continues to be narrated as a momentary blemish in the "exceptional" history of the United States. The result is a wholesale denial of the centuries of abuse inflicted on a targeted population group—African Americans—and the metamorphosis of these abuses in the post-emancipation nation. It is easy to ignore the connections when on both ends of this history— that is, enslavement and post-enslavement—we silence and muffle the voices of the victimized.

Just as the outcome for sampling in music is the final mix, which consists of selected samples arranged to convey a narrative or impression, the mix in *Francis* is the arrangement of archival sources to tell a story that by conventional scholarly methodologies would be dismissed as unknowable. Progressing primarily through a cache of sundry sampled sources, this narrative conveys the story of Francis Sistrunk and her family and the legacy they left for their posterity. The opening chapter, "Francis in Georgia: Kinship and Family Formation in the Black Antebellum South," shows that while we do not find Francis named during the decades of her life when enslaved by Jacob Sistrunk

Jr, there is evidence of her presence. In conventional histories of the South, the larger population of enslaved persons are dismissed as unknowable. Where are the records that name them and how do we verify their existence in the absence of officially sanctioned documentation? Without explicit records noting their names, date of birth, parents' names, and other personal–individual evidence of existence, the presumption is that we cannot know them. In this focus on Francis in Georgia the unnamed enslaved girl on the 1840 Census comes out of the shadow of the archives. Her remarkable story takes shape and finds voice from the very records that silenced her for more than a century. Layering the antebellum records with samplings of post-emancipation records and archives, her name and narrative emerge to tell the story of a young girl catapulted into motherhood while she was still herself a child. From 1844 to 1855 Francis gave birth to five of her six children. While her youngest was probably still breastfeeding, at the behest of their enslaver, Jacob Jr., Francis and children were forced to migrate out of Georgia.[19]

At the close of the war, Francis and her six children—John, Hillman, Shadrick, Willis, Lucretia, and Robert—emerge as named entities. Chapter 2, "Neshoba to Noxubee: Pre-Civil War to Reconstruction" explores this journey to freedom. A view of the Civil War through the post-Reconstruction period is presented through the lens of Francis and her family. Aligning Cistrunk family history with and against archival and official records underscores the tensions that can emerge when engaging formal and informal archives. This is particularly evident when published narratives that read Jacob Jr. as independent, self-sustained farmer are revisited to read the narrative of Jacob, the enslaver, whose wealth and aspirations rested in large part on the valuation of the enslaved people he held. Forced to migrate with Jacob Jr. and his family, Francis and her family arrived in Mississippi around 1856. In 1861, during the start of the war, Francis would give birth to her sixth child, Robert, likely fathered by Jacob Jr. Francis set her family's roots in the formative postwar years of Noxubee's newly freed Black communities. It was here that she anchored her children in a collective identity. No matter who may have fathered her children, all took on the surname she adopted—Sistrunk. As Sistrunks, three sons—John, Hillman, and Shadrick—would later make one spelling alteration for themselves and their posterity, spelling their name with a *C* instead of an *S*. The family story that continues to date explains that this was a deliberate and defiant proclamation on the part of the brothers and reflects a spirit that would survive generations.

The story of the early decades of the post-emancipation Cistrunks is one of optimism and hopefulness, but it is also one of great struggle that ties to the larger political and economic struggles of Black southerners during this era. Chapter 3, "Post-Reconstruction and a New Century: Anxious and Audacious

Times (1870s–1910)," examines their struggle through the converging elements of Mississippi's postwar racist policies and challenges of other natural and social forces that culminated in the state's return to white rule that mirrored the antebellum South. Despite the great Compromise of 1877 just as their urban and northern peers, Black rural southerners embraced a vision of Black uplift that included the pursuit of economic, political, and social advancement. Conventional and unconventional archives tell this story, and this chapter samples these resources to hear this story through the version of Francis and her lineage. Francis's youngest son, Robert, died sometime between the 1870 and 1880 Census; The fourth oldest, Willis, left Noxubee County by 1880, and Francis died sometime after the 1880 Census and before the 1900 enumeration. Remaining were the Noxubee Four—John, Hillman, Shadrick, and Lucretia— who were part of the story of Blacks building post-emancipation communities in the rural southern county of Noxubee, MS. Their story also reveals the dynamics of the infrastructure that made it so difficult for many of these families to hold on to their land or to stand their ground and establish a place of home for their future generations.

Chapter 4, "Hillman: A Man's Story Bookended by Women," follows Francis Sistrunk's last living son, Hillman. By 1920 when 19-year-old Carl Cistrunk appears in Jasper County, his father, Noah, stepmother, Luella, and their children had moved to Winston County, where the once landowning Noah of Noxubee County, now farmed on rented land. Carl's grandparents, Shad and Susan had died years earlier, and Hillman, his great-uncle, the remaining Noxubee County patriarch, had been admitted to the State Hospital for the Insane, in Hinds County, more than one hundred miles away. Within three months of his admission, Hillman died and was buried on the asylum grounds. It is a story with years of heightened distress for the Cistrunk family that eerily presages the continued health, financial, and social instability still prevalent in African American communities throughout the nation. The eruption of the COVID-19 virus pandemic in the spring of 2020 was a century removed from the Spanish flu, which raged across the globe from 1918 to 1920. The circumstances of Hillman's death in March 1920 echo those of many Blacks during the 2020 pandemic period that was marked by heightened health crises, economic distress, and increased incidences of racial violence. If landownership were the only measure of Cistrunk resilience, perhaps this may be considered a dismal ending. However, the dedication to education, industry, family, and community held by Hillman and his brothers lived into future generations to the present. The writing of this narrative is a testament to that legacy.

The coda reflects on the methodology and ideological framework that was foundational to the writing and conceptualization of *Francis*. I offer it to those who may have an interest in the process.

Chapter 1

FRANCIS IN GEORGIA

Kinship and Family Formation
in the Black Antebellum South

Everybody's Business Ain't Nobody's Business
    Cistrunk/Black southern maxim

While post-emancipation census reports suggest that Francis Sistrunk was born in Georgia, I have found no document to confirm this record.[1] During her life, Annie Cistrunk passed on the story that the Cistrunk ancestors came into Mississippi by way of Virginia. Annie often told the family story through a fused history of her parents—Carl and Anna Denson Cistrunk. As a result, it was not always clear whether she was giving the account of Cistrunks, Densons, or both. Given expanding settlement patterns in the early nineteenth century, Francis could have been transported into Georgia from bordering North or South Carolina, or even from the more distant state of Virginia. Like most enslaved people, Francis was not acknowledged by name in pre-emancipation census records or in the personal accounts of her enslavers. and she nor her parents would have been permitted to keep a written record of their family lineage. This historical reality underscores the difficult, and in most cases unlikely chance of affirming birth and childhood information on enslaved African Americans. Despite the absence of basic social identity markers such as name, birthday, and parentage the story of Francis from childhood and even her parentage can be deduced or approximated. Working from a range of records such as oral histories, DNA evidence, census records, tax records, and slave importation accounts from the Colonial period to the twenty-first century, a more visible portrait of young Francis comes to light. Employing scholar Christina Sharpe's description of indigo in Julie Dash's fictional *Daughters of the Dust*, each record used to tell Francis's story is akin to "a trace of slavery," that lives well into "the afterlives of slavery."[2] Just as trace elements are present only in minute amounts but are vital to an organism's growth, these traces of slavery are vital for reconstructions of histories and memories that speak with greater clarity to the present.

FRANCIS: TRACES—SPECULATIVE AND AFFIRMATIVE

The "trace" of slavery that I sample early in my search for Francis is the un-detailed family summary of Cistrunk Virginia origins. While Francis may have been born in Georgia as post-emancipation census reports suggest, I had to consider the possibility that she was transported into the state as a young child. Colonial Georgia's early growth in slave population was significantly fueled by importations from South Carolina via the port of Charleston where captured Africans were delivered from the African continent or the Caribbean islands. After the banning of the slave trade, antebellum Georgia grew its slave population by childbirth, but interstate importations remained a key source, and South Carolina remained a significant passageway for enslaved people entering Georgia.[3] These importations were often the result of white planters moving south and westward, forcing enslaved people to join them in the migration. Some planters purchased enslaved people outside Georgia and added them to their enslaved population, and some traveled through Georgia with enslaved possessions they were transporting into the farther western territories of Alabama and Mississippi where they were settling. Many enslaved were also introduced into the state via slave traders—some who were farmers or planters and some who dealt in the purchase, transportation, and selling of enslaved people as their primary financial venture. The scenarios varied, but the result was the same: a constant flow of enslaved African Americans living the trauma of forced migration and separation from kin and family.

If Francis was imported into the state of Georgia, she likely entered across the South Carolina-Georgia border. Sampling a range of official documents such as tax, estate, wills, census, land grants, and bill of sales records around and prior to Francis's birth-year range, I have found no record to date that shows how or when she became Jacob Sistrunk Jr.'s legal property. Before his death in 1762 in present-day Orangeburg County, SC, Jacob's immigrant great-grandfather, Heinrich, had come into ownership of an enslaved woman and child. This mother and child were probably remanded to the ownership of Heinrich's oldest son, Henry, and their descendants may very well be among present-day Black Sistrunks whose ancestral lines point to South Carolina. It is not clear whether Henry's younger brother, Gasper, was a slaveowner, but Gasper's son, Jacob Sr., does not appear to have entered Georgia owning enslaved persons. There appears to be no enslaved people inventoried as part of Jacob Sr.'s estate after his death in 1841. It is unlikely then that Jacob Jr. came to own Francis through inheritance from his own family, and no evidence to date suggests that Francis was brought into the household through inheritance via Jacob Jr.'s wife, Martha. The likelihood is that he bought Francis, and the combination of her sex and age suggest that he could have afforded this purchase during the 1830–1840 period before she appears as a teenager in his possession on the Census.[4]

Definitive evidence of how and from whom Jacob Jr. purchased Francis remains undiscovered. One possibility is that he purchased her from a trader bringing Blacks into the state for his own use and/or to sell. In Dawn Watson's *Slave Importation Affidavit Registers for Nine Georgia Counties, 1818–1847*, five enslaved Black females with the name Francis/Frances are listed as being transported into the nine county jurisdictions of Georgia for the thirty-year period covered in this work. Watson's compilation is by no means a comprehensive list, but it is a substantive one, particularly when considering importations into upper and middle Georgia counties, where Francis would likely have entered, and Georgia's relatively late entry into the slaving economy of the colonial United States. Founded as a British colony in 1732, Georgia prohibited slavery until 1751; however, after legalization of slavery, Georgia's enslaved population grew from a few hundred to an estimated 18,000 by 1775.[5] Land grants to settlers from South Carolina accounted for significant numbers of early Georgia settlements: "Most of those moving to Georgia after the first several years were from other colonies, especially South Carolina. These settlers viewed restrictions on the size of individual land holdings as a sure pathway to poverty. They also opposed restrictions on land sales and the prohibition against slavery for the same reason."[6] The second- and third-generation descendants of the immigrant, Heinrich Süsstrunk, were among the many South Carolinians who crossed into Georgia in the decades after the slave ban was lifted. Heinrich's grandsons, Jacob Sr. and his older brother, John, moved from their birthplace in Orangeburgh District, SC, to the Georgia border county of Lincoln in the closing decade of the 1700s.[7] Their quest for financial fortune would be tied to the slaving economy that flourished into the nineteenth-century antebellum era after Georgia's removal of the ban.

The five Francis/Frances listings in Watson's compilation are introduced into Georgia between the years 1830–1833 along the state's eastern boundaries and they include infants, toddlers, and young girls who were in the age range of young Francis Sistrunk. Given this possibility I considered each case individually to determine who among the five could be identified as the Francis that would be delivered into the hands of Jacob Jr by 1840. The Frances who appears in the record in 1830 is among a group of twenty-seven enslaved persons registered in Camden County, GA, in the interest/ownership of Jane B. Robinson.[8] The lack of age and physical description leave it difficult to affirm or rule out the possibility, but the spelling of the name and the location in southeastern coastal Georgia suggest that this is not Francis Sistrunk.

In an 1831 Franklin County (GA) affidavit, Dozier and N. M. Thornton declare a young girl Francis, "8 months old yellow," and her mother Mary, "a woman 21 years old dark," along with more than a dozen other "field hands" they are importing into the state.[9] A case can be made for considering that this is Francis Sistrunk. In 1833 in Elbert County, GA, "Frances a girl about 10 years old" enters the state with a group of enslaved persons, "all dark complexion," and Frances is noted as belonging to Alexander Spur of South Carolina."[10] The age and complexion of this Frances suggests that it is unlikely that she is Francis Sistrunk. In that same year, two additional enslaved girls with names spelled Francis are introduced into Elbert County. Francis, 2 years old, is among the more than twenty enslaved persons declared by Rufus Haywood who reports entering Georgia with them for the expressed purpose of "carrying them to Alabama."[11] The deposition offers no physical description of the 2-year-old girl, so whether she is of light-skin complexion like Francis Sistrunk is unknown. However, if the deponent, Haywood, is truthful in his assertion that he is traveling through Georgia en route to Alabama, it is unlikely that this is Francis Sistrunk.

Deponent Jeptha Harris declares in his 1833 Elbert County affidavit, that he is introducing "negro slaves . . . all common servants 'including Weaver, Spinster, Seamstress, &c," and among the enslaved declared by Harris is "Francis a girl 5 [years] old fair."[12] While no document definitively marks Francis Sistrunk's date of birth, the 40-year period of records from 1840–1880 help to narrow her birth year to a probable range. The 1840 Census lists her in the age range of 10 to 24, which corresponds to a birth-year range from 1816 to 1830.[13] In the 1850 (October) Slave Schedule, she is listed as 23 years old.[14] A decade later in the 1860 (September) schedule, she is listed as 33 years old.[15] These two successive census documents suggest her birth year was 1827, or, depending on the month of birth, in the range of years 1826 to 1828. This further indicates that she was approximately age 13 at the time of the 1840 Census. The 1880 Census (June) shows Francis Sistrunk as 58 years old, suggesting however that she was born between the years 1821 and 1822.[16] If we consider the consistency of the 1850 and 1860 Census record of her age, the 5-year-old Francis listed in Harris's 1833 Elbert County affidavit could have been Francis Sistrunk. The description of her light complexion and that she was among a group of enslaved people classified as skilled laborers is consistent with the 1860 description of her as "mulatto," and that she may have been a domestic rather than field laborer. If Jacob Jr. came into possession of Francis through a sale, her young age suggests that with limited funds he speculated that this young girl, whom he could purchase for a much lower cost than an enslaved adult woman or man, could be initially useful as a household servant and would ultimately through bearing children increase his financial fortunes. At age five in 1833, this Francis would have been born around the year 1828. Census reports show a significant decrease in Harris's holding of enslaved persons from 116 in 1830 to eighty-eight in 1840.[17] Francis may have been among the twenty-eight enslaved people whom Harris sold during this time. To date, no records of sales or asset transfers related to Harris's reduced number of slaves has been found. The trail goes cold here, signifying that Harris cannot be confirmed or eliminated as the enslaver of Francis during her girlhood. This point of indeterminacy represents a possibility and thus must be revisited if related archival records emerge to shed definitive light on Harris's possible link.

A return to the Francis listed in Thorntons's 1831 affidavit also leads to a trail that ends cold, but, as with the case of Jeptha Harris, suggests a reasonable possibility and in fact appears a stronger case. Although Dozier and NM Thornton are listed on the affidavit, it is Dozier who is enumerated on the 1830 census in Franklin County where his age is noted in the 70- to 80-year-old range. A second Dozier Thornton (probably Dozier Jr) is listed in the 40- to 50-year-old age group on the 1830 census in Muscogee County, and yet another and younger Dozier Thornton is listed in the 20- to 30-year-old age group in adjacent Harris County for the same year's census. The census records do not show any of the Doziers as senior or junior, but the age group and the migration path from the northeastern to the recently formed midwestern border counties of the state was reflective of the period. The enslaved Francis listed in Thornton's affidavit is again described as having a light complexion and is being transported into the upper South Carolina-Georgia border area that was a busy traffic route for slave transportations into interior Georgia and Alabama. When considering that the Francis in Thornton's possession may have been Francis Sistrunk, the matter of age calls for pause in what is an otherwise compelling possibility. This Francis was only 8 months old when listed on Thornton's affidavit, so she would have been born in 1830 instead of 1827, the year suggested in the 1850 and 1860 Slave Schedules. If this is Francis Sistrunk, she would have been about 14 years old when she gave birth to her first son, John. While childbirth at this age in the twenty-first century is unthinkable, this was not the case for much of the ninetieth century. It is even less extraordinary among enslaved populations, where Black girls and women were unprotected from rape and sexual exploitation. The 1840 Census shows Francis in the 10 to 14 year age range, but given the overlap with the 0–10 age range we cannot discount that a 10-year-old Francis may have been listed in the upper range instead of the younger age range. This may have been the result of an entry error on the part of the Census enumerator, but if the child Francis was being sexually violated, listing her in an older age group may have been a safeguard against such accusations should she become pregnant. While whites were not threatened with the possibility of criminal charges for sexual violation of enslaved people, they created and maintained a culture of denial. Numerous well-known white planters and statesmen were the biological fathers of enslaved children born of forced sexual relations with enslaved women and girls. In our modern era, Thomas Jefferson has probably emerged as the most well-known of these figures. The reality of these sexual violations and the children born out of them was an unspoken element of the facade of the southern plantocracy. While this was an accepted practice of plantation culture, it was generally ignored, and if acknowledged, the charge that Black women were jezebels turned them into the aggressors who seduced their white enslavers. Jezebels were women, but the sexual violence of girls, even Black girls, was less palatable for the white public that generally looked away from the atrocities of the plantation. Harriet Jacobs captures this aspect of plantation culture in her account of her enslaver, Mr. Flint, who awaited her emergence from childhood before initiating his sexual pursuit.[18] As Jacobs reached age 15, Flint, who was 40 years her senior, explained that as his property, she had no choice.[19] While Flint began his pursuit of Jacobs when she came of age, there was custom that informed both his boldness and his wait. Jacobs explains that before the age of 12 enslaved girls learn this custom and come to learn as well that their mistress may be angered by the custom, but they do not stand in its way.[20] While few if anyone in Jacob Sistrunk Jr.'s circle would have made a stir about an enslaved girl giving birth to a mixed-race child, an enslaved 13-year-old pregnant girl would ensure that apathy, and a 10-year-old pregnant child might prove more difficult to dismiss. In the slaving Americas, the age of the enslaved was often manipulated for the benefit of masters and slave traders; therefore, assigning a false age to an enslaved child to veil the common practice of sexual violence would not have been extraordinary.

The possibility that the infant Francis in Thornton's affidavit is Francis Sistrunk becomes more compelling when one considers the migration pattern of the early nineteenth-century Thornton families from Elbert and Franklin Counties, who settled in areas near Georgia's western boundary. While Jeptha Harris cannot be omitted as the enslaver who possibly brought young Francis Sistrunk into Georgia, his migration to the interior areas of Athens, GA, and Marietta, GA, from the counties bordering South Carolina do not connect as directly to Jacob Jr.'s migration path.[21] By the 1830 Census, he had moved westward with his parents from the eastern border county of Lincoln County, GA, and after his father's death in 1841, Jacob Jr. moves from Marion to neighboring Harris County, GA. This path reflects that of the east-Georgia Thorntons who also moved westward from the South Carolina-bordering counties into Harris County and the boundary counties of the Georgia-Alabama state line. Dozier Thornton Jr.'s residence in Muscogee County, GA, placed him adjacent to Marion County, GA, where the Sistrunks lived and in the newly formed Harris County, where Jacob Jr. would move after his father's death.[22] The location and the timeline make a strong argument that Jacob Jr. purchased Francis from Dozier Jr. In 1831 Thornton entered Georgia with seventeen enslaved people that were described as field hands: thirteen were children ages 8 months to 15 years old, six were under the age of 10, three were under the age of 2.[23] Few of these seventeen were at an age to be immediately assigned field labor that would contribute to high levels of productivity. Three of the four adults were women with two suckling infants and a toddler, and five additional children were less than 10 years old. Clearly Thornton was engaging in some financial speculation with these human assets that were not yet matured or in the case of the mothers recovered to a point of being fully fledged workers. This would mean then that if Thornton decided to sell them, he would not receive the price that adults could command. It also would mean that for would-be enslavers, such as Jacob Sr. and Jr., they might be afforded entry into the world of slaveholding. If the 8-month-old Francis, daughter of Mary, was the Francis purchased by Jacob Jr., she was not born in Georgia as the 1870 and 1880 Census records show.

In the post-emancipation era Francis appears in two census reports—1870 and 1880—and both show Georgia as her place of birth.[24] However even if Francis was not brought into the state by Thornton, whether she was born in Georgia as suggested in the Census reports remains uncertain. It was not uncommon in post-emancipation census records that when asked their place of birth and that of their parents, respondents often named a prior state of residence rather than what may have been the actual birth state. This is not altogether remarkable when one considers that throughout the antebellum period, enslaved people were in great numbers separated from birth parents, and this practice regularly occurred generationally. The confiscation of native territories in the early 1800s not only fueled mass removals and murders of Native Americans, but with the ensuing rapid expansion of settlers across the South inter- and intra-state slave trading escalated. The result for many enslaved people was the horror of serial migrations and separations and a complex perhaps confusing sense of familial roots and origins. For example, an enslaved child born in South Carolina with a mother born in Virginia could be carried into Georgia with or without her mother. Later after that child is sold and forced to migrate to Mississippi, she might report that her mother was born in Georgia and not Virginia, and when she becomes a mother, her children may report that she was born in Mississippi rather than Georgia. With so much movement and separation of families, many enslaved did not know their parents' or their own place of birth; however, while this was often the case, we must consider that many did know the history of their own and their parents' nativity. In numerous cases then, inaccurate reports of birthplaces may not have been a result of enslaved parents not sharing birth and childhood stories with their children. In many cases the inaccuracies were the consequence of enslaved people having resided in multiple states during their lifetime and thus reporting any one of those states as their birthplace. Inaccurate reports of birthplaces also oftentimes reflect one of many language idioms among African Americans in the South. Throughout Black southern communities the phrases "where [are] you from" and "where [were] you born" are understood to be interchangeable, and it is the nature of the conversation that drives the response. In some cases, it is a matter of whether the question is asking where a person lived prior to their current address, where they grew up as a child, or where they were born. Hence, a Census enumerator asking for the parents' birthplaces may get an answer that depends on the respondent's assessment of the interrogator and/or the implications of the answer. So, the respondent may indicate the previous state where their parent lived, or they may indicate what they believe is the parent's actual state of birth.

This varying report of parent birthplaces across census reports is exemplified in the case of the Cistrunk siblings, John, Hillman, Shadrick, and Lucretia. In the 1880 and 1900 Censuses Shadrick reports that his father (Shadrick Dowdell) was born in Alabama.[25] In 1880 Hillman and Lucretia (Cistrunk Dobbins) report their father's birthplace as Georgia, while John reports Virginia.[26] As with Shadrick on the 1900 Census, Hillman and John report their father's birthplace as Alabama, while Lucretia (Cistrunk Dobbins McDaniel) reports Georgia.[27] John and Shadrick seemed to have died before the 1910 Census, but Hillman and Lucretia report their father's birthplace in Georgia in that year's census, and by 1920 Lucretia reports Mississippi, which is clearly not the case.[28] In the 1920 Census Lucretia does make a curious change. She is recorded as listing Mississippi as her birthplace and that of her mother and father.[29] This could have been a case of Lucretia misreporting, but it seems unlikely since she consistently reported Georgia as her birthplace for the previous three census reports. The error is more likely on the part of the enumerator. With the exception of the 1920 Census, Lucretia and Shadrick are consistent in their statements of their father's birthplace: Shadrick reports Alabama, and Lucretia reports Georgia. While Shadrick seems to maintain that his father was born in Alabama, he probably also knew that his father had lived in Georgia. He may not have known, however, that his father was transported into Georgia possibly from Kentucky or Virginia—states where his enslaver, James Dowdell, lived before coming to Georgia.

The Cistrunk siblings reported different birthplaces for their father across census reports, but they were consistent in reporting that their mother, Francis, was born in Georgia. They may have assumed that because they were born in Georgia and since the family moved to Mississippi from Georgia, their mother was as well born in Georgia. Francis may have told them that she was born in Georgia either because she knew this for a fact or because she assumed this based on the best information she had. Returning to the two young, enslaved girls named Francis in the slave affidavit records for Harris and Thornton, we see how Francis may have been born in a state other than Georgia but concluded or simply declared Georgia as her birth state. In the case that Francis was brought into Georgia by Harris at 5 years old, having been uprooted and separated from her mother, the trauma of the experience at such a young age may have impacted her willingness or ability to remember the past. Georgia may have represented in her psyche the point of her awakening of place and self. The 8-month-old infant Francis who may have been transported along with her mother into Georgia by Thornton would know of her birthplace only through information shared by others. If either of the two possible Francis children is Francis Sistrunk, she would have been transferred to Jacob Sistrunk Jr.'s ownership before or during her early teenage years. She may have been too young and too traumatized to hold on to either her own or secondhand memory of her birthplace and origins. Again as well, even if the young Francis did know her place of birth or that she came into Georgia as a young child, she may have simply begun the story of her origins at the point of her consciousness of self and at a moment of recognizable community, family, and belonging. Though there are no enslaved companions for her in Jacob Jr.'s household, her emergence into adulthood and community is facilitated by the community of enslaved on Jacob Sr.'s adjacent plantation. Francis's place of birth remains an unanswered question, and in this speculative biohistoriography of Francis, I leaned toward the vision of Francis as that infant child, with her mother, Mary, being brought into the state of Georgia in 1831, by enslaver and trader Dozier Thornton. Sometime between 1831 and 1840, 10-year-old Francis was forcibly separated from her mother and delivered over to Jacob Sistrunk Jr. As the subsequent sections of this chapter will reveal, I would have to reconsider this narrative version—or at least the players— as I looked more closely at the affairs of the Sistrunks in Marion County and those of Jacob Jr. during the years in Harris County.

BUILDING LEGACIES OF BLACK MOTHERING
AGAINST PARADIGMS OF ERASURE

In 1841 when Ralph W. Emerson published "Self-Reliance," the romanticized myth of rugged American individualism that anchors citizenship and democracy to assertions of individual rights and freedom, Francis and millions like her are ironically in the possession of enslavers under a government that does not recognize them as citizens or whole human beings. Around age 10 at that time, Francis is the lone enslaved and unnamed person listed on the 1840 Census in Jacob Jr.'s household in Marion County, GA.[30] I think about her as a contemporary of some of the nineteenth-century African American authors and figures that I regularly teach: Frances Harper, Harriet Wilson, Frederick Douglass, Harriet Tubman, and Harriet Jacobs. Wilson's fictionalized auto-biographical heroine, Frado, who would have been Francis's peer in age, also closely parallels Francis in the circumstances of her younger years.[31] Just as Wilson's heroine, Francis is a young, enslaved girl with no family or fellow enslaved persons as company in the white household where she is forced to reside and labor. In the case of Wilson's heroine, the result is tragic: Frado grows into a confused, self-denigrating, and isolated young woman who, though ultimately freed from indenture, succumbs to poverty and death at a young age. Wilson narrates a story of failed conversion that seats Frado's fate in the failure of Christianity: Anglo Christianity and its conversion ritual that promises entry into the "community of saints" offers no place for the would-be Black convert. Frado is therefore left on her own, and no hearty dose of Emersonian self-reliance is available for this young, Black woman, isolated in a world of whiteness.

There are clear distinctions between my ancestor Francis and Wilson's autobiographical protagonist: Frado is an indentured servant in the free North and the "mulatto" offspring of a white woman and a Black man.[32] On the contrary, while she is identified in the 1860 Slave Schedule as mulatto, Francis is probably the offspring of an enslaved woman and an unnamed white man who may have been her enslaver.[33] This difference in the condition of the mother underscores the condition of Francis in the eyes of the law as slave. By the dawn of the eighteenth century, laws throughout the colonies sealed the generational fate of Blacks. With the legal decree that children followed the condition of the mother, children fathered by white men and enslaved women were not only not white, they were also not free. The most pernicious outcome of the sexual license given to white men over Black women was that the rape of Black women and girls by their enslavers perpetuated single Black motherhood to the economic benefit of the enslaver and the continued dis-paragement of Black women. In a striking contrast, sexual unions between white women and Black men were criminalized and could readily lead to death for enslaved Black men. This then diminished unions between Black men and white women, but not so for the contrasting case. This license for white ex-ploitation of Black enslaved women paved the way for generations of white "baby daddies" that this nation continues to ignore in its historical narrative. Unlike the servitude of Wilson's 1850 fictional character, the story of freedom for Francis is not an individual story of fulfillment of indenture, but rather part of the collective experience of freedom for Black southerners after the Civil War. Francis may have lived in Jacob Jr.'s household as his lone slave; however, unlike Frado, who was similarly isolated in a white New England household where she was forced into servitude, Francis was not alone. She was part of an enslaved community that existed beyond the constructs of the master narrative propagated by whites to erase the meaningful presence and humanity of Blacks.

While the enslavers may not have acknowledged the personhood or any meaningful power of their "property," enslaved people themselves operated within and around power structures to shape and control their lives where they could. The communities that they built were informed by their forced engagement with whites and legally sanctioned white rule, but they also shaped their communities and ethos from African traditions and sensibilities that they refashioned to respond to their diasporic experience. The evolution of African ways of knowing and being into African American culture has been examined across areas of study such as spirituality, family, language, music, art, dance, and cuisine.[34] It is the matter of family as concept and practice in African American culture that is especially relevant to understanding and knowing Francis, her children, and their legacy. Simply looking at Francis and family through the prism of the white/western paradigm of the nuclear family leads very quickly to the all too often recited saga of the failed Black single mother. This stigma on Black motherhood is seated in America's vision of the nuclear family that was seeded in the nineteenth century interlocking emergence of capitalism and individualism. This period injected into the free citizenry a belief in the power of and the equal opportunity for economic prosperity guaranteed through democracy, thereby promising a potential to gain wealth that is only limited by individual capacity.

Arguably cemented into public discourse through sociologist Daniel Patrick Moynihan's 1965 report on Black poverty, *The Negro Family: The Case For National Action,* the denigrating trope of the single Black mother has become an all too common default explanation for the continued struggles of Blacks in America.[35] Moynihan's report concluded that Black poverty grew out of the higher percentages of single parentage, that is, women-led households among Blacks. Moynihan's theory rests in a normalization of white patriarchal constructions of culture and family, and the assumption that assimilation into white culture is the road to Black uplift. In his estimation, Blacks needed to emulate the nuclear family model to both integrate themselves into the social corpus of America and to enjoy the fruits of economic prosperity. The logical supposition to Moynihan's study was that Black advancement and prosperity hinged on Black transformations to male-led households and childbirth restricted to marriage. While he acknowledged that slavery had facilitated what he labeled a Black matriarchal legacy, Moynihan nevertheless centered Black women as the source of Black poverty and sluggish improvement in the lives of Blacks in general. Moynihan failed to examine the historical exploitation of Black people and their labor—and thus Black economic survival—that was centuries in the making and clearly not by the design of Black women. He further neglected to consider that Blacks themselves did not recognize white-derived constructs of humanity and society as a universal normal.

Moynihan's report also hinged on his dismissal of African American ways of knowing and living that grounded Black communities in a different model than the white patriarchal blueprint that he imposed. His theory conveniently overlooked the reality that white-constructed models of civilization and society had been the bedrock of the nation's violence and exploitation of enslaved people and their descendants. Blacks survived enslavement and the ensuing era of Jim Crow because they did not submit to American myths of rugged individualism and the nuclear family. Blacks could not survive social- and state-sanctioned racial discrimination operating out of an ethos that held individuals and individual parent–children units as self-sustaining and self-interested entities. Survival and advancement for African Americans in and out of enslavement occurred from an ethos of community and kinship, and Black women—married and unmarried—were anchors. Blacks did not vilify the generations of Black women and mothers who were the glue that held communities together, assuming responsibility and connection not only to those they birthed into life but to those of extended blood lineage and to surrogate connections outside of bloodlines.

By design enslavement was an ongoing obstacle to building and sustaining nuclear households with a father as head. Enslaved parents were often separated through sales of any members of the immediate family—parents and children. Women were often left with their own children and/or assumed responsibility for other young children who may have been separated from both parents. Without question these practices left a generational sense of instability and anxiety among African Americans. However, while the splintering of families necessitated that Black enslaved women head households, this role was not anathema to Black culture: enslaved societies were informed by pre–Middle Passage African societies where Black women held a place "relatively higher in the family than that of European women."[36] Therefore, when Francis Sistrunk emerges on the 1850 Slave Schedule as mother of three with no apparent male spouse, she would not have been regarded as an anomaly or a pariah. She represented part of an antebellum world where "slaves lived in families, legally recognized or not, and the majority of slave children grew up with their mothers and—somewhat less often—their fathers."[37] In the slaving South, despite the enslaved husbands' inability to perform the patriarchal role of economic head, Black families with both parents was the dominant familial template. But again, "mother-headed households" were not uncommon, and slave women were the primary source for "basic continuity to families—and communities—faced with disruption."[38]

FRANCIS: MOTHERED AND MOTHERING

Francis was born into the unspoken and sadistic tradition of slaving that granted white men free reign to rape and sexually exploit enslaved Black girls and women. If Francis is the infant declared in Thornton's 1831 importation deposition, she entered Georgia with her mother, Mary, who in contrast to Francis, is described as dark-complexioned. Whether her mother is Mary or an unnamed enslaved woman already living on a Georgia plantation, the 1831 description of Francis as "yellow" and the description of Francis as "mulatto" on the 1860 Slave Schedule indicate that her mother had likely conceived her through a forced sexual encounter with her enslaver or other white male.[39] An enslaved child torn from her family unit, Francis Sistrunk experienced the need to be supported and nurtured, and in turn as an adult, she came to know the responsibility of an enslaved mother navigating the ever-present threat of separation from her children. Unless her mother was among the two adult enslaved women listed on Jacob Sr.'s 1840 Census count, Francis had been separated from her mother by this point.[40] Like many enslaved children separated from their mothers, Francis would have become the charge of a surrogate mother. The process was necessary and commonplace throughout enslaved communities: The surrogate was usually a woman and a relative, "usually an aunt or a sister, but in the absence of female relatives, nonkin women assumed the responsibility."[41] For the most part, whether the ties were built from biological relations or not, kinship relationships reflected the broad nuclear concept of adult-child delineations, but not with the restrictive Anglo-derived notion of parents and children as nuclear entity. No assignment of gradations such as "step," "half," or "adopted" were employed to signal hierarchies of belonging: "In friendships and dependency relationships women often treated nonblood kin as if a consanguineous tie existed. This is why older women were called Aunt and Granny, and why unrelated women sometimes called each other sister."[42]

Enslaved women worked closely, both in their labor for the enslavers and in those off-hours when they had to manage the matters of everyday living.[43] They built close knit female societies where they shared common duties such as child-rearing, cooking, sewing, gardening, and tending the sick.[44] If neither of the two women on Jacob Sr.'s farm was Francis's biological mother, one or both would have nevertheless stepped in as surrogate to care for and guide her through adolescence. It is this kind of relationship structure that again marks kinship formations in African American communities during slaving and remains integral into the twenty-first century. These women would have exemplified and taught Francis a kinship model shaped beyond immediate biological relationships and built around a belief in the duty of individuals to make a place for, that is to embrace into their circle, those who may be alone. Examples of the imprint of this cultural ethos abound throughout generations of Francis's lineage. This generational ethos of kinship care and support is exemplified for example in her son Shadrick, who extended his family beyond the singular mark of direct bloodline. When Shadrick married Susan Landrum, he folded her young relative (probably her daughter), Aggie, into their newly established household.[45] In the generation that followed, his daughter-in-law, Luella (Noah Cistrunk's wife) would assume the role of matriarch for the family of her stepson, Carl Cistrunk, whose mother had died in his toddler years. In his own household, Carl would take in and help raise the niece of his wife, Anna, after her mother died. As an adult, this niece would in turn take in two neighboring children and raise them along with her own three.

Francis's time in Marion County was formative. In 1840 the children in her community circle on Jacob Sr.'s farm were two girls and four boys under age 10, and a boy like Francis, who was listed in the age category 10–24.[46] With the large range in each age category, the children under age 10 could have been her playmates or even her charges to help care for. The one enslaved man noted in age group 24–36 may have been husband to one of the two enslaved women in the same age group. As well, he may have been the biological father to some of the children and surrogate to those with whom he had no biological connection. This would have been the kinship world that shaped her young foundation of family and community. As she was entering the early stage of puberty in 1840, the women of her community would advise her what that meant for a young Black enslaved female. While 19 was the average age for enslaved women giving birth to their first child, the onset of puberty placed enslaved girls in immediate danger of sexual violence and thus teenage pregnancy.[47] The well-known autobiography of Harriet Jacobs as well as Thomas Jefferson's sexual exploitation of his teenaged, enslaved girl, Sally Hemings, underscore the sexual license that some enslavers could and did assume with enslaved females starting from childhood. Enslavers and white men in general were protected by law and practice so deeply rooted in the nation that "from the beginning of the eighteenth century through the Civil War, there is no record in American courts of any white man's conviction for raping an enslaved woman."[48] Francis's course was like the many enslaved women who endured sexual violation and/or the threat while having to navigate the everyday perils of enslavement. Her trauma would not have spared her from the rudimentary work responsibilities that increased as she grew near adulthood. By the time she gave birth to her first child, her days of playing and working alongside both her girl and boy peers shifted to the more gendered path of the community of enslaved women. The adult women would have taught her the basics of cooking, sewing, childcare, and logistics of the female community that helped Black women sustain their own and their community's humanity.

Francis's oldest child (and perhaps her first), John, was born in 1844.[49] If Francis was born in 1827 as the 1850 and 1860 Census suggests, she would have been 17 at the time of John's birth. If she is the Francis reported by Thornton in 1831, she would have been 14 years old. In either case, she became a mother at an age younger than the average (19 years old) for enslaved women, which was two years earlier than the average age of 21 for white women. By the time she gave birth to John, the community of Francis and the ten enslaved on Jacob Sr.'s farm had been dissolved for three or more years; therefore, it is unlikely that John's father was from among her earlier peer group of Black enslaved males. In 1848 Jacob Jr., his brother Samuel, and his sister, Nancy, received the final disbursement from their father's estate from their brother Lemuel, and Jacob Jr. signed a document acknowledging receipt of this disbursement in Harris County.[50] This is the first written record found to date verifying Jacob Jr.'s residence in Harris County, but he likely moved there before that year.

It is not clear why Jacob Jr. moved from Marion County after his father's death, nor why he chose Harris County as his destination. The family had resided in Marion County for fifteen years at the time of Jacob Sr.'s death in 1841. Jacob Sr. and his brother John had migrated from South Carolina into the border county of Lincoln County, GA, in the first decade of the nineteenth century—they are said to have arrived in Lincoln in 1807 and 1808 respectively.[51] Within twenty years of establishing his home in Lincoln County, Jacob Sr. migrated to Marion County. In the 1818 *Tax Digests for Lincoln County,* John and Jacob Sr. appear as landowners with property near the Savannah River.[52] Jacob Sr. purchased one hundred acres of land in 1815 that was "bounded to the North on Chamberlain's [his in-laws] tract of land."[53] In 1826 Jacob sold 250 acres that he owned in nearby Early County, GA. He then moved his family to Marion County sometime between the sale of this land in 1826 and his appearance there on the 1830 Census.[54] Their movement into Georgia reflected the westward expansion in South Carolina that left fewer opportunities for acquiring land bounties as their immigrant ancestor, Heinrich, and his first-generation Sistrunk sons had done. The Sistrunks's

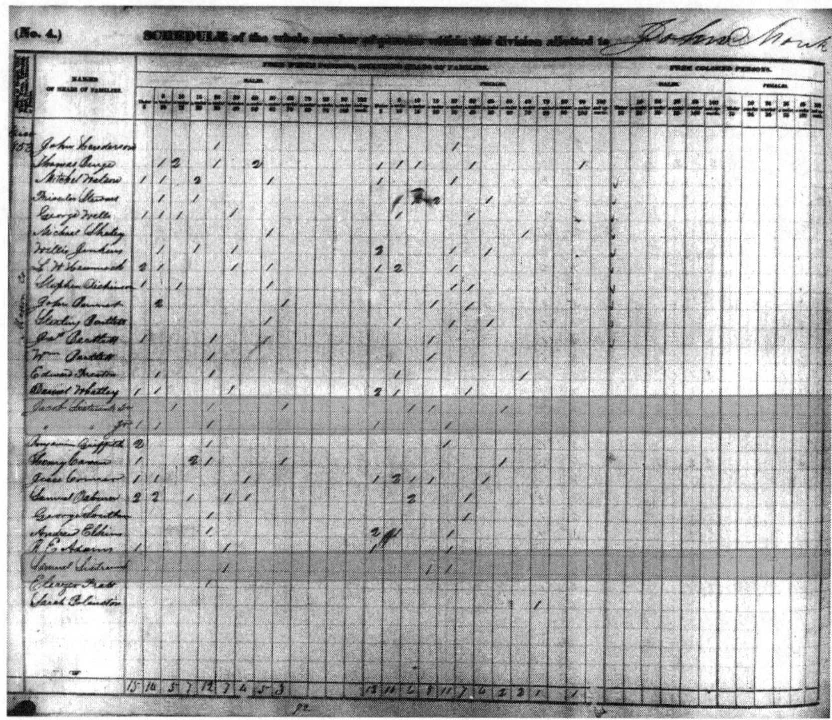

1840 Census, Marion County, GA

movements seem to be informed by a pursuit for wealth, and the vision was tied to the southern symbol of wealth and prosperity: the plantation and the enslaved labor that fueled it.

Record of Jacob's holdings in enslaved people surfaces in Marion County. While Jacob is not recorded as owning slaves on the 1830 Census, ten years later he appears on the 1840 Census holding ten enslaved people: four males under 10 years old; one male 10–24 years old; one male 24–36 years old; two females under 10 years old; and two females 24–36 years old.[55] In this same year, the Census lists one female slave, aged 10 to 24 years old in the household of his son, Jacob Jr.[56] Jacob Sr. died in 1841, and although the inventory of his goods reported after his death do not show much of value, his offspring would have inherited his property if his finances were clear.[57] Included in the property that was divided would have been any enslaved people that Jacob owned. An 1845 fire in the Marion County Courthouse has made it unlikely that probate records from Jacob's estate survived. It is, therefore, unclear how the enslaved people held by Jacob Sr. were utilized to settle his estate after his death, but they were not transferred to his children.

Jacob Sr.'s death seems to have precipitated Jacob Jr.'s move from Marion to Harris County, but how soon he left after his father's death remains unclear. The ten enslaved people in his father's possession by 1840 suggest that Jacob Sr. had planter aspirations. The greater number of children in his enslaved ownings indicates his eye on the future. However, by the time of his death, Jacob Sr.'s finances may have been strained, and the chance that his offspring would improve their lot by his holdings did not appear to have materialized. In their speculation of why Jacob's three sons did not purchase any of the items for sale from their deceased father's estate, *The Sistrunk Families* authors propose that "some division of property had already been made before the inventory was taken and the sale conducted."[58] This is perhaps not the likeliest answer. I have found no extant record showing sales of enslaved persons from Jacob Sr.'s estate. However, if he had been legal owner of the ten enslaved, they must have been sold to settle his estate because neither his children nor his wife inherited them. If he had been leasing them, then his death would still have precipitated the settlement of debt to the lessor and the return of the enslaved that were legally their property. The more likely circumstance was that Jacob Sr. had borrowed money and suffered financially from the fallout of the 1837–1843 economic depression.[59] If Jacob had borrowed with the expectation of repaying debtors based on his income from crop sales, he may have gotten caught in the dropped prices for cotton during this period and the large-scale panic that began four years before his death and lasted two years after.

While the authors of *The Sistrunk Families* report that Jacob and family raised cattle and hogs and grew the grains to feed them, they conceded that they may have grown some cotton.[60] Their gloss over the likelihood that Jacob Sr. and family had committed resources to cotton farming may have been informed by their own personal investment in the story they were telling. The authors are twentieth-century white male descendants of immigrant, Heinrich Sistrunk, and the history they convey of their ancestors rests in the all too familiar paradigm that sums up America's greatness as the outcome of white male industriousness and independence. Their account of Jacob Sr. and his sons overlooks the matter of the eleven enslaved people in the collective family—ten enslaved by Jacob Sr., one enslaved by Jacob Jr., specifically Francis —and the cotton boom that had set off in Georgia and other Deep South states by the 1830s. During the Depression, cotton prices fell and "in the South [where] all loans made by a local bank would depend ultimately on the value of a single crop" lower-than-anticipated sale prices would result in runs on the bank for those wanting to liquidate.[61] For those smaller farmers like Jacob Sr. and sons, lower prices on a cash crop such as cotton could mean severe financial loss. Again, if Jacob had owned outright the ten enslaved people in his possession, it would have been unlikely that all would have to be sold to settle his estate. In the 1841 appraisal for Jacob Sr.'s estate, the total assessment value of his personal property was less than $400, and the estate sale ledger showed a total sale amount of $336.[62] When all was settled out in 1848, the heirs were awarded $87.75 each.[63]

With his father's death, Jacob Jr.'s subsequent migrations in Georgia and Mississippi would dictate the movements of Francis and her children through the end of the Civil War. Jacob Jr.'s search for that American gold mine would be elusive, and he would be reminded of his relatively common financial status by some of his more fortunate cousins who would find prosperity as slaveholding planters. Consider for example, Jacob's cousin Samuel Oliver, an Alabama planter and physician who appears in the Georgia slave importation registers in 1831, crossing into Georgia from South Carolina with twenty-two enslaved persons.[64] Samuel entered and registered these enslaved persons in Elbert County, GA, and would likely have passed through the counties in which his Sistrunk cousins resided. Maps of federal routes during this period show that Samuel, who was headed to his home in Montgomery, AL, would have traveled on these roads as he journeyed home. Samuel had Sistrunk cousins in Lincoln, Marion, and Houston Counties: all destinations along his route. He appears on the record as well years earlier crossing over state lines with an enslaved woman, Lucy. [65] Samuel Oliver was clearly familiar with these roads and was not a one-time transporter of enslaved people across state lines. Jacob Jr. would have been aware of his cousin's wealth, and it certainly would have served as inspiration for his own aspirations. Similarly, Jacob Jr.'s cousin Samuel H. J. Sistrunk, migrated to Houston County, GA, married into a wealthy family whose fortunes would lead to his local prominence and wealth as a planter with more than sixty enslaved people.[66] One of his twentieth-century descendants would become a US senator and be recognized as one of the state's favored sons.[67] Jacob never realized the wealth and acclaim of his cousins Samuel Oliver and Samuel H. J. Sistrunk. In his social disposition as landless, his financial worth would hinge upon the financial valuation of the enslaved girl Francis, as she became an adult and mother of six. Without Francis and her children, who constituted the foundation of his comfortable financial standing years later in 1860, Jacob Jr. would likely have been among the "substantial landless white population in Mississippi," the great percentage of whom had migrated in search of improving their economic conditions.[68]

In 1841 Francis entered a period where she was the lone enslaved person under Jacob Jr.'s rule. Her time in the house where Jacob and his family resided may have significantly increased: If she had been allowed to sleep in the slave quarters on Jacob Sr.'s property, a number of factors would have made it more to Jacob Jr.'s liking to have her nearer to his family residence. With no children and her childhood community dissolved, the young Francis may have been tempted to escape, especially given that her community had been severed. Without his father's enslaved laborers to help on his farm, Jacob Jr. and his family would expect Francis to take on more work and to be nearby. Perhaps this was the period that Jacob became more alert to the potential benefit that Francis could bring to his future financial fortunes. As a young, enslaved girl with no immediate community, Francis would have become more susceptible to sexual advances by Jacob Jr. or any number of white males in his circle. In less than two years after the December 1841 sale of Jacob Sr.'s estate possessions, Francis became pregnant, giving birth to a son, John, in 1844.

Whether John was fathered by a white man is not made clear in extant written records that I have found. I have heard repeated stories passed down from Shadrick Cistrunk's descendants who maintain that there were Cistrunk ancestors fathered by white men and that this difference in paternal origins was at one point a source of family division. Some maintain that in the early twentieth century, a rift in the Cistrunk family occurred, and it stemmed from colorism within the family. The names of the persons involved in the family conflict did not get passed down, so I have never heard specific names connected to either side of the light-dark divide. A look at census records, however, specifically the 1920 Census, shows that some family members were identified as mulatto and others as Black. John and Shadrick had died a decade earlier, but Hillman and Lucretia were alive at the time of the Census enumeration. Shown still residing in Noxubee County, Lucretia and her granddaughter Bertha are identified as mulatto. Hillman, who appeared on the Hinds County Census, was identified as Black. Still residing in Noxubee, John's grandson Elisha was identified as mulatto. It was Elisha who would remain in Noxubee County to raise the next generation of Francis's lineage and whose descendants can be found in Noxubee today. Elisha's dark-skinned cousin Noah, the lone son of Shadrick and Susan, left the county sometime between 1910 and 1917. Although no photographs of Noah appear to have survived in the family, Bunnie Cistrunk described Noah as dark-skinned: He explained that if I remembered the image of Carl (my grandfather, Noah's firstborn) then I had seen a replica of Noah. I saw my grandfather a few times in my life, and his complexion was a dark hue like that of his brothers and, according to Bunnie, like their father, Noah. Noah's 1918 military draft registration indicates that he was living in Winston County as early as 1917, thus suggesting that the split had occurred by this time. The matter of Elisha's brother, Dossie, complicates the story. Dossie appears on the Census that year in Winston County and is identified as Black. While he and Elisha were brothers, he may not have been as fair-skinned as Elisha. In addition to the potential impact of colorism in the family conflict, Dossie would end up in a land dispute with his aunt, Lucretia, and this appears as well to have informed his move from Noxubee County. While no Cistrunks today know the details beyond the general assertion that colorism influenced the divide that ensued, this early twentieth-century split of the families signals that while Shadrick's paternal line was Black, the paternal line of his brother John may have been white.

As with John, whether Hillman had been fathered by a white man is not clear. Reporting his birth year as 1846 in later census reports, Hillman, like John, may have been born in Marion County. How long Jacob Jr. had resided in Harris County before he appears on record in 1848 is, again, not certain. When Jacob Sr. moved his family from Lincoln County to Marion in 1826, Jacob Jr, age 15, was the oldest and was a minor. In 1830, the three sons still appear on the Census in their father's household. Jacob Jr. married in 1833, so it would have been after that date that he established his family household independently of his father's home.[69] Although the 1840 Census shows them as heads of their own households, the fact that Jacob Jr. lived adjacent to his father suggests that he probably settled his family onto his father's land without a formal transfer of property in his name.[70] With the loss of land and enslaved people and the sale of Jacob Sr.'s personal property in December 1841, the brothers may have had to promptly vacate the property and begin life with the assets they possessed at that moment.

Not knowing the year Jacob Jr. moved after the death of his father leaves it difficult to determine whether John and Hillman were born in Marion or Harris County. However, it is the paternal lineage of Francis's third child, Shadrick, that significantly anchors the story of the family's location in Harris County, GA. Shadrick's racial paternity and his paternal family line were confirmed through the expanded narrative that can emerge from sampling DNA and ancestral accounts available through online ancestry databases. Drawing from two DNA tests (conducted through 23andMe and African Ancestry Inc.) taken by a second-generation male descendant of Shadrick, I was able to determine that Shadrick was not fathered by a white man. Shadrick would have passed down to his sons and direct male descendants the Y-chromosome haplogroup that he inherited from his father. DNA results show that Haplogroup pointing to West Africa, specifically the Yoruba in present-day Nigeria.[71] Through additional sampling of DNA matches and ancestry trees from Ancestry.com and FamilySearch.org, the story of Francis and family in Georgia took on new dimensions. In particular, as these resources helped affirm that Shadrick's father was Black, this fact revealed that as an enslaved woman and mother, Francis dared to find ways to assert her autonomy.[72] A combination of census records, showing Jacob Sistrunk residing adjacent to the wealthy planter James Dowdell in Harris County, GA, and slave importation records, showing that an enslaved boy named Shadrack was brought into Georgia in 1821 by Dowdell, make the case that this was Shadrick Cistrunk's father, or that Shadrick Dowdell was a biological relation of Shadrick Cistrunk.[73] An additional DNA match between present-day Cistrunk and Dowdell descendants whose lineage point to 1850s Harris County further make the case for Shadrick Cistrunk's lineage to Shadrick Dowdell.[74]

In June 1821, James Dowdell signed an affidavit signaling that he was introducing "Twelve negroes Slaves," into the state of Georgia, in the county of Jasper.[75] He lists "Shadrach about Seventeen years old" among the group of twelve that excluding the children, he identifies as field hands.[76] A Virginia native, Dowdell had by this time been living in Georgia since at least 1820, the year he is recorded in the Census for Putnam County.[77] Dowdell eventually settled into the western boundary of Georgia, bordering Alabama counties of Lee and Chambers, where he owned thousands of acres, in addition to the thousands he owned in Harris County, GA. He is recorded on the 1850 Harris County Non-Population Schedule for Agriculture, where he is listed six entries below Jacob Sistrunk Jr.[78] The $14,000 cash value of his farm and the $3,000 for fellow plantation elite, S. J. Whatley, are a striking contrast to Jacob's valuation of $250—a difference that exemplifies the magnitude of wealth distance between Jacob and these nearby wealthy residents. Jacob may have in fact been the manager of the farm where he resided. On the Non-Population Schedule, the entry line for owner specifies that an agent or manager can be entered in lieu of owner. That Jacob was probably serving in this alternate capacity is echoed in the 1850 Census of Free Inhabitants in Harris County, in the area recorded as Dowdells District.[79] In this Census Jacob and three other adult men are listed below Whatley who is reported to have $3,500 in real estate. That the three men are listed directly below Whatley with no reported value in real estate suggests that they were in some type of work arrangement with the landowner, Whatley. On the 1850 Slave Schedule, Jacob is shown again sandwiched between Whatley and Dowdell, whose list of enslaved adults contrasts that of Jacob who has possession of one adult enslaved person—Francis.[80] This contrast is not insignificant: Jacob may claim ownership of four enslaved persons, but he does not have the land or the labor force to muster a high level of farm production. Francis and family represent future wealth for Jacob: Their value for him will increase as the children grow.

In his position in Harris County, Jacob was little more than a farm laborer, sandwiched between men who had great wealth and wielded significant influence in and around Harris County. Summarizing the 1850 Agricultural

	NAMES OF SLAVE OWNERS	Number of Slaves	DESCRIPTION — Age	Sex	Colour	Fugitives from the State	Number manumitted	Deaf & dumb, blind, insane, or idiotic			NAMES OF SLAVE OWNERS	Number of Slaves	DESCRIPTION — Age	Sex	Colour	Fugitives from the State	Number manumitted	Deaf & dumb, blind, insane, or idiotic
	1	2	3	4	5	6	7	8			1	2	3	4	5	6	7	8
1	Joseph Fitzpatrick	1	13	M	B				1	1	Hillery Whitehead	1	55	F	B			
2		1	30	M	M				2	2		1	20	F	B			
3		1	22	M	B				3	3		1	17	F	B			
4		1	20	M	B				4	4		1	14	F	B			
5		1	18	M	B				5	5		1	6	F	B			
6		1	16	M	B				6	6		1	3	F	B			
7		1	16	M	M				7	7		1	3	F	B			
8		1	10	M	B				8	8		1	1	F	B			
9		1	55	F	B				9	9		1	3	F	B			
10		1	35	F	B				10	10		1	4	F	B			
11		1	13	F	B				11	11		1	1	M	B			
12		1	13	F	B				12	12	William Haughton	1	15	M	B			
13		1	13	F	B				13	13		1	13	F	B			
14		1	13	F	B				14	14		1	20	M	B			
15		1	11	F	B				15	15		1	10	F	B			
16		1	9	F	B				16	16		1	10	F	B			
17		1	4	M	B				17	17		1	8	M	B			
18		1	2	F	B				18	18		1	6	F	B			
19	O. B. Black	1	45	M	B				19	19		1	5	F	B			
20		1	45	M	B				20	20		1	3	F	B			
21		1	24	M	B				21	21	J. M. Fuchar	1	30	M	B			
22		1	23	M	B				22	22	B. G. Whaley	1	20	M	B			
23		1	45	F	B				23	23		1	13	M	B			
24		1	23	F	B				24	24		1	10	M	B			
25		1	21	F	B				25	25		1	6	M	B			
26		1	10	F	B				26	26		1	35	F	B			
27		1	10	F	B				27	27		1	14	F	B			
28		1	16	F	B				28	28		1	11	F	B			
29		1	16	F	B				29	29		1	2	F	B			
30		1	12	M	B				30	30		1	1	F	B			
31		1	4	M	B				31	31	Jacob Intrech	1	13	F	B			
32		1	4	M	B				32	32		1	8	M	B			
33		1	3	M	B				33	33		1	8	M	B			
34		1	7	F	B				34	34		1	1	M	B			
35		1	2	F	B				35	35	Hepsen Milner	1	1	F	B			
36		1	1	M	B				36	36	James Powell	1	50	M	B			
37	Hillery Whitehead	1	40	M	B				37	37		1	45	M	B			
38		1	1	F	B				38	38		1	45	M	B			
39		1	6	M	B				39	39		1	45	M	B			
40		1	12	M	B				40	40		1	40	M	B			
41		1	3	M	B				41	41		1	30	M	M			
42		1	2	M	B				42	42		1	23	M	B			

1850 Slave Schedule, Harris County, GA. Jacob listed with four unnamed enslaved people (Francis, John, Hillman, and Shadrick). Source: www.family search.org.

Census record of Jacob and his brother, Samuel (living in Macon County), *The Sistrunk Families* authors represented the brothers as commonplace, that is white, farmers of the mid-nineteenth century, whose livelihood had no direct ties to the slaving economy of the South. They summarize the brothers' farming ventures as follows, "It seems clear that both Jacob Sistrunk II and Samuel were growing corn and sweet potatoes as their major crops. The corn and potatoes were then used to feed to hogs which were their cash source. They reported no cotton so they apparently were not in that business."[81] The conclusion that Jacob and his brother were not in "that" business suggests that if they were not growing cotton, they were not involved in the business of slavery. However, by 1850, Francis had given birth to three children—sons—who, along with Francis, were recorded on the slave schedule as Jacob Jr.'s property. He is shown as an enslaver of four unnamed (as was the custom on slave schedules) slaves with the following reported ages: 23-year-old female (Francis); 6-year-old male (John); 4-year-old male (Hillman); and 1-year-old male (Shadrick).[82] Jacob was clearly not wealthy; however, with his inventory of four enslaved people, he had surpassed his first-generation immigrant ancestor, Heinrich, who upon his death was shown to be in the possession of a slave girl and infant.

It is unlikely that Francis was unaware of Jacob's lower status among the more financially endowed white planters in the area. It is also unlikely that enslaved persons on neighboring farms and plantations were not clear on the local planter hierarchy, and any who knew Jacob would have understood that he was not a power player. On the contrary, the influence of James Dowdell and his thousands of acres in the northeastern area of Harris County, along with the holdings of his brother Lewis Jefferson Dowdell in the same area, are exemplified in the naming of "Dowdell's Knob," the highest geographical point of the Pine Mountain area where their Harris County plantations were located. Similarly, the tributary that ran through James Dowdell and Seaborn Whatley's properties was called Dowdell's Creek. These landmarks still bear the Dowdell name today, along with a road that runs through Dowdell's nineteenth-century lots.[83] Nineteenth-century Whatley family members—including Seaborn Whatley—were buried on Seaborn's 1850 Harris County lot where Jacob lived and held Francis and children. These graves are still prominently marked in the now overgrown Whatley cemetery section of the property. Jacob was a pauper in comparison to men like the Dowdells and Whatleys who hired landless and poor white farmers to help manage and farm their large plantations. Living on and farming land owned by Whatley and in proximity to Dowdell's estates, Jacob must have felt overwhelmingly outclassed.

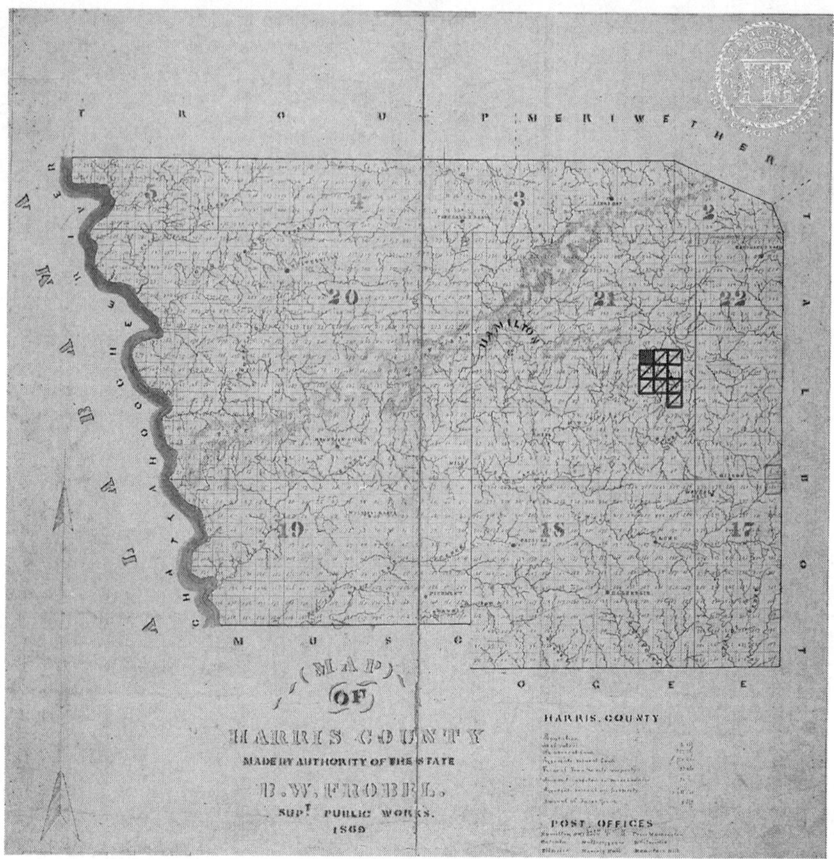

Map of Harris County, GA. Courtesy, Georgia Archives, County Map File, cmf0177.

With the larger population of enslaved on Whatley and Dowdell's plantations alone, Francis, now an adult, would have found opportunities to create a larger community and kinship circle. Enslaved people developed and sustained families and communities across plantations. If they could travel "from one farm to the next on a regular basis and within a reasonable amount of time, they could and did re-create a distinctive culture," and this included formations of kinship and family networks.[84] In this world of plantation powerbrokers where Jacob Sistrunk was in pursuit of greater financial fortunes, Francis Sistrunk and Shadrack Dowdell encountered one another, and at least one child, Shadrick, was a product of the relationship that developed between them. James Dowdell held two enslaved men named Shadrack during the period that Francis lived in Harris County. They, along with their wives and offspring, are named in Dowdell's 1855 will as part of the possessions he conveys to his daughters.[85] Dowdell bestowed to his daughter Susan land in Chambers County, AL, and among the enslaved for her inheritance were "Shadrack and his wife Mirah and their Cherry."[86] This Shadrack (hereafter noted as Shadrack I) and family would be removed to the plantation bequeathed to Susan in Chambers County and enveloped into the estate of Susan and Andrew Lipscomb after they married. To his daughter Louisa, Dowdell granted co-ownership of 2,500 acres in Harris County and shared use of his plantation in Macon County, AL. He also granted Louisa for her sole ownership twenty-two enslaved persons, among whom were "Shadrack and his wife Lucinda and their children Eliza, Joe, Henry, and Silas."[87] With Louisa's properties located both in Harris County, GA, and Macon County, AL, the enslaved that she owned might readily be moved to either locations depending on her preference or the labor needs at each plantation. The Shadrack (hereafter noted as Shadrack II) who had been willed to Louisa likely worked on both the Alabama and Georgia plantations; however, prior to Dowdell's death and the assignment of Shadrack I to Dowdell's daughter Susan, the elder Shadrick had also likely labored on the plantations in both states.

It is in the 1870 Census that the age of Shadrack II is revealed and also the probable relationship between the two Shadrack Dowdells. That Shadrack II, his wife, Lucinda, and their family appear on the 1870 population census in nearby Sumter County, GA, suggests that they lived on Louisa Dowdell's Harris County plantation after they became her legal property in 1855.[88] It is not clear what prompted the family's move from Harris County to Sumter County, but the move may have been influenced by events of the Civil War or its aftermath. Shadrack II appears to be listed in the Freedmen's Bureau records, Americus, GA, in the 1868 "Register of the Sick and Wounded."[89] Although his age is not revealed in Dowdell's 1855 will, Shadrack II is listed as 45 years old in the 1870 Census. He and Francis were peers in age: He would have been approximately 23 years old and Francis between the ages of 18 and 21 when she gave birth to Shadrick. The 17-year-old Shadrach I, who entered Georgia in 1821, would have been 44 years old in 1848 when Francis gave birth to Shadrick. He would have been more than 20 twenty years her senior, old enough to be her father. That Shadrack I was more than 20 years older than Shadrack II, and that their families were born and held on Dowdell's plantations, suggests that Shadracks I and II were father and son. While either could have fathered Francis's son, as Francis's peer, Shadrack II was more probably father of Francis's son, Shadrick Cistrunk. While I will then refer to Shadrack II as father, and Shadrack I as grandfather of Shadrick Cistrunk, I do so acknowledging that Shadrack I could just as well have been the father. In this case Shadrack II would have been Shadrick Cistrunk's sibling rather than his father.

Shadrick Cistrunk consistently pointed to Alabama as his father's place of birth, and this may lead to the assumption that Shadrack of Chambers County (Shadrack I) was his father. However, if Shadrack II was his father, Shadrick Cistrunk may have identified Alabama as his father's place of birth from memory of his alternating assignments on James Dowdell's Alabama and Georgia plantations. A year or two after Dowdell's death, Jacob Jr. moved his family from Harris County, GA, to Neshoba County, MS, forcing Francis and her family to migrate with them.[90] If Shadrick's father and/or grandfather were laboring on an Alabama Dowdell plantation during this time, Alabama might have been the last point of memory that he would hold of his paternal relations. This move would have effectively ended communication between Francis and the father of her son Shadrick. While their relationship could not be sustained, it reveals a moment in which Francis was able to exercise autonomy, and the decisions she made during that time regarding partnering and naming of her third son, Shadrick, would prove key to the survival of her legacy. To understand the self-empowerment exercised by Francis at this moment it is useful to reflect on the well-known autobiographical narrative of Harriet Jacobs. Jacobs tells the story of her emergence into young adulthood when her enslaver began to make sexual advances toward her. Jacobs explains that she knew that her fate would be sexual violation by her enslaver or some other white man, so she chose to thwart this power of her enslaver, Flint, by choosing a white man of power equal to Flint.[91] It was this man with whom Jacobs would establish a relationship and give birth to two children. Francis appears to invoke a similar act of self-authority for a period in Harris County. While her son John may have been fathered by Jacob Sistrunk or another white male through sexual relation without her consent, Francis may have, like Harriet Jacobs, seized a moment to declare her power over her own body.

In contrast to Harriet Jacobs whose defiance was enacted through her selection of a white man, Francis declared her autonomy by forging a relationship with an enslaved Black man. Although the relationship was not long lived, if Francis consented, it was a rare moment in which she was able to exercise authority over one of the most important expressions of one's human connectedness. That Shadrack II was probably married to Lucinda at the time of his relationship with Francis further speaks to her boldness.[92] Her pregnancy and birth to a darker-skinned son would have also made it clear to Jacob Jr., her enslaver, that when exercising her will, she placed greater value on those from the community into which she was born. The birth of this child also would have signaled to Jacob Jr. that neither Francis nor the enslaved on neighboring plantations held a particular respect for his power or authority over her. If Jacob Jr. had exerted full authority to determine whether Francis could enter into a partnering or sexual relationship with an enslaved person on another plantation, Shadrack II and Francis may have been deterred. It appears that they were not. It further reveals that at least once during her time as enslaved, Francis demonstrated an open defiance to Jacob Jr.'s presumed authority over her body and will.

The lasting imprint of Francis's connection with Shadrack II is in the name of their son. By naming her son Shadrick, Francis created a family and kinship line for her son and for future generations, and ironically for her story. She could not imagine that her story and that of her son would be recorded in writing, but she could and did rely on the tradition of naming to memorialize their legacy for their posterity. Francis and Shadrack II lived on separate plantations in a world where enslavers at any moment could and often did exercise their power to separate Black families and communities. Enslaved people often conferred names to children to help them maintain knowledge of their family connections and origins, especially considering the probability that they may be separated. The naming of Shadrick Cistrunk was akin to the African American practice of burying the newborn's umbilical cord in the aftermath of birth. In her novel, *Jonah's Gourdvine,* Zora Neale Hurston captures this cultural practice in the episode describing the birth of the story's hero, John. In the immediate aftermath of John's birth, his grandmother, Pheemy, buries his umbilical cord in a tree in their front yard: In this act she hopes to secure John's anchor to home and his knowledge of his origins. When John returns years later, she references his "nable string" buried under the chinaberry tree in her yard as affirmation that he is her grandson.[93] Hurston reveals in this fiction the awareness and commitment of African Americans, during and beyond enslavement, to tie their children to home and to their familial lineage. Naming her son Shadrick, Francis reflects this ethos and suggests that she may have acted similarly in naming one or more of her other children.

While the sheer matter of proximity suggests that Jacob likely fathered one or more of her children, Francis did not bestow the name Jacob on any of her sons. An obvious deterrent would have been the wrath of Jacob's wife that Francis would have invited by such an act. Although wives of enslavers were familiar with the sexual license they took with those they held in bondage, these women regularly inflicted harsh treatment upon the enslaved women who their husbands sexually abused. As an alternative to naming a son Jacob if he had been fathered by Jacob, Francis might have adopted names from Jacob's family line. Hillman, Willis, and Robert do not appear to be names that link to Jacob Jr.'s immediate parental line; however, a sampling from Jacob's life in the post–Civil War era raises the possibility that Francis may have been familiar with a relative of Jacob whose name was John. According to *The Sistrunk Families,* Jacob's information on the 1870 Census was incorrect to such an extreme that one could only surmise that "someone else gave the census taker the grossly wrong information or, else, Jacob deliberately gave false information for whatever reasons he may have had for doing so."[94] What is clear about Jacob's appearance on the 1870 Census for Noxubee County is that he borrowed the name of his uncle, John Sistrunk, and his aunt, Elizabeth Sistrunk, who were his neighbors during the first decades of Jacob Jr.'s life, when the family had moved to Lincoln County, Georgia from South Carolina.[95] Jacob Jr.'s attempt to conceal his real identity from the government would distance him from military records that showed his less-than-honorable service. Civil War records show that Jacob Jr. was absent from duty much of the time, that he signed an allegiance to the US government while a prisoner of war, and that he then reenlisted in the Confederate army after swearing that he would not take up arms again against the Union.[96] Fearing that the government may punish Confederates like himself who reneged on their oaths, Jacob Jr. assumed the name of his uncle, John Sistrunk, and assigned the name, Elizabeth (John's wife's name) to his own wife, Martha. This story reveals that among names of his close relatives, John was foremost in Jacob Jr.'s mind. John and Jacob Sistrunk Sr. were close during their early settlement period in Lincoln County. John may have visited his brother and family during their years in Marion County, and Francis would have been familiar with the name and Jacob Jr.'s connection to it. If Jacob Jr. was the biological father of Francis's son John, her choice in naming him may have been to signal her son's biological lineage to Jacob Jr.

The argument for the deliberateness of naming her son John is perhaps not as compelling a case as Shadrick's naming; however, that the two names link to probable paternal lines, speaks to Francis's determination to control aspects of her family life and history when and where she could. Again, it is not unlikely that Francis assumed this cultural protocol in naming all her children, but the archives have not yet led me to as clear a trail as in the case of Shadrick. With this indeterminacy around the names of her other children, Francis's purposefulness in naming Shadrick proved an especially impactful mechanism for placing herself in the memories of her descendants. Francis was rediscoverable in the twenty-first centurybecause she left defining markers. Reading these markers is a reminder that just as we must read the codes embedded in early Black writings, we must as well read those embedded in the everyday lived experiences that are unwritten. With the relative uncommonness of the name Shadrick, and Shadrick Cistrunk's consistent reference to his father's place of birth as Alabama, Francis planted traces that were seemingly small, but generations later would prove central to resurrecting her story from near erasure. We see and hear Francis today because despite the trauma of enslavement, she understood that there were ways, no matter how small, to preserve and narrate one's identity and existence. Her children and their descendants would themselves maintain key practices and ideals that were markers pointing back to the ancestral trail that Francis paved. Thus, they would become living archives of her life.

MATRICES OF PATERNAL POSSIBILITIES

On Census Schedules for the year 1850, James Dowdell was enumerated on slave schedules and Non-Population Schedules for Agriculture in both Alabama and Georgia. He is listed in Chambers County for the Population Census of Free Inhabitants, suggesting that he had established his primary residence in Alabama.[97] This perhaps explains Shadrick Cistrunk's consistent designation of his father's birthplace as Alabama. If one or both Shadracks and their minor children were resettled to Dowdell's Alabama estate by 1850, this would have been Shadrick's earliest memories of familial connections to the state. Shadrack Dowdell seems to have fathered only one of Francis's children. Given the closeness of age (about one year) between Hillman and Shadrick however, the possibility that Hillman may have been fathered by Shadrack Dowdell remains one to be answered. With no physical description of Hillman and no DNA or other ancestry links that connect him to a paternal line, there is no means to determine whether his father was Black or white.

Before the migration to Mississippi, Francis would give birth to two more children, Willis and Lucretia. As with the case of John and perhaps Hillman, Jacob Jr. stands out as the probable paternal progenitor of Francis's two youngest children. It is Willis's name that calls for revisiting the possibility that it may have been someone other than Jacob. The connection of Willis to a likelier paternal line becomes clearer with a return to the 1841 estate sale of Jacob Sistrunk Sr. in Marion County. Beginning here and tracing the long association of Jacob Sr. with the Whatleys, it appears that Francis and her children were also tied to the Whatleys. This is signaled not only in two of her children's names, but in Francis's name as well. The appearance of Whatleys at the estate sale and Jacob Jr.'s later residence on S. J. Whatley's plantation in 1850 are likely more than coincidence. In 1840, Daniel Whatley Jr., his wife, and five minor children are recorded directly above Jacob Sistrunk on the Marion County Census. They are neighbors.[98] In the following year, Daniel and younger brother Willis Whatley are recorded purchasing a considerable number of items in the estate sale records of Jacob Sr.'s personal properties.[99] In 1850, S. J. Whatley appears directly above Jacob Jr. on the Harris County Slave Schedule, three spaces above Jacob Jr. on the Non-Population Schedule for Agriculture, and two lines above him on the Census of Free Persons.[100] In 1860, Jacob Jr. and Daniel Whatley Jr. appear on the Census for Neshoba County, MS: Perhaps the death of Daniel Sr. in 1857 prompted the decision of his son to seek his fortunes westward, and it appears that he and Jacob may have migrated to Neshoba together or within a short period of one another. They are not bordering neighbors, but they both reside within Township 11.[101]

Daniel Jr. and his brother Willis bought a considerable number of items at Jacob Sr.'s estate sale, with the younger brother making the greater number of purchases.[102] Approximately 25 years old and probably not long from under his father's roof, Willis's purchase of livestock and farm tools would help build his inventory and his farming capacity. It likely took some wind out of the sails of 29-year-old Jacob to see assets that represented his father's lifetime of work and aspirations being bought by someone just starting to make his way in the world. In his move to neighboring Harris County Jacob Jr.'s fate would be tied again to a Whatley. He would spend several years here living on property owned by Seaborn J. Whatley, a second-half cousin of Jacob's Marion County neighbor Daniel Whatley Jr. They were descendants of Shirley Whatley (1685–1783), a Virginian who migrated into North Carolina and whose children would migrate into the northeastern counties of Georgia in the latter decades of the eighteenth century.[103] Daniel Whatley Sr. descended from the line of Shirley and his second wife, and Seaborn from the line of Shirley and his first wife. Settling into Georgia after the slavery ban was lifted in 1751, these early generations of Whatleys quickly acquired land in a westward movement across the state.

Daniel Whatley Sr. was born in 1744 in Virginia but by the last decade of the eighteenth century he, along with his father, Michael Sr. and siblings, John and Michael Jr., appear on records in Greene County, GA.[104] By 1840 Daniel Whatley Sr. and his sons had settled into the cluster territory that would become Marion, Macon, Houston, and Taylor Counties, while Seaborn settled in Harris County.[105] In 1830 the Census shows Daniel Whatley Sr. as head of his Houston County household with three sons (probably the three younger sons: John, Daniel Jr., and Willis) and two enslaved females: one in age group 10–24; the other in age group 24–36. Ten years later in the 1840 Census at eighty-plus years, Daniel Sr. is the only white male listed in his household (now listed as Macon County). Additionally listed in the household are a white female, 60-plus years of age, and three enslaved people (noted in categories of sex and age as "male, 55–99; females 24–35, and 55–99"). At this time Daniel Whatley Sr.'s four sons—William, John, Daniel Jr., and Willis are listed as heads of their own households in Macon County (which in 1837 was created by combining sections from Houston and Marion County).

As revealed in the will of his father, Michael Whatley Sr., Daniel Sr. came from a slaveholding household. Michael Sr. awarded six enslaved people to his wife and some to his other children.[106] Neither Daniel Sr. nor his brother John Whatley were among the heirs who inherited human property from

Michael Sr., but a transaction between the two brothers a year before their father filed his will reveals that they are active participants in the market of enslavement. In a deed recorded in 1799 Daniel Sr. is shown purchasing from John a "negro fellow named Jo for the sum of six thousand weight of tobacco."[107] Jo could be the unnamed enslaved male listed in Daniel Sr.'s household on the 1840 Census, though he is curiously not recorded in the household on the 1830 Census. No female enslaved child is listed in Daniel Sr.'s household on the 1830 Census, but either of the two enslaved females listed between ages 10–24 and 24–36 could have given birth to Francis in 1827—the birth year consistent with the age reported for her in the 1850 and 1860 Slave Schedules. Jo and Francis's absence on the 1830 Census may have been an oversight of the enumerator and may as well have been Daniel Sr.'s deliberate exclusion. Daniel may have purposefully undercounted the number of enslaved people he held. Although the Census is not used for calculation of taxes, he may not have been clear on this. Daniel Sr. was not above engaging in illegal or unscrupulous behavior, which is evidenced in the 1829 Houston County Superior Court case of Michael Whatley Jr. v. Daniel Whatley Sr. In this case the injured brother sought to recover damages "for certain improper conduct alleged to have been had by the said Daniel Whatley with the wife of said Michael Whatley—and for abduction and harboring her the wife of said Michael Whatley and for criminal conversation with her."[108] Michael settled and withdrew the case for payment of $5.00 from his brother. It is both remarkable that Daniel Sr. would abduct and engage in adultery (if not rape) with his brother's wife and that they settled the matter with a payment of $5.00 from Daniel Sr. The significance of this incident in connection to Francis is that it reveals the savage standards out of which Daniel Sr., his family, and the court operated. If these parties considered $5.00 an acceptable resolution to this matter, then clearly enslaved girls and women were subject to unimaginable treatment at the whims of their enslavers.

From 1840 to the time Jacob Jr. migrated to Harris County, the four Whatley sons and their father lived in close proximity to Jacob Jr. Before his departure from Marion County, Jacob Jr. may have even lived on the land of Daniel Jr., his neighbor. Jacob Jr. may have purchased Francis from Daniel Sr. or from Seaborn J. Whatley, on whose land he appears to be living during his time in Harris County. Jacob Jr. probably landed on Seaborn's property through an introduction or recommendation of his Whatley neighbors in Marion County, and he may have as well been introduced through a business relationship between his father and Seaborn. It is perhaps not coincidental that Seaborn's count of enslaved persons increased from five to twenty-six between the 1840 and 1860 Censuses.[109] If Jacob Sr. was indebted to Seaborn at the time of his death in 1841, the ten enslaved persons on Jacob Sr.'s plantation in 1840 may have been remanded to Seaborn to reconcile that. Even if Seaborn sold some of the enslaved people returned to his possession, it is conceivable that his increased holdings from fifteen to twenty-six enslaved people in that 20-year span resulted from some of those additional ten and their increases from childbirths. If this were the case, Francis would not have been separated from the community that she had known in Marion County. While the circumstances that dictated the more than two decades connection between Jacob and the Whatleys cannot be determined with certainty, the significance is that the timeline confirms that Francis would have encountered the Whatleys during this period. This then calls for closer examination of Willis Whatley and the lineage of Daniel Whatley Sr. for a connection to Francis's choice to name her fourth son Willis.

Willis Sistrunk (who does not appear to change the spelling of his surname as his four siblings did) was born in 1852, four to five years after the birth of Shadrick.[110] While records do not indicate whether he is mixed-race, the extended time between the births of Willis and Shadrick suggest that Francis's relationship with Shadrack Dowdell had waned if not ended and that he did not father Willis. This may have occurred for any number of reasons: the logistics of sustaining a relationship if Shadrack was moved frequently between plantations, the possibility that Jacob intervened and placed obstacles to their relationship, the likelihood that Shadrack's marriage was his primary familial obligation, and the simple possibility that one or both may have decided to end the relationship. Three years following Willis's birth, Francis's only daughter, Lucretia, was born. When she appears on the slave schedule in Mississippi five years later, her designation as mulatto makes clear that she was fathered by a white male in her birthplace, Harris County, GA.[111] That Lucretia consistently shows her father's place of birth as Georgia also suggests that she had knowledge that the man who fathered her lived at some time in Georgia. Whether she and Willis were fathered by the same man is unknown. I have had conversation with one descendant of Lucretia who assumes that Jacob Jr. was Lucretia's father, but her assumption is derived from the simple case that Jacob Jr. was the enslaver and that historically the case of enslavers raping and forcing Black women into ongoing sexual relations was not uncommon. This alone is not sufficient evidence to conclusively assert that Jacob Jr. is father of Lucretia or Francis's other mixed-race children.

Returning to Daniel Whatley Sr. and an inventory of his children's names, particularly three that appear in Francis's family and in multiple generations of Shirley Whatley's lineages, a stronger case emerges that one or more Whatleys fathered one or more of Francis's children. John and Willis are names shared by Daniel Sr.'s sons as well as Francis's sons. While John is a name common throughout lineages of Heinrich Süsstrunk descendants, Willis is not, particularly not in Jacob Sistrunk's lines. A more striking case is made in the matter of the name Francis in the Whatley family. Among Daniel Sr.'s siblings were brothers named Willis and John and a sister named Frankey (Frances). Daniel Sr. would also name his one daughter Frances.[112] The matter of the shared names and the proximity of Whatleys to Francis make a compelling case, but one other record further supports this hypothesis. In a nonexhaustive search through my own ancestry DNA matches, I found matches to three descendants of late eighteenth-century Whatleys, two pointing directly to Greene County, GA, and one to Augusta, GA.[113] That I am a descendant of Francis with a DNA connection to Whatleys of the late eighteenth century in northeastern Georgia raises the probability that Francis and her sons John and Willis were biologically related to the Whatleys. John, Willis, and Shadrick were siblings through their maternal line, that is, Francis. Shadrick would not have had a biological connection to the Whatleys through a paternal line, as he was fathered by Shadrick Dowdell. Therefore, as a descendant of Shadrick, any DNA connection I might have to the Whatley line would come through Francis, Shadrick's mother. It is unlikely then that Francis is any of the young, enslaved girls reported in Watson's *Slave Importation Affidavit Registers for Nine Georgia Counties, 1818–1847*.

While the young Francis brought into the state by Dozier Thornton seemed to me for some time to be the Francis I was in search of, the stronger evidence points to a Whatley male as Francis Sistrunk's biological father. Her mother was probably enslaved by a Whatley, and while Daniel Sr. was in his mid-60s in 1827, he could have fathered a child at this age. Either of the two enslaved women recorded in Daniel Sr.'s household with his three sons in 1830 would have been at the age of conception in 1827. What the 1829 court case between Michael Jr. and Daniel Sr. demonstrates is that neither age nor honor would have restrained Daniel Sr. from forcing a woman, particularly an enslaved woman, to engage in a sexual act with him. Ironically, his older sons William, John, and Daniel Jr. who would have been in their teens to early twenties in 1827, could have as well been the biological father of Francis. Fourteen years later in 1844 when Francis named her first son John and then later in 1852 when she named her fourth Willis, she may have been recording their paternal connection to the Whatley line. It could also mean that Francis was raped by and conceived children from one or more Whatleys to whom she was biologically related. It is chilling to consider how often the individual histories of enslaved Black women were enveloped in experiences of sexual violation that they endured as children and later as mothers. It is hard to think that this level of horror could be surpassed; however, the intergenerational sexual violence that Francis likely experienced is a reminder that the horrors of enslavement ran deep. Francis was likely born to a mother who had conceived under similar circumstances. Despite these abuses, enslaved women like Francis signaled to their children that they had a history and a lineage. Naming was one way of asserting their link to a knowable past. While they bore the imprint of the inhumanity inflicted upon them, they found ways to mark their presence and their stories. Francis named her sons to mark the trail for any who would come later and want to know their story.

Sometime after Lucretia's birth, Francis and family would be forced to migrate to Mississippi with their enslaver, Jacob Jr. who was following a wave of Heinrich Süsstrunk's descendants, who since the early 1800s, had moved into Mississippi and other westward territories.[114] Jacob Jr. and his brother, Samuel, would move in the mid-1850s and begin their farming endeavors in the central eastern county of Neshoba, MS.[115] Francis was between 25–27 years old by the time she and children were forced to make this move. The older sons, John, Hillman, and Shadrick were around ages 12, 10, and 8 respectively. In a matter of five to seven years they would be reaching an age and labor capacity that would increase Jacob Jr.'s financial worth. He could either use them as laborers on his own farm or lease them out as laborers on other farms. Their increased valuation would improve Jacob's ability to borrow money should he need. The two younger children, Willis and Lucretia, no older than 5 years, were still too young to work, but Jacob could speculate that in total Francis and her children would position him for a higher standard of living than he had known in Harris County.

Well aware of the ongoing threat of rupture to her family that could be precipitated by Jacob Jr.'s circumstances, Francis, nevertheless, continued to build a foundation of familial connectedness. It is in Mississippi that these bonds would become more evident. By the time the family was removed from Georgia, the three oldest children—John, Hillman, and Shadrick—had spent their formative years in Harris County. It was there that their ethos, their sense of being, their appreciation of relationships with others in their community were formed, and it was there where they learned the many incarnations of family. Whether they had significant opportunities for interaction with the one or two known Black father figures that have been revealed through the archives—that is, Shadrack II (or Shadrack I)—they left Georgia with a sense of the reality of how enslaved communities built families and kinship groups despite the racist-informed world of slaving that was invested in denying them their fundamental level of humanness. In the midst of the plantations of wealthy enslavers, such as Whatley and Dowdell, and the more common farmers, like Jacob, the multitude of enslaved people who labored in these spaces also built families and communities—this included both co-parented and single (primarily women-led) parent households. Though they may not have been able to articulate the sentiment at their young ages, Francis's children were part of an African American generation that understood the folk proverb, "Everybody's business ain't nobody's business." This adage that I heard often from my mother was a teaching from generations before, and it was a simple warning against the practice of gossip and the imposition of one's values onto others. If enslaved Blacks had internalized white-imposed constructs of the nuclear family, particularly, the assumption that kinship units operating outside this structure are somehow unrecognized or "illegitimate," they perhaps might have suffered the mythical "social death" that some scholars insist represents the condition of the enslaved. While many may continue to float this myth, Black experience, Black culture, and the ethos that has anchored generations continue to defy such reductive readings. Francis illustrates that while the enslaved lived under pressing physical and mental persecution, they nevertheless demonstrated "the remarkable capacity to forge fragile communities, preserve cultural inheritance, and resist the predations of slaveholders."[116] The erasures of Francis in antebellum census and official records and in the twentieth-century narratives of white Sistrunk descendants glaringly contrast the sampling of those same documents through the perspective of the enslaved and their descendants. The difference in interpretation underscores the destructive narratives of African Americans that predominate from an Anglocentric gaze. Women like Francis—single Black mothers—were present throughout the plantation South, and they existed alongside co-parenting households. Woman households were for the most part designs of necessity to respond to ongoing disruptions of families. They were also, however, familiar in their similarity to family and kinship designs that Africans brought with them to the Americas. Francis Sistrunk was the matriarch of her family: She was not a social or moral oddity. She was among generations of enslaved Black women whose purposefulness and wit and love were products of previous generations who tended family under harrowing circumstances, believing that better days would come.

Chapter 2

NESHOBA TO NOXUBEE

Pre-Civil War to Reconstruction

You learn what you need to know as you grow in age.
   Bunnie Cistrunk

The forced move to Neshoba County, MS, around 1855 may have been a more despairing experience for Francis than the decade-earlier displacement from Marion to Harris County, GA. While Francis had been removed from her childhood community in Marion County, in Harris County she encountered a more populated area with an enslaved population double that of Marion.[1] The striking demographic contrast between the majority white and smaller total population in Neshoba could not have gone unnoticed by Francis.

NESHOBA COUNTY

In the year before the start of the Civil War, the 1860 Census recorded a total population of just more than 8,300 for Neshoba County, with a near three-to-one ratio of whites to enslaved inhabitants.[2] In contrast, the total population of Harris County ten years earlier was more than 14,000, with Blacks numbering nearly 8,000. Undoubtedly, Francis was struck by the smaller population, particularly that of the enslaved. What this may have meant for her adjustment is uncertain: Whether a smaller population offered a better or more expedient opportunity to develop friendships is not certain. It is a matter that may depend on any number of variables, especially in the world of slaving. In 1840s and 1850s Mississippi, the state had a "substantial landless white population" and an enslaved labor system where "more slaves worked on larger plantations."[3] Therefore, while Jacob may have been in search of greater fortunes, Mississippi's wealth structure was in large part a mirror of what he had known in Georgia. For Francis, then, it may have meant proximity to larger plantations and thus a still substantially populated and intricate enslaved community network. She would have encountered a community of enslaved women much like those she had known in Georgia as enslaved people across territories faced similar labor and social struggles. As in Georgia, enslaved women in Mississippi also saw their long days of labor concluding with the transition to evenings filled with the fundamental tasks of living. There were still responsibilities of family life that included necessities such as food preparation, tending the sick, sewing and mending, and caring for children. Over time, Francis likely found her way into a circle of women reminiscent of her previous communities. Although a young woman—mid- to late-20s—at the time of the move, Francis was mother of five children, with the youngest still an infant in 1855. By this time, she would have understood clearly, if for no more than practical reasons, the importance of finding community.

The 1860 Census shows 48-year-old Jacob Sistrunk Jr. living in Township 11 Range 13 of Neshoba County, MS.[4] In contrast to the $250 valuation of Jacob Jr.'s assets in 1850 in Harris County, the 1860 Census shows $6,250 for Jacob in the category of personal estate value.[5] As in 1850 Harris County, he still appears to hold no land. Clearly, Jacob Jr.'s ownership claim to Francis and her five children accounted for this remarkable escalation in his estimated financial worth. For more than 20 years he had yoked his aspirations for wealth to Francis and her increase, and in Mississippi it appeared that the dream was unfolding into reality. Worth noting is *The Sistrunk Families*'s gloss over the question of this unexplained growth in Jacob Jr.'s financial worth. There is no consideration that perhaps Jacob Jr.'s wealth rested in his active participation in slaving, that Jacob Jr.'s wealth hinged upon ownership of an enslaved woman and her children. In their detailed genealogical publication on the Swiss German patriarch and his descendants, these Sistrunk descendants and authors summarized the oddity of Jacob's wealth with the following: "No slaves were shown although the value of his personal property was listed as $6250."[6] Similarly, with no consideration that Jacob's notable financial comfort may have rested in a legal claim to enslaved people, twentieth-century descendant Thomas Sistrunk estimates that Jacob's $6,250 asset valuation would be approximately $180,000 in 2018. He then notes with a hint of admiration, "It would appear that Jacob II and family did live quite well in the years prior to the war."[7] While Jacob claimed ownership of Francis and her children, and benefitted financially from this claim, he was not as inclined to claim them on the tax roll that same year. On this record, he claims ownership of only two slaves, thereby reducing his tax obligation.[8] Jacob was clearly in the business of slaving, and as the 1860 Census confirms, within a decade, his ownership claim to Francis, her five children, and unborn child would account for the greater percentage of his estimated financial wealth. The 1860 Slave Schedule shows that he maintained Francis, the older son, John, and the two younger children, Willis and Lucretia, in his possession while he leased out for hire the middle children—sons Hillman and Shadrick. Francis and her family were maturing into the stage where they could render the kind of income that would allow Jacob and his family to "live quite well."[9]

In 1860, when Jacob leases out 14-year-old Hillman and 12-year-old Shad, it is noteworthy that he retains 16-year-old John, the oldest brother, with him. Though Hillman and Shadrick are two years apart in age, the slave schedule shows them both at Hillman's age.[10] Apparently 12-year-old Shadrick was of sufficient size and stature to pass for older, and though still children, he and Hillman were seen by enslavers as fit for adult labor. Perhaps Jacob's choice to lease Shadrick instead of John was driven from a desire to maximize labor and skill for his own farming needs: John was probably a more capable field hand and craftsman than his 12- year-old brother. Jacob likely did the math to determine the option that would net him the most profit. While this seems the more likely motive for Jacob's decision, his choice may as well have been informed by a more deep-seated disregard for Shadrick, Francis's clearly Black offspring. Might this suggest also that Jacob's choice to lease Hillman points to a Black paternal lineage for Hillman as well? Was Hillman fathered by Shadrack Dowdell? These questions are more difficult to answer in the case of Hillman. Unlike Shadrick, Hillman does not appear to have had children. There are no direct male descendants from Hillman, so there is no living DNA source to help answer this question. With no descriptions or extant image of Hillman, the question of his racial paternity will remain unanswered.

The 1860 Slave Schedule identifies Francis's sons as Black, while listing Francis and daughter, Lucretia, as mulatto.[11] Her sons not identified as mulatto cannot be taken as evidence that the male progenitor of John, Hillman, and/or Willis was not white. There was monetary value in identifying enslaved women as mulatto as this distinction marked another avenue of marketability in the world of slave trading. Enslaved women identified as mulatto, quadroon, or octoroon—terms regularly used to suggest degrees of Black ancestry—could command higher prices and special interest beyond field work. The southern plantocracy was rooted in the exploitation of Black labor, but it also became a playing field for white male sexual violence. The female products of that violence—mixed-race enslaved women—were commonly sought by white men who usurped their bodies for labor and sex. The designation of mulatto for an enslaved female was as good as an advertisement for her enslaver.

WARTIME MIGRATIONS: NESHOBA, WINSTON, NOIUBEE

The year 1861 marked the beginning of the Civil War, and in that year Francis would give birth to her last child, Robert. The war would precipitate a period once again where Francis would find herself with infant and children in tow, being forced to migrate and set new roots. Lincoln issued the preliminary

SCHEDULE 2.—Slave Inhabitants in Township 11 Range 13 **in the County of** Noxubee **State of** Mississippi **, enumerated by me, on the** 20 **day of** Sept **, 1860.** C. S. Cockrell **Ass't Marshal.**

NAMES OF SLAVE OWNERS	No. of Slaves	Age	Sex	Color	Fugitives	No. manumitted	Deaf & dumb, blind, insane, or idiotic	No. of Slave houses	NAMES OF SLAVE OWNERS	No. of Slaves	Age	Sex	Color	Fugitives	No. manumitted	Deaf & dumb, blind, insane, or idiotic	No. of Slave houses
James Wilkinson	1	43	m	B				1		1	17	m	B				
Jacob Sistrunk	1	33	f	M						1	2	f	M				
	1	16	m	B						1	1/2	f	M				
	1	7	m	B					David L. Seale	1	37	f	B				
	1	5	f	M						1	11	f	B				
Marion V. Rea	1	12	m	B						1	6	m	B				
Barbry Greer	1	70	m	B						1	3	m	B				
	1	50	f	B					John H. Gray	1	14	m	B				
	1	30	f	B					Sophronia Williamson	1	16	m	B				1
	1	4	f	M					Thomas Gray June 23rd 1860	1	60	f	B				
	1	2	m	B				2		1	50	m	B				
June 21st 1860										1	24	m	B				
Daniel Clements	1	38	f	B						1	23	m	B				
	1	19	m	B						1	31	m	M				
	1	9	m	B						1	20	f	B				
	1	7	f	B						1	18	f	B				
	1	5	f	B						1	9	m	B				
	1	2	m	B						1	6	m	B				
	1	1/52	m	B						1	5	m	B				
H. C. Greer	1	43	f	B						1	5	m	B				
	1	36	m	M						1	4	f	B				
	1	26	m	B						1	2	m	B				
	1	22	f	B						1	1	f	B				
	1	19	f	B						1	1/2	f	B				
	1	11	f	B						1	1/2	f	B				
	1	5	m	B						1	1/13	f	B				3
	1	1	f	B					Badith Clements	1	52	m	B				
	1	1	f	B						1	20	m	B				
	1	4/12	f	B				2		1	13	f	M				2
John E. Seale	1	34	f	B					W. C. Seale	1	30	m	B				
	1	21	m	M						1	16	m	B				
	1	15	m	B						1	13	f	B				
	1	13	m	B					Isaac Whitton gard	1	24	f	B				
	1	11	f	M						1	1/2	m	B				
	1	9	m	M					W. S. Daniel	1	13	f	B				
	1	6	m	B					Agnes Moses	1	43	m	B				
	1	4	m	B					Thomas Samuels	1	46	f	B				
	1	1	f	B				2		1	30	f	B				
Jane Seale	1	52	m	B						1	24	f	B				
Amy E. Seale guardian of Elizabeth L. Seale	1	19	f	B						1	17	f	B				

No. of owners,		No. of male slaves, 132	38	No. fugitives,	No. deaf and dumb,	No. insane,
No. of houses, 65		No. of female slaves, 124	39	No. manumitted,	No. blind,	No. idiotic,
		Total slaves, 342				

1860 Noxubee County Slave Schedule showing unnamed Francis, John, Willis, and Lucretia, with Jacob named as slaveowner. 1860 Census.

SCHEDULE 2.—Slave Inhabitants in *Township 11 Range 12* in the County of *Noxubee* State of *Mississippi*, enumerated by me, on the *18th* day of *June*, 1860. *E S Crockett* Ass't Marshal.

NAMES OF SLAVE OWNERS.	Number of Slaves.	Age.	Sex.	Color.	Fugitives from the State.	Number manumitted.	Deaf & dumb, blind, insane, or idiotic.		NAMES OF SLAVE OWNERS.	Number of Slaves.	Age.	Sex.	Color.	Fugitives from the State.	Number manumitted.	Deaf & dumb, blind, insane, or idiotic.	No. of Slave houses.
1									Township 11th Range 13 June 18th 1860									
	1	9	f	B					Lydia Jones	1	58	m	B				
	1	8	m	B						1	59	f	B				
	1	6	f	B						1	55	f	B				
	1	5	m	B						1	42	f	B				
	1	3	m	B						1	35	m	B				
MyFamily.com	1	3	f	m	1					1	26	m	B				
	1	2	m	B						1	23	m	m	1			
	1	1	m	m	1					1	13	f	B				
	1	1	m	B						1	12	m	m	1			
	1	1/2	m	B			4			1	10	f	B				
E Crockett	1	55	f	B					E Seale for the Estate of	1	18	m	B				
	1	35	f	B					Wm H Seale								
	1	18	f	B					Bartholomew Long	1	30	f	B				
	1	18	m	B						1	13	f	B				
	1	14	m	B						1	8	m	B				
	1	14	f	B						1	6	f	B				
	1	13	m	B						1	3/65	f	B			1	
	1	12	f	B													
	1	12	f	B													
	1	10	m	B						June 13th 1860								
	1	10	m	m	1				Cynetha Jackson	1	38	f	B				
	1	8	f	B						1	38	f	B				
	1	6	f	B						1	30	f	B				
	1	4	f	B						1	15	f	B				
	1	1	m	B						1	1	m	B			1	
	1	1/2	f	m	1		3		Samuel Taylor	1	65	m	B				
E Crockett for Estate	1	38	m	B						1	21	f	B				
of L H Cooper	1	30	f	B						1	12	f	B				
	1	3	f	B						1	10	f	B				
	1	1/2	m	B						1	1	m	B			1	
Lewis Pigg	1	22	f	B					E N C Hayward for	1	14	m	B				
	1	1	f	B					Jacob Sistrunk	1	64	m	B				
Marg F Wilkinson	1	44	f	B					Lewis guardian								
	1	17	m	B					Percilla Barrett for	1	14	m	B				
	1	5	m	B					Jacob Sistrunk								
Ann E Crockett	1	20	f	B													
	1	13	f	B													
E S Lewis	1	25	m	B	1												
J W Ellison	1	4	f	B													
Township 11 Range 12 Concluded																	

No. of owners, ___ No. of male slaves, 152 No. of fugitives, ___
No. of houses, 82 No. of female slaves, 152 Re. manumitted, ___ Total slaves, 304

1860 Noxubee County Slave Schedule showing unnamed Hillman and Shadrick, both listed as age 14, with Jacob Sistrunk as slaveowner on behalf of the individuals who had leased the two teenagers. 1860 Census.

Emancipation Proclamation in 1862, and in this same year "Natchez surrendered without resistance to Union naval forces," portending the sentiment of many Mississippians by the end of the year that "the war was lost."[12] While the Confederate army in Mississippi buckled early to Union forces, white citizens were still encouraged to enlist and fight. Jacob and his oldest son, William, would answer this call in 1862. Mississippians continued to enlist in 1862 and afterward, but they also began a trend of deserting their Confederate posts.[13] Confederate muster rolls show that soon after their enlistments, both Jacob and his son would be among the vast numbers of Mississippi soldiers who were absent from duty as much as they were present.[14] These records show that Jacob had a continued pattern of absence from duty—some explained as sickness, while others show him as missing without permission. His son William was also regularly absent without leave. He eventually deserted the Confederacy and enlisted in the Union Army in 1864.[15] Jacob's apathy over the war and the Confederate's proclaimed great cause, however, did not deter him from his self-interested cause to maintain ownership of Francis and her children—the Black family that was the bedrock of his financial worth and aspirations. Claiming four slaves on the Noxubee County Tax Rolls in 1864, Jacob clearly was left uninspired by Lincoln's declaration of freedom for the nation's Black population.[16] Francis and some, if not all, of her children remained tied to Jacob and his migrations until the war's end.

Unlike enslaved people who worked on large plantations with larger enslaved populations, Francis had less distance from her enslaver. From childhood, this close proximity to Jacob—psychologically and physically—would have conditioned Francis to a heightened scrutiny of her enslaver. Whites historically assumed that because they dismissed the presence and power of the "Black gaze," enslaved people had no capacity to critically eye them. White terrorism operated throughout the plantation South around white control of the Black gaze, demanding the downward gaze of Blacks in encounters with whites.[17] However, beneath the imposed deference Blacks were made to perform, they watched and critically assessed white people and the world they constructed. Blacks came out of enslavement with their humanity. They survived the heinous institution for generations, and they resisted in varied and creative ways, which speaks to their capacity to critically gaze whites despite the uneven playing field. Their strength in this area guided them in determining or assessing how their lives would be impacted by the circumstances and whims of their enslavers and moreover what inner powers they may access to affect the course of their own lives. Francis would have been listening for news on the war, and she would have been closely watching Jacob's actions and with ears alert, listening to ascertain how the intersections of war and Jacob's self-interests were impacting her life and options.

Neshoba remained the county of residence for Francis and family and enslaver, Jacob Jr., during the first year of the war. Confederate muster rolls show Jacob Jr.'s county of residence as Neshoba when he enlisted during the second year of the war.[18] By the war's end, however, Jacob crossed over into adjacent Winston County and established residence there before finally settling in Noxubee County. Per the historic roll showing that he reenlisted in the Confederate army, Jacob doesn't seem to formally declare Winston as his county of residence until 1864; however, he may have moved there as early as summer 1862.[19] In the very month that he enlists, the muster roll lists Jacob as sick and absent. He may very well have relocated to Winston County to evade Confederate authorities who would return him to his military post. After being captured by Union forces in 1863, Jacob Jr. was released on his oath swearing that he would not again bear arms against the US government.[20] Jacob Jr. breaks this oath in 1864 when he enlists again in the Confederate army. This time he enlists in Noxubee County, and while he declared residence in Fearns Springs (Winston County), he appears on the 1864 Mississippi Tax Roll for Noxubee County where his surname is spelled "Cistrunk."[21] This dual county residency seems to have continued into the year 1865, and perhaps two years beyond. In her application for widow's pension years after the war, Jennie Sistrunk, the widow of Jacob Jr.'s son, William, would report that when she and William married in 1865, "William was living with his father in Winston County."[22] She also reported that she and William returned to Winston County around 1867 and lived near Jacob Jr.[23] Jacob Jr. either maintained households in both Winston and Noxubee or lived in one county while maintaining a cover residence in the other. The conflicting 1864 tax records exemplify this, and the 1867 Tax Roll suggests that this deception continued into that year.[24] While his daughter-in-law reports that Jacob Jr. was in Winston County in 1867, the county tax roll shows a John Cystrunk in Noxubee.[25] This enumerated resident was likely Jacob Jr., and this time he not only changed the spelling of his surname but also assumed a different first name—John. In the 1870 Census, this evolution would culminate into his assumption of the name John Sistrunk.[26]

The world must have seemed a whirlwind to Francis and her children during the war years. With Jacob Jr.'s numerous absences from military duty and frequent returns home where he would continue exploring schemes to avoid active military duty, Francis was surely living in a heightened state of anxiety. Jacob was desperate, and his desperation could spill over into dire consequences for Francis and her children. Throughout the South during the war, civilians competed with the military for manpower and resources. Farming was interrupted and thus resulted in food scarcity, and incomes were interrupted leaving many in desperate financial states. Although the enslaved population had been freed by law, some were still forced or coerced to work on plantations of former enslavers. Some enslavers like Jacob Jr. would insist that they still had claim to people they once legally held in bondage, and with this presumption would also assert the right to treat them as possessions. This meant they would continue to demand the free labor of these now free people, and would assume the authority to sell, lease, and use them as they saw fit. Without question, Jacob Jr.'s financial straits were a threat to Francis. As the presumed "owner" of Francis and her family, Jacob could sell any one of them to bring in money if circumstances turned desperate enough. It could have been somewhat of a standoff. As a freed person Francis could leave, and with the war's end Jacob surely was aware that freedom meant that she could exercise her legal right to uproot her family. With six children, however, moving would have presented some practical challenges. With the ongoing war travel was dangerous, and there were questions such as where they would live and how they would make a living. Between the choice to strike out and navigate the chaos of the war while seeking a home and income or navigating the chaos of Jacob's world, Francis at least had years of experience with the latter. Staying under the umbrella of Jacob's household structure provided a location to maintain her family unit. With that Francis could then manage the logistics of surviving through the war period.

Firsthand written accounts of the Civil War experience of Francis and her children do not exist. However, probable narratives can be formed in part through the worldview of the era and the structure that defined their lives and continued its impact into their posterity. Generations after Francis, Cistrunk descendants have been shaped from the legacy of her resilience through enslavement, war, and the first half century of the post-slaving South. Thrust into a society that denied them the fundamental right to build sustainable and autonomous families and communities, enslaved Blacks had to build cultural mechanisms of survival. These would range from strategies for everyday engagement with whites to how they fed and sheltered their families and communities and how they maintained the essence of their humanity. Many of these early African American survival strategies and practices carried over into post–Civil War Black culture and remain into the twenty first century as traces from enslavement. We may for example consider African American cuisine as a portal to envision the Cistrunks's experience during the Civil War era. Beginning first with the knowledge that in addition to growing food on their own farms or small lots in rural and later in urban areas where they migrated, generations of post-emancipation Cistrunks hunted, fished, picked foods from the wild and preserved food for storage. I grew up hearing stories of how my grandparents and their generation fed their children in rural Mississippi through the foods they planted and the livestock they raised. But when years were lean, my grandparents fed their family from food sources in nature that they had learned about through their parents and elders—knowledge that dated back to the era of enslavement. They knew the greens, roots, nuts and other vegetation that were favorable for human consumption; and they knew how to catch animals in the wild and prepare them for meals. Like many southern Blacks, they developed cuisine around the available foods and resources within their realm. Just as they did not have the luxury of fine cuts of meat for entrees or for flavoring their meals, Black southerners did not have the choice of deciding that certain meat options were not to their liking. It was not uncommon to find rabbit, squirrel, or racoon as mealtime meats. These could be captured with or without a gun, and children could easily assist in these captures.

Francis and children would have eaten meals created from whatever rations they received, but like their descendants, they would also supplement these limited rations through their own resourcefulness. Much of the rations that Francis received for her family probably came from crops raised through Jacob Jr.'s farming ventures. The 1850 Agricultural Census shows Jacob raising wheat, corn, beans, peas, white and sweet potatoes and highlights what were likely the dietary staples for Jacob and his family as well as for Francis and her children.[27] Dishes such as cornbread, grits, mashed potatoes, and beans and peas flavored with a small, non-select piece of pork were meals Francis would have prepared from the crops Jacob is shown raising. These meals were dietary staples throughout enslaved communities and remain embedded in Black southern culture and its diaspora to date.[28]

If Francis was not herself adept at trapping wild animals to supplement meat rations, by start of the war her older sons had reached the age where they would have learned. If the twentieth-century Cistrunk descendants serve as examples, Francis would have certainly relied on fish as a supplemental food resource. The many creek tributaries of Neshoba, Winston, and Noxubee offered a dependable meat source for mealtime. I am reminded of the historical importance of waterways in the lives of Black southerners when I consider how fishing was central in my childhood years in Mississippi. In summers during the May to August period when school was out, teachers received no pay. My teachers, my mother, and our neighbor supplemented dinner meals with fresh fish that we regularly caught on morning outings. Only later as an adult did I learn that we fished not only because my mother and her friends enjoyed it, but also because it provided food at almost no cost during a period when our household finances were strained. In the small town where we lived, teachers' pay was low and the system of economic survival for teachers was eerily close to sharecropping. Aware that teachers' salaries were low and limited to a nine-month period, many businesses established summer credit for teachers. Just as with sharecroppers, teachers would begin their work season, academic year, in debt before receiving their first paycheck. And of course, the credit was granted at a rate and terms dictated by the business owners. My mother, along with other teachers, minimized the amount they borrowed by going directly to nature to feed their families. Just as her parents and foreparents, my mother grew fresh vegetables, canned fruits that we picked, and prepared wild game that neighbors were kind enough to offer. My mother earned a college degree, but it was my parents' knowledge from Black folk traditions dating to pre-emancipation times that kept food on our table. Throughout small towns and rural areas in Mississippi at the dawn of the of the civil rights movement, Black families still relied heavily on the wisdom and skills that their enslaved ancestors had passed along to successive generations. Again, Francis drew from these ways of knowing to bring her family through the Civil War period and its aftermath, and while enslavement had ended, her descendants would depend on the legacy of living and surviving that had helped Blacks survive generational slaving.

Although Lincoln's 1863 Emancipation Proclamation declared that enslaved people were free, freedom did not arrive immediately for all who had been enslaved. In the case of Francis and her children, freedom does not appear to have come until the war's end in 1865. Jacob Jr.'s continued assumption to ownership of Francis and her children is evinced on the 1864 Noxubee Tax Roll that shows him liable for taxes on four enslaved people.[29] His claim to Francis and her children at this point suggest that they had still been in his possession during his time in Winston County, his location before his final settlement in Noxubee. Forced to move from Neshoba to Winston around 1862 or 1863, Francis and family would have been there before the move to Noxubee by 1864. The tax roll records one female slave between the age 15–45 (Francis), one male slave between age 15–45, and two slaves under age 15 (Lucretia and Robert). The one male slave listed was probably Willis, although he was 12 years old—not yet 15. With only Francis and the three younger children recorded on the tax record, the three oldest, John (age 20), Hillman (age 18), and Shadrick (age 16), may have assumed their rights as freedmen by this time. They may have remained in Winston County where they would have been located in 1863, the year of Lincoln's emancipation decree. Whether the older sons were in Noxubee County at the end of the war in 1865 is not clear. Although I have not found him on records in that county either, John's absence on the 1870 Census in Noxubee suggests that he spent the first postwar years in Winston.[30] John appears to have married his wife, Chany, in 1864 or 1865, as their oldest child, Caroline, was born in 1865.[31] To date, it is unclear where John and Chany lived or whether Chany was from Winston County. Although the Cistrunk sons were teens at the start of the war, by 1864, at age

20, John may have been among the increasing numbers of freed Blacks in Mississippi who joined the Union forces. He also may have remained in Winston County after the war, contracted out to work for wages on the plantations that were under the supervision of the Freedmen's Bureau. If Hillman and Shadrick remained in Winston in 1862, they undoubtedly joined their mother and siblings in Noxubee in the early aftermath of the war. The brothers would have known that their mother and younger siblings needed them, and unlike John, they had no marital obligations to complicate their decision.

NOXUBEE COUNTY POSTWAR

The post-emancipation era spawned a surge in marriages of formerly enslaved couples, including those with children as well as newly formed unions of freed persons. For many women like Francis, there was little opportunity to build a family structure reflecting the white-contrived myth of the nuclear family. While some African American leaders would tie racial uplift to a politics of respectability anchored to this myth, unmarried mothers had to envision themselves and their families as legitimate, worthy, and equitable members of their communities. For many newly emancipated mothers, remaining unmarried may have been a practical and self-interested decision—despite the social pressure to marry. Formerly enslaved Black mothers held a fresh memory of their lives on slaving plantations where they "labored in a variety of roles on plantation fields, farms, and white households, and they also performed the bulk of domestic chores for their own families at the end of the working day. Slave mothers were also disproportionately more likely to have to undertake additional work after 'sundown,' including typically gendered tasks such as sewing and weaving."[32] As enslaved mothers they carried a workload that arguably exceeded that of all parties on the plantation.[33] What then would make marriage necessarily desirable as freed women?

Having endured a system that overtaxed their labors, newly freed Black mothers may have chosen not to marry to spare themselves the extra burdens that marriage had brought to enslaved women. In 1865 at the war's end, Francis, in her late 30s, was the mother of six children fathered by men who were absent and unavailable as possible marriage prospects. At least four of her children were likely fathered by one or more white enslavers, and Shadrick Dowdell II, the Black man who likely fathered her middle son, Shadrick, was married with children, living more than 300 miles away in Georgia.[34] Francis may not have been without marriage prospects, but her set of circumstances probably left her hesitant to marry. She could not be certain that marriage would result in a spouse who would accept the role of surrogate father to her children, particularly given the tensions that could arise over colorism. This intraracial tension among African Americans over skin tone and white ancestry dates back to slavery and survives into the twenty-first century. Countless works by early to contemporary Black authors speak to this ongoing and sometimes divisive element of Black identity.[35] Cistrunk family accounts that attribute the family's early twentieth-century split to tensions rooted in colorism exemplify the extreme division that could result around issues of skin tone. It was Noah Cistrunk's grandson, Noah, who first shared the story with me.

While many formerly enslaved people married and thus confirmed their place within the rubric of Anglo-patriarchal respectability, numerous households resembled that headed by Francis. The challenges and circumstances faced by freed people were rooted in the centuries of slaving that had influenced the evolution of Black culture and community. The centuries-old practice of separating enslaved parents resulted in generations of family units headed by women. The prevalence of Black female-led households in the antebellum South was a striking contrast to Anglo-American households that reflected the framework of white male patriarchal power. It is a structure that legitimates and places higher values on those households recognized through legally sanctioned marriage and offspring born from these unions. The matter of the nuclear family was not one that simply played out in ideology or myth. Whether married or single, Black women faced the added challenges that women face in a heavy-handed patriarchal society—that is, the matter of financial autonomy. This was particularly manifested in a practice that made it difficult for women in farming to secure independent wages. In a move that was clearly designed to benefit the planters, they "eliminated contracts with women and began contracting only with freedmen, who took responsibility for their families and thereby gained more control over them."[36] Planters could then secure the labor of entire families while only having to negotiate pay with a single adult worker—the male head of household. While this practice left laboring wives dependent on their husbands' goodwill for equitable power in household finances, it put single mothers under added duress. Without a male figure to negotiate and contract with planters, single mothers could be left to the whims of planters who might refuse to contract with them. Planters who might contract directly with freedwomen likely drew from the legacy of a slaving economy where enslaved men were assessed in dollar values higher than enslaved women and children. Therefore, in the shadow of this gendered paradigm, Black women in the postbellum era attempting to contract work agreements with planters would certainly have to anticipate a system in which their labor worth was undervalued. Mothers who had sons old enough to present themselves as head of household could have an older or adult son assume the role of negotiator, and thus subvert the threat of lower wages. This rocky course that single mothers navigated illustrates that beyond a show of deference to social mores, marriage was a means for economic sustainability throughout newly freed Black communities.

Despite the many potential threats to the cohesiveness of Black female-led households in the postwar South, Francis maintained her children under her roof in the early years of freedom. In 1870, she was perhaps fortunate that even though she had two young children—ages 10 and 4—the four others were teenagers and older. The oldest, 21-year-old John, was an adult, and does not appear to be living in the family household in 1870.[37] The three middle sons, ages 13–19, were old enough to make substantial contributions to the family's farming obligations. With all working together, they could avoid the fate of some families with children who were forced into indentured servitude. Children as young as 5 could be—and were—contracted to service for fifteen years.[38] This kind of arrangement, perhaps unimaginable in our twenty-first century minds, was justified in contracts of a standard template that asserted the child had "voluntarily expressed a willingness to live with and be bound" to the planter named in the contract.[39] While these contracts made the assurance that the Black child would not be required to work more than any white child bound by indenture, no legal or historical precedent suggested that this promise would be kept. The brief explanations for turning these children over to planters seem to originate from a scripted list. Throughout these files the recurring claims were that the child was abandoned, the parents were deceased, or the mother (and sometimes both mother and father) was unable to support the child. There was no regard given to the question of the child's family or kinship relation to others in the community or whether other arrangements could have been made to maintain the child with their family or community. In cases where the child's parent(s) was acknowledged, the claim was that the parent was in agreement, and the child concurred.[40] The Macon office Freedmen's records of indentures reveal that in Noxubee County primary-school-age children were indentured to white planters with years of servitude—with the number of years dependent on the age of the child.[41] Once indentured, children were bound to the contract until they reached age eighteen. This looming threat would deepen the weight of the pressing concerns of survival in these early years after the war. The irony of this new reality could not have gone unnoticed by Francis. That is the stinging realization that in their newfound freedom, Blacks still faced the threat of separation that had lurked so prominently during the slaving era. Francis knew, as her older sons knew as well, that she must be able to provide for her family and to avoid financial ensnarement with planters who could then force Francis into signing over her children.

The family likely hired out as laborers on planter estates where this business was overseen in many cases by the Freedmen's Bureau. Like many freed people hoping to move beyond the status of refugee and to find stable financial and living circumstances, Francis either negotiated work contracts on her own or through the bureau. Her ability to independently negotiate was undoubtedly obstructed, however, when planters shifted to contracting only with freedmen. At that point she may have resorted to employing her former enslaver, Jacob Jr., to witness or to endorse her position as head of household. Jacob's appearance as a witness on an 1867 Freedmen's labor contract suggests that if he were not hiring Francis and her children himself, he cannot be ruled out as an involved party in contracts the family may have made.[42]

Although the bureau was established to help the newly freed population establish a footing into their new lives, the effectiveness of the bureau was neither extensive nor long-lasting. If the Freedmen's office report of complaints (1865–1872) in Macon, MS (Noxubee County), exemplifies the tenor of contracts and relationships orchestrated and managed by the bureau, it suggests an operation that did not serve the newly freed population well. Snapshots from this report in 1865 depict a bureau that oversaw the interest of the planters more than that of the freed community it was enacted to serve. One of the most recurring charges by planters was against workers who refused to respond to orders: In these cases, the crime was most often noted as "insolence" or "disobedience."[43] The common penalty for this infraction was a jail sentence that ranged between two to five days with a diet of bread and water. Similarly, this report also shows that the contracted laborers were held to the grounds of the plantation much like they had been during enslavement. Another recurring charge against Black workers was leaving the plantation without permission, and this too brought a jail sentence with a bread-and-water diet. In circumstances where jail was not an elected penalty, the punishment would be meted out on the plantation grounds. A notable punishment reminiscent of enslavement was to restrain the charged worker by tying them up.[44] While no record of beatings is recorded, the antebellum practice of tying up enslaved persons and applying the whip was not lost in this new South. Freed people very quickly learned that not only did whites still presume that Blacks had no rights, but also that the very government that had declared them free was delivering them up once again for the benefit of white men's wealth.

The charge of stealing—especially theft of food—also echoes dynamics of the antebellum plantation. Enslaved people were often accused of stealing, and the charge was regularly theft of food. Enslavers had the power to demand long hours of labor from those they enslaved, and they had the power to determine food allotments for those they forced to work. The result was that hunger and malnutrition was not uncommon among enslaved people, and neither was confiscation of food when they found a way. Frederick Douglass's well-known nineteenth-century autobiography describes in detail the anguishing hunger that was ongoing in his life as a slave. He explains that the meager rations that he was provided were never enough. The result, as Douglass explains, was the choice of either "begging or stealing, whichever came handy in the time of need, the one being considered as legitimate as the other."[45] While enslavers called it theft, those enslaved were clear that the theft was the labor they were forced to render without choice or compensation. If they could acquire food from the plantation to quell their hunger, it was right and just. This ethos of righteous confiscation in an unrighteous society was needed in the postwar period as much as it had been during the antebellum era. The Freedmen's Bureau contract system portends the financial trap that ensnared many Black workers during the post-emancipation era of sharecropping. Having no money at the start, great numbers of freed people entered into labor contracts borrowing money or the cost of food and supplies that would be provided at the onset of the contract. The planters and merchants were given the controlling voice on prices and terms of repayment, leaving Black workers with little control of their financial state. Food quantities and selections were determined by the planters, and just as the result of this practice during enslavement, freed people under contract with planters were left to the options for the enslaved Douglass outlined in his narrative.

It is not surprising to see numerous charges of theft on the Macon Freedmen's Bureau complaint reports. The choice between hunger and jail can become blurred and equally unbearable, and the reports of theft in the Freedmen's reports reveal this dehumanizing dilemma that was quickly becoming part of the experience of freedom for Blacks in the South. A case that caught my attention was the ledger entry showing a contracted worker named Shedrach who was charged with "stealing a chicken."[46] Shedrach was given a three-day sentence that included the customary bread-and-water diet. The record does not offer sufficient information to verify that the Shedrach on this ledger is Shadrick Cistrunk. I felt a sense of awe at the boldness of Shedrach, wanting to claim him as my ancestor Shadrick Cistrunk; however, I had to consider that this may not have been Francis's son. Shadrick was not a common name, but there were at least eight Shadricks in Noxubee County who could have been the Shadrach recorded on the 1865 complaints report. The scant information on the report is not enough to affirm whether the accused on the ledger was Francis's son Shadrick. That this could have been Shadrick Cistrunk does, however, present an identity—a known person—to the many people throughout freed communities who were subjected to the looming threat of unjust encounters with the law. Imagining a17-year-old Shadrick stealing a chicken portends the present for many young Black teenage males who, whether out of need or want, engage in nonviolent actions that put them at much greater risk of prosecution and persecution. Whether the threat is actual or presumed, the results can be fatal for them.

If one considers the devastation and shortage of resources and food in the aftermath of Hurricane Katrina in 2005, the parallel to the Civil War aftermath is striking. When whites were seen in grocery stores and drug stores helping themselves to supplies they needed, the news media did not report these occurrences as looting or theft. In the case of Blacks who acted similarly, we saw their images plastered across newspapers and videocasts, painting them not as hungry, desperate, and in need, but again as vagrants.[47] Much like Black mothers more than a century and a half after her, Francis had to live with the looming threat of encounters with a legal system that systematically regarded Blacks, especially Black males, as innately violent and criminal. Francis had to instill in her children an awareness of situations that could put their lives and fates in the hands of whites who had the full force of the law to wield against them. This state of heightened alert that informed her consciousness represents a generational state of trauma that to date continues to engulf Black life across the United States. In the throes of the prominent twenty-first century cases of police and white vigilante violence against Blacks—especially against Black youth, we hear considerable discussion about the coming-of-age talk that Black parents have with their children about the high risk they face for this kind of violent encounter. While many who are not African American seem astonished by this necessary practice of child-rearing, this cautionary ritual predates our contemporary enlightenment to this reality. Dating back to enslavement, and arguably escalated in the post–Civil War era, Blacks have had to give their children the talk that they hoped would keep them alive in confrontational encounters with any white person—whether a legal agent of the law or just a random white who feels authorized to question or charge them with a wrongful act. Francis would not have been unlike freed people throughout the South who imparted to their children the wisdom of how to best navigate life in a world where white rule was sanctioned on the premise of Black submission. The talk was not rooted in an acceptance of white rule or claims to superiority but was instead a severe look at the racial power structure to clarify for Black children emerging into adulthood the predatory nature of white supremacy. Newly freed Black southerners were filled with hope for a brighter future, but that future required ensuring some level of safety for Black children. The talk was a safeguard ritual to equip Black children with knowledge to minimize the potential for harm in their encounters with whiteness, and it remains an element of child-rearing in Black households to the present. This was brought to the forefront in Ta-Nehisi Coates's 2015 book, *Between the World and Me*, in which he tells his young son that "In America, it is traditional to destroy the Black body—it is heritage."[48] Similarly in Kiese Laymon's 2018 memoir, *Heavy,* this message is conveyed throughout the work. An early and poignant example is advice given to young Kiese from his grandmother. When he asks whether Black people could evade the law in the celebratory and heroic fashion of the heroic Bo and Luke on the 1980s television series *The Dukes of Hazzard,* with great severity his grandmother warns him, "Nope. Not at all. Never. You better never try that mess either."[49]

Francis and her family, like all in their community, faced the ongoing resistance of whites who refused to acknowledge Blacks as citizens. White resistance operated in many forms, particularly violence, intimidation, and political foul play. As the Macon Freedmen's report of complaints reveals, when Blacks charged whites with crimes against them, the weight of the punishment made it clear that the courtroom would bring little justice for the newly freed. Charges that range from "beating negro woman," "cutting negro with knife," "running negro with hounds," "cruelty to freedmen," and "refusing to pay just dues," were in all cases presented as resolved with the repeated notation that reads "responded and settled satisfactorily."[50] Of course the document gives no details of what actions were taken to arrive at satisfaction, and more importantly there is no indication of which party found the results satisfactory. All the absences in this report speak louder than words could. Even if the accused white person was made to offer some token of reparation, it was not considered worthy of entry into the records, and the reputation of the white assailant would not be marked by a record of a legal offense. Notable in this excerpt from the report is the continued threat of violence that Black women faced. The record shows that white men's mythical defense of the weaker sex would continue to exclude Black women. Black women in the free South still lived under the threat of unanswered violence against them and a court system that continued to offer them little to no protection. While the cases referenced above do not include any allegations of sexual violence, they simply reflect the loopholes in a legal system that refused to acknowledge the rape of Black women as a punishable act.[51] In general, Black freed women continued to live under the threat of white men's license to predatory sexual actions against Black women.[52] While Black women lived cautiously in general as they navigated their encounters with white men, single Black women heading their own households probably operated in a more heightened state of alert over this threat.

Like many counties in Mississippi, nineteenth-century Noxubee was a majority Black population district: In 1860 Blacks were seventy-five percent of the more than 20,000 persons counted in that year's census.[53] This did not however translate into long-standing political power. Despite the constitutional declaration of Black citizenship, the majority of white Mississippians rejected the participation of Blacks as equal citizens, and as early as 1865, state officials, led by the governor himself, declared that there would be no equal society.[54] What followed swiftly was an attack on all fronts to prevent Blacks from asserting the rights bestowed on them by the federal government. This came in forms such as Black code laws that denied Blacks fundamental economic and legal rights. For example, denying Blacks the right to lease farmland and denying their right to bring charges against whites in court.[55] These legal obstacles exemplify the legal methods implanted to diminish opportunities for Blacks to build an autonomous economic future and to render them powerless to combat the white violence that was mounting throughout postwar Mississippi. While many Americans envision the postwar Reconstruction era as a period when Black southerners were granted full engagement as citizens of the nation, the reality was quite the contrary. In many ways Reconstruction represented the period in which the white supremacist South would dig its heels in deeper to resist the government's attempt to steer the South to a more racially equitable society. While Black men had gained the right the vote and even to hold office, white resistance to these freedoms was mounting before the ink dried on these constitutional declarations. The Ku Klux Klan is the more well-known white supremacist group that spread throughout the South after the Civil War, but other secret societies emerged as well. The White Line of Mississippi was among these vigilante organizations that employed "tactics of terrorist groups" to end the government promotion of a racial equality in the South.[56]

The 1869 race riot in Noxubee County reveals the level of violence that whites would employ in pursuit of the apartheid culture they were determined to establish. On Wednesday August 25, 1869, the *Memphis Ledger* provided "a true statement of the difficulty that had occurred at Macon between the negroes and the whites of that place."[57] The report describes a mob of seventy-five to one hundred armed Blacks who on Monday had demanded that a young white man (whom the paper names) be delivered to them to answer for killing a Black (whom the paper does not name) the previous day.[58] When confronted by the sheriff and ordered by a "negro preacher" to fire their arms, the Black rioters were said to have run off after the shooters were wounded. The report ends with a tone as flippant as the plantation narratives that would become popular at the turn of the century. The preacher who had given the order to fire disappeared after the confrontation and by the time of the newspaper account, all was reportedly quiet "in and about the battlefield."[59] The armed Black men had been apprehended by the sheriff's men who had not fired according to the newspaper's account because they were unarmed. The article has a demeaningly comical ring to it, as it suggests that

Blacks feared the presence of white authority, even when unarmed. Much like the silences in the record of the Freedmen's report of complaints about white violence against Blacks, this news account offers no serious details of white violent aggression nor the complicity of the law. It is probable that the unarmed sheriff and his men negotiated with the group of armed Black men, perhaps promising that the killer would be prosecuted or at least questioned. Once a truce was established the condition of the agreement may have hinged on the agreement of those armed to drop their weapons. This is clearly the more probable scenario since precedence shows that law enforcement with guns did not feel inclined to tolerate armed Black threats. Evidence of law enforcement as the second arm of white supremacist rule dates back to the antebellum period when slave rebellions were not just answered by armed planters protecting their property. Planters could depend on law enforcement and militias to take up arms against enslaved people who dared to fight for their freedom. With its summary of the Black "mob" as unlawful, the *Ledger's* 1869 account of the Macon riot echoes the tenets of a legal system still unwilling to recognize white violence against Blacks as unlawful.[60] Whether the preacher or other Blacks were killed is left to the reader's imagination, but again, what is clear in the tone of the article is the disregard for Black life and the presumption of unchecked white rule.

In a matter of years after the war, violence and racial hatred against Blacks would be replanted in southern culture, but this did not deter the first generation of free Black southerners who enthusiastically embraced the future. In Noxubee, as elsewhere in the South, Blacks built their own churches, built their own social organizations, built their own schools, promoted education in their communities, fought to exercise their political rights, and despite the odds many became landowners. Despite the representation of even Black leaders such as Alexander Crummell who saw the newly freed Black population as "wretchedly ignorant," after centuries of "being an unthinking labor-machine," this depiction is a severe contradiction to the activities of the period.[61] Throughout Mississippi, education was one of the immediate goals for freed Blacks, but white responses to Black enthusiasm for education was one of the early indicators of the Jim Crow South of the future: "Whites did burn many Black schools, some repeatedly when they were rebuilt."[62] Despite the all-out war that whites waged against Black education, freed people made this quest a priority. This determination for literacy was no less a priority for Blacks in Noxubee County where the Cistrunks were establishing their roots. Like elsewhere in Mississippi, Blacks in Noxubee County would not be welcomed or admitted into white schools, so separate schools for Blacks had to be built. In many instances the interim solution for time needed to plan and construct schools was to repurpose abandoned or available buildings. This would allow for the newly freed population to immediately begin educational programs for adults and school-age children. This was a practice in postwar Noxubee County where the demand for educational facilities for Blacks was answered in part through usage agreements for existing available buildings.[63] The Freedmen's Bureau managed at least some if not most of these usage agreements and also oversaw the establishment of some schools. While the Freedmen's Bureau is often seen as the driving force of Black education in the immediate years after the war, "until creation of the public school system, the majority of Black schools drew their financial support from their students and their families." [64] Though their financial resources were slim, first-generation freed people took on the mission of self-help and as indicated in the Freedmen's report on building usages for freedmen's education, Blacks in Noxubee were creative and persistent in their quest for Black education and literacy.

As quickly and as enthusiastically as freed people embraced opportunities for literacy, they also claimed their religious autonomy. In present day Noxubee County St. Paul Methodist Church and Second Baptist Church engrave their 1867 founding date on the cornerstone of their buildings. These inscriptions are a reminder of the churches' post-emancipation beginnings and metamorphosis from the more clandestine worship of the antebellum era. Blacks had few opportunities in the antebellum South to build physical or permanent worship structures, but they maintained spiritual and religious practices through hush harbors where they worshipped in secret away from the scrutiny of enslavers or other whites.[65] The hush harbors generated pathways for continuation of African spiritual carryovers that would be foundational to African American spirituality and culture: The ring shout, water baptism, and the homegoing are well-known examples of African carryovers that were maintained as sacred through the hush harbor tradition.[66] Even as African Americans aligned their formal rituals and affiliations to Anglo-Christian conventions, they would Africanize their Christianity with pre-Middle Passage practices such as these. The more conservative Black denominations such as Episcopal, Presbyterian, Lutheran, and even the early A.M.E. Church concerned themselves with mirroring the stoicism and customs of the Anglo-Christian church. On the contrary, Methodist, Baptist, and independent Black denominations did not develop around a fixation on or deference to Anglo Christianity. When emancipation was confirmed, hush harbors would be transformed into material structures, built by and for Black worshippers. In these new houses of worship, Blacks could more formally and openly pay tribute to their deceased in ways of honor and celebration that date back to burial practices of pre-Middle Passage Africans. The homegoing—the celebration of the life of the deceased and the send-off to the eternal world of the

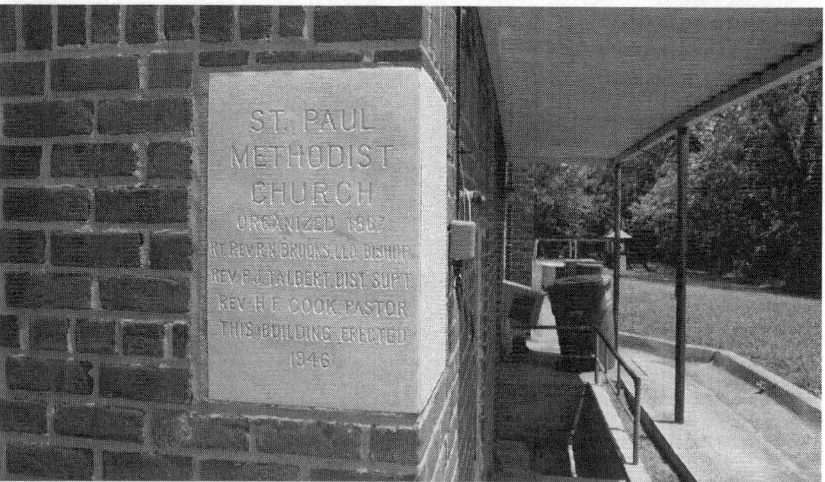

St. Paul Methodist Church and cornerstone showing founding date of 1867

spirits—must be part of the death ritual. Showing one's love and respect for the dead and celebrating their life is ingrained in African American culture, and it is a spiritual and social ill to leave the dead unattended and uncelebrated. During enslavement, family and kin were often separated and enslavers did not feel obligated to respect the need of the enslaved to grieve their deceased or to bury them with honor and respect. As freed people, African

Second Baptist Church marker showing founding of 1867

Americans could reclaim the centuries old tradition of Africans honoring the dead to receive the blessings of the ancestors.

It is not clear where Francis and her children first worshipped after the war, but Shadrick Cistrunk's son Noah, was a member of Brushfork Baptist Church where, according to family members, he served as deacon, even after his move to Winston County around 1918.[67] Brushfork Church still stands today not far from its earlier location on a two-acre parcel of land purchased in 1890.[68] The deed contract shows the purchaser as "Brushfork Baptist Church (Colored)," thereby recognizing the sale to an established church entity at the time of the signing. The church was established before 1890 and, like St. Paul Methodist Church and Second Baptist Church, Brushfork may have been organized within the first years of emancipation and from a community that worshipped together in the pre-emancipation era. The church's own record states that "Back in 1880, a small church was located on what is now Howard Triplett's place off of Hwy 14."[69] The record identifies the church as already in existence in 1880, rather than being founded in that year, which suggests that its origins predate the year 1880. Originally known as Friendship, the church had been a "gift from the Whites to the Blacks," and had existed at the Triplett location for some time until a fire forced its relocation. During the aftermath of the fire the church congregation met in the "'brushes'—under a brush harbor," that was "relocated several times," until the congregation purchased a lot in 1890. The first permanent building was completed in 1930, and over the years and decades the one room was expanded and improved until 1990 when "another idea came to mind . . . to rebuild Brushfork on Highway 14." The church history does not explain who proposed the idea and why it was thought to be advantageous; however, it is perhaps remarkable if not curious that the church was able to convince a giant business corporation to assist. The challenge of a new location was solved when "Georgia Pacific agreed to exchange" the property on the Brushfork Rd. location to its present day location on Highway 14 where it is now called Brushfork Missionary Baptist Church.[70] If the record is accurate, this would mean that much of the Cistrunk family history in the church would have been during its era of the brush harbors, with services held outdoors.

Having arrived in Noxubee County during the war, the Cistrunks's relationship with the Black spiritual communities of the area did not go back very far. As new arrivals to the community around 1864, they had to establish their spiritual footing, and the early Brushfork community may have been the place where Francis anchored her family. Noah was a member of Brushfork, which suggests that his parents, Shadrick and Susan, were members—perhaps founding members. Noah's homegoing at Brushfork points to his burial on or near the church grounds, and perhaps his remains were returned to Noxubee to be placed near his father, Shadrick, and grandmother, Francis, who both may have been buried there. In the conversations I had with Noah's son, Bunnie, he insisted that despite the death certificate identifying Mt. Pleasant in Winston County as the site of burial, he recalls Brushfork cemetery as the place of his father's burial. When Noah died in 1937, the family was not financially able to purchase a headstone for his grave, so the location of his remains cannot be determined by a physical marker. The return of Noah to his home church in his county of birth brought him back to family and kin for the celebration of his life and his spiritual transformation to ancestor. His return to Noxubee marked a geographical point of Cistrunk origins that helps to trace the family's long arc from enslavement to freedom. It is the history of his birth and years in Noxubee that direct his descendants to the family's pre-Winston County roots, which can be traced by way of Noxubee to the family's history that predates entry into Mississippi. The family may have been financially poor at the time of Noah's death, but they were still enriched by the legacy of Black burial rites that have been anchored in the imperative of bringing the body home for its final return to the earth. This rite, which is also central to reaffirming family and kinship ties, was for centuries denied many enslaved people. It is an element of family and ancestral connectedness that is manifested today in Black families that often takes on the extra expense of transporting the remains of their loved ones for burial in the places that were their family or childhood homes.

Emancipation issued in a new religious era for Blacks to build their own churches and to worship independently of white oversight. This seeming signal of emerging autonomy was quelled by the sobering realization that the political and economic climate of the postwar South was reminiscent of the old South. The world that framed the future for Francis and her family was on the one hand promising a new era for Black citizenship and prosperity, but on the other hand, was fraught with signs of a past era not entirely past. Reconstruction did little to temper white assumptions of dominance over Blacks and their willingness to engage in violence to assert that power. The political rights promised the newly freed dissipated within years after the war as laws were installed to diminish Black enfranchisement. Despite efforts to strip Blacks of a political voice and representation, Blacks remained engaged in politics. During the Reconstruction era Blacks in Mississippi not only voted and voiced their interests, but some held political offices. Among Blacks in Mississippi who held political offices was A. K. Davis, "an obscure Black Republican from Noxubee County" who served as lieutenant governor to Adelbert Ames, who was elected governor in 1874 .[71] Whether today's predominantly Black population of Noxubee County is aware that one of their own brought this historical distinction to an otherwise little-known community, in 1874, this Noxubee representation in government probably fueled a wave of hopefulness for Black residents.

Even as Reconstruction was nearing its official end by 1876, the future for the Cistrunks looked promising. Brothers John, Hillman, and Shadrick were establishing themselves as farmers.[72] Farming was not a guaranteed path to reliable or predictable income, but to work one's own land was at least a labor investment in one's own future. While Black laborers in greater numbers worked on land owned by white planters, the Cistrunks were representative of a smaller percentage of freed persons who bought land. While I have heard the story from one senior family member that land was given to our Cistrunk ancestors from a former enslaver, I have not found evidence that this is the case. The 1900 deed records show the full conveyance of ownership to Hillman and Shadrick the parcels of land in the Bottom (the southwestern corner of the county where the family lived) that they had farmed for decades. They each mortgaged their properties in 1879 through the Farmers' Loan and Trust Company, confirming that they purchased their land.[73] This does not, however, fully negate the story passed down by some family members. Official records show that the Cistrunk brothers bought their land, but this does not mean that they were not in some way indebted to a white planter or person of influence. To this point I am reminded of an account of a landowning freedman in Noxubee County who would have been a contemporary of the Cistrunks. While there were cases of former enslavers giving land to Blacks in the aftermath of the Civil War, James Bridges, a Noxubee County resident whose lineage dates back to antebellum Noxubee, recounts the deal his ancestor made with the former enslaver. Bridges described the arrangement of his ancestor with the former enslaver as "indentured servitude" as the arrangement required the newly freed to bind himself to work for his former enslaver. Bridges's ancestor worked for a prescribed period in payment for land that would be turned over to him after the period of indenture. Bridges stressed to me that early Black landowners sacrificed a great deal to purchase land. The account of his ancestor reminded me that many stories of whites giving freedmen land after emancipation may be thinly veiled tales of a system of transactional "giving" that had a glaring resemblance to enslavement.

James Bridges reminded me that in some instances, planters gifted land with no strings attached to some Blacks they had formerly enslaved. He also noted that these were cases of formerly enslaved who for varied reasons were favored by their former enslavers. In the case of his ancestor and mine, however, what is revealed is the neglected story of the industry and determination of freed people to purchase and work their own land. The story of "generous" former enslavers "giving" land to those they formerly enslaved not only maintains a narrative legacy that literally whitewashes the centuries and generations of theft of Black labor, but also harmfully fuels ongoing stereotypes of Blacks as historical recipients of government or philanthropic "gifts." Before and after emancipation, the Cistrunks were industrious, proud, and resourceful, and this is revealed in both the family's own accounts as well as official records where they and Blacks of this era have been presumed absent. Despite facing times that were challenging and uncertain, within the first decade after the war, the Cistrunks showed signs of building their pathway to better circumstances for themselves and their posterity. As landowners, the Cistrunks were susceptible to the difficult economy of the war period and the decades that followed. This was a period of falling prices, but "agricultural prices (especially cotton) fell faster and further than non-agricultural prices," and the result was deeper hardships for southerners.[74] The crisis nature of this phenomenon was that farmers who borrowed annually to purchase supplies they needed for crop cultivation could see the season readily turn to a loss if prices fell so severely that the revenue from crop sales would not cover loans incurred. As was the case with most in their community under threat by escalating white resistance to racial equality, the Cistrunks would learn to also operate under the ongoing threat of uncontrollable and unpredictable economic elements that could upend their hopeful look to the future.

Although Francis was a single mother, any stigma that she may have experienced from that marker was certainly lightened as her children grew older and married. With the exception of the oldest child, John, the 1870 Census shows Francis and family together in Noxubee County.[75] This census also reveals the assertion on Francis's part to establish the unity of her family through their shared surname. While her six children did not all share the same biological father, as a freedwoman Francis assumed the surname Sistrunk. Her role as matriarch was established by the assignment of that surname to all her children. Francis was head of household, and by virtue of their shared surnames, she and her children were a unified, cohesive family. With unity in name, there was no marker of degrees of relation as found in the nuclear family model—that is, "half-brother," or "half-sister." The three oldest sons—John, Hillman, and Shadrick—would marry, and the lineages from John and Shadrick would pass on the surname with one alteration. As early as 1871, the brothers began to change the spelling from "Sistrunk" to "Cistrunk," distinguishing themselves from their previous enslavers.[76] An 1877 deed of trust showing the surname spelled "Scistrunk," suggests that they explored or contemplated versions before settling into the spelling that stands to date.[77] A number of factors may have influenced the change in spelling, but the story that has been passed down for generations maintains that this was a deliberate decision to thwart the insistence of the local post office to convey mail for the Black Sistrunks to the household of white Sistrunks. The new spelling not only marked the Black Cistrunks by the change in the beginning letter, but the more emphatic allusion was what the "C" denoted. "C" in the new spelling carried the insinuation of "colored," and the Black Cistrunks were well aware that no white man would invite speculation that they may have family ties to Blacks. Therefore, the postmaster was clear that mail for Cistrunks was not to be delivered to a white Sistrunk household. To this date Cistrunk family members share hearty laughter over this account of their ancestors' wittiness.

While John does not appear on the 1870 Census, the birth years of his children on the 1880 Census show that he married first among the six siblings. His first two children were born at the close and aftermath of the war thereby indicating that John and his wife, Chany, met during the war period. Their first child, Charity, was born in 1865, daughter Caroline in 1866, and Annie in 1870.[78] Where the family resided at the time of the 1870 Census is not revealed on records found to date, but by the late 1870s they are in Noxubee and in the family fold.[79] John's return as a married man by the close of the Reconstruction era marked the opening of a new and expanding kinship circle for Francis and her children. The era and legacy of Francis's children in Noxubee would begin. John's siblings would follow his lead before the close of the 1870 decade. Most notable, the year 1871 was a year of marriages for the Cistrunks. In February, 16-year-old Lucretia married Alfred Dobbins, and her 19-year-old brother, Willis, signed the marriage bond.[80] In April, 25-year-old Hillman married Harriet Harden, and later that year younger brother Willis married Hopea Brown.[81] It is on Hillman's marriage license that we see one of the first occurrences of the surname spelled with a "C" rather than an "S."[82] In 1876 when 28-year-old Shadrick married Susan Landrum, he would be the last of the siblings to marry.[83] If still alive, the youngest sibling, Robert, would have been 16 years old in 1876. Robert's last appearance on census records is in 1870, suggesting that he died sometime between that year and the 1880 Census.[84]

Francis was now matriarch of a kinship circle that was extended through the marriage of her children. Her son Shadrick exemplified through his marriage how post-emancipation kinship ties among African Americans continued to be built through biological and surrogate networks. His wife, Susan, would bring a minor dependent into their marriage, and the child would be enveloped into the household.[85] The Bottom would be the place where Francis's children, with the exception of Willis, would take their stand, claiming their place and part in the making of their American South. Having lived the consequences of forced migration, enslavement, and motherhood absent of full autonomy, Francis witnessed her living adult children married in their own household units and connected as a family as they forged their way into the future.

Chapter 3

POST-RECONSTRUCTION AND A NEW CENTURY

Anxious and Audacious Times (1870s–1910)

If your head ain't itching, don't scratch it.
  Noah Cistrunk

The story of the early decades of the post-emancipation Cistrunks is one of optimism and hopefulness, but it is also one of great struggle. In addition to the everyday, ubiquitous struggles of the era informed by elements such as politics, labor, economics, and health, their reality was still framed by the ongoing racist campaign for white rule in the South. The white violence directed toward freed people in the aftermath of the Civil War did not extinguish Black people's expectations for full citizenry and better lives. Even with white resistance to Black citizenry, "the first legislature under the new constitution convened in 1870," and Blacks made up thirty-five of the total 140 legislators.[1] This year also marked the first Census that recognized Francis and her children by name, no longer as nameless possessions on the slave schedules. What seemed the promise of a new South for the formerly enslaved would, however, by the end of the century, be a return to white rule that mirrored the antebellum era. With the installment of poll taxes, state-sanctioned violence and intimidation, inequity in education, and criminalization as a new source of free Black labor, Black landowners faced almost impossible odds for maintaining economic autonomy. In 1879, Hillman and Shadrick bought their tracts of land in the Bottom area of Noxubee County.[2] In that same year of a yellow fever surge, eroding civil rights across the South helped fuel an exodus of Blacks who hoped to find better circumstances outside the southern vortex of escalating racial oppression. Many, like the Cistrunk siblings would remain and work for the future that emancipation had promised. Despite the great Compromise of 1877 as with Blacks outside the South, Black rural southerners continued the struggle for Black uplift. It was a pursuit fueled by the expectation that Blacks deserved and would find a pathway to economic, political, and social advancement. Conventional and unconventional archives tell this story, and this chapter samples these resources to hear this story through the experiences of Francis and her lineage. It is difficult to imagine what it meant to Francis to be free of Jacob Sistrunk Jr., the man who had for decades enslaved Francis and her children and claimed them as his possession. Jacob Jr. and his oldest son, William, resided in Noxubee, Township 13, where Francis and her children established roots as freed people.[3] The 1870 Census shows Jacob Jr. and William still residing in Noxubee, but by 1880 William and family are living in Leake County, and Jacob Jr. and wife, Martha, do not appear on the Census.[4] It appears then that sometime before 1880, Francis and her family were finally free of the Sistrunks. Their departure this time would not include the company of Francis and family. This time Francis would make a choice, would set her roots in a place, and declare it home.

Within the first decades of freedom, Francis would lose two of her children —one to death, the other to migration. The absence of her youngest son, Robert, on the Census in 1880—when he would have been 20 years old—suggests that Robert died sometime between the 1870 and 1880 Census.[5] He does not appear on the 1880 or subsequent census reports, and his name is missing in public records such as trust deeds and enumerations of educable children where we find his brothers and their family members for four more decades. What some deem the most fateful curse of motherhood, to be preceded in death by one's child, could not have been easy to accept. During this period the fourth oldest, Willis, left Noxubee County, probably among the wave of rural Black southerners who migrated to urban areas after the end of Reconstruction. Though two members were gone, in 1880 the remaining Noxubee four—John, Hillman, Shadrick, and Lucretia—along with their mother, Francis, were settled into their lives as first-generation freed Blacks.[6] They were part of the story of Blacks building post-emancipation communities in the rural southern county of Noxubee, MS. Their story reveals the dynamics of the infrastructure that made it so difficult for many of these families to hold on to their land and to stand their ground to make a home for their future generations. Buttressed by an infrastructure of racism at the end of the war, "freed African-American slaves generally had no resources or access to credit to purchase land."[7] Thus, the future was predictable: "Most of Mississippi's Black population that worked in agriculture in the late 19th and early 20th centuries became sharecroppers."[8] It is therefore noteworthy and did not likely go unnoticed in their community that Francis's children carved out a path to landownership in such a hostile climate.

The oldest son, John, seems to have been the sibling who from the earliest, struggled most financially. While trust deeds show that John owned livestock and farming assets, there is no evidence that he ever purchased land.[9] He and

Inquiries numbered 7, 16, and 17 are not to be asked in respect to infants. Inquiries numbered 11, 12, 15, 16, 17, 19, and 20 are to be answered (if at all) merely by an affirmative mark, as /.

SCHEDULE 1.—Inhabitants in *13th Township*, in the County of *Noxubee*, State of *Miss*, enumerated by me on the *13* day of *July*, 1870.

Post Office: *Shuqualak Miss*   *A J Simmons* Ass't Marshal.

1	2	3 — The name of every person whose place of abode on the first day of June, 1870, was in this family.	4 — Age	5 — Sex	6 — Color	7 — Profession, Occupation, or Trade of each person, male or female.	8 — Value of Real Estate	9 — Value of Personal Estate	10 — Place of Birth	11	12	13	14	15	16	17	18 — Whether deaf and dumb, blind, insane, or idiotic	19	20
244	239	Sistrunk Francis	65	F	B	Farm Hand			Ga						/	/			/
		" Hillman	23	M	B	"			"						/	/		/	
		" Shedd	21	M	B	"			"						/	/		/	
		" Willie	18	M	B	"			"						/	/			
		" Lucretia	15	F	B	"			"						/	/			
		" Robt	9	M	B				Miss						/				
244	240	Harrison Fann	63	M	B	Farm Hand			Ala						/	/		/	
		" Leah	63	F	B				"						/	/			
		" William	40	M	B				"						/	/		/	
		" Richd	8	M	B				Miss						/	/			
		" Virginia	16	F	B				"						/	/			/
245	241	Dunham Rose M	45	M	B	Farm Hand									/	/			/
		Hoghey Ruby	22	F	B										/	/			
		" Annie	3	F	B														
	242	" Savannah	25	F	B	Farm Hand									/	/			
		" John	5	M	B				"										
		" Mattie	3	F	B				"										
		" Sarah	2	F	B				"										
246	243	Richards Geo	64	M	W	Farmer	1240	884	Ga					—					/
		" Lucinda	60	F	W									—					
		" William S	23	M	W				Ala					—			Idiotic	/	/
		" Warren Jr	21	M	W				"					—				/	
		" Thos W	18	M	W				Miss					—					
247	244	Schooler Isaac	26	M	B	Farm Hand			Ala						/	/		/	
248	245	Burrage John H	55	M	W	Farmer	2700	900	D.C.					—				/	
		" Mary	42	F	W				Ala					—					
		" Washington P	17	M	W				Miss					—					
		" Rosalee	14	F	W				"					—					
		" Joseph	10	M	W				"					—					
		" Sarah	7	F	W				"										
		" Martha	5	F	W				"										
		" Anna	4	F	W				"										
		" Lucy	2	F	W				"										
		" Mary	3/12	F	W				"			Mar							
349	246	Matthews Stephen	58	M	W	Painter	700	500	Ala					—				/	
		" Elizabeth	52	F	W				N.C.					—					
		" Mary	18	F	W				Miss					—					
		" Emma	27	F	W	Cook			"						/	/			
		Bell Nan	22	F	W				"						/	/			
350	247	Harris George	50	M	B	Farm Hand			Ala						/	/		/	

No. of dwellings 8   No. of white females 10   No. of males, foreign born ——
" " families 7   " colored males 11   " " females ——   No. of insane —— Idiots 1
" " white males 5   " females 11   " " blind ——

1870 Census, Noxubee County. Francis and children named, with incorrect age for Francis. Oldest son, John, is married with children, so he is not enumerated in Francis's household.

his wife, Chany, had three daughters who died by 1900, and these deaths left them with the added responsibility of providing for the grandchildren that were orphaned.[10] They had no sons and the children's father does not appear to have assumed responsibility for their care. Shadrick faced ongoing financial challenges as well, but he and his son, Noah, are landowners at the dawn of the twentieth century.[11] By the decade's end, however, sometime around 1910, Shadrick's land would be lost, and his wife, Susan, appears in Tallahatchie County, MS, on the 1910 Census as a widow.[12] Remaining in possession of his land, Hillman would live another decade after the death of his brothers, but as the next and final chapter reveals, his final years would not bring ease.

Two Cistrunk brothers were among early Blacks in postwar Noxubee to purchase and farm their own land, and their sister, Lucretia, who married at a young age a man more than a decade her senior, maintained ownership of their land after her husband's death.[13] Until she remarried, she would, like her mother, assume the role of household head. Land and farming were the source of economic stability for the Cistrunks, but they recognized that education was central to Black uplift. While the 1870 Census showed Francis and all members of her household unable to read or write, ten years later in the 1880 Census Hillman, Shadrick, and Lucretia were recorded as able to read and write.[14] Hillman and Shadrick appear to have been committed to the education of children in their own family as well as others in their community. This is illustrated in several enumerations of educable children in Noxubee County where we see the brothers registering their own family members and children that do not appear to be from their immediate households or blood relations.[15]

As discussed in the previous chapter, with her grandson Noah, a member of Brushfork Baptist Church, and son Shadrick, likely a member, Francis was probably among the church's early members. The earliest extant records of Brushfork's operations and members extend back to the entries in their 1944 records in the *Boyd National Baptist Sunday School Minute, Roll and Record Book* that were part of recordkeeping in Baptist churches. Noah Cistrunk was the last Cistrunk member of the church, and by 1944, he had been deceased for seven years. His Hunt in-laws and their descendants would remain members to the present, but in the extant church history that was first committed to writing by member Ethel Mosley before her death in 2013, there is no mention of Cistrunks among the list of past and present deacons and leaders of the church.[16] Ethel Mosley was born in 1924; she would have been 13 years old at the time of Noah's death. When she recorded names of church leaders she would have been working from her memory and from the earliest record book of the church which only went as far back as 1944. Noah's son, Bunnie

Cistrunk, who was Ms. Mosley's contemporary, passed on his memory of Noah's membership at Brushfork and his burial service there. It is haunting to think how easily an aspect of life that was so central to Noah and his family's memory so easily disappeared in the collective memory of the church. Current Brushfork secretary, Ms. Jeanette Parks, informed me that her mother, Ms. Mosley, who had been church secretary for twenty to thirty years, had told her that early records had been destroyed in early damage to the old church. She could not recall whether the cause had been fire or some other hazard, but the result is that while details of the church's beginning are known and still retold today, Noah is among those early members whose names have been lost to the church's written history. The Brushfork Church like so many rural churches had limited monthly services, which may have created a disconnect between members like Noah who resided outside the community and those who were locals.[17] Until the 1990s Brushfork held one monthly Sunday service and Noah probably attended local churches in Winston County when he did not travel to Brushfork for the monthly service on each fourth Sunday.

While the family's remembrance of Brushfork Baptist Church is tied to Noah's membership and service there, it is again not unlikely that his devotion to the church was spawned from that of the family matriarch, Francis. Historian Evelyn Higginbotham reminds us of the importance of Black women in the history of the Black church: "Women were crucial to broadening the public arm of the church and making it the most powerful institution of racial self-help in the African-American community" and representing the largest African American denomination, the Black Baptist Church was leader in this regard.[18] Brushfork has a new location and building since its 1890 location, but the church bell that was either purchased for the new construction in 1890 or moved from a previous location, stands today at the entrance to the church grounds. When the Brushfork congregation purchased land in 1890 for its then new location, they were among the more than "1.3 million Black Baptists in the South," and again women were the majority demographic among that membership.[19] As with the collective body of Black churches, Black Baptist churches continued the legacy of the hush harbors, responding to the ongoing and new challenges for African Americans in the post-enslavement era. Throughout the South, these churches served as "critical communication hubs, meeting places and sites for dissemination of information," and were "instrumental in maintaining morale, providing material support," and helping to build future leadership.[20] The Black church fed the spirit, but it also was the anchor of family and community solidarity and survival. The continuation of this legacy is seen today for example in the biennial Noah Cistrunk family reunion, which centers its celebration around prayer and worship, and from a long historical legacy, still recognizes the Black church as the anchor of their historical survival.

The lives of Black southerners intersected the everyday world of southern society in which whites presumed that Blacks had no equal place. In matters that may be considered the building blocks of society, the post-reconstructed South had been "redeemed" by whites in the interest of white rule. In their everyday lives Blacks intersected a world of white redemption politics, economics, and social mores that compounded the difficulties of building a secure life during the harsh economic times for the nation's farmers at the close of the nineteenth century. No less than the case had been during centuries of enslavement, Blacks found that solidarity and cooperation remained central to their survival. Black churches were the axis upon which Black southerners navigated this dynamic whirlwind. The ethos of religious devotion and commitment to community advancement that became a driving force for the early Noxubee Cistrunks was consistent with "the nationalist consciousness of the Black Baptist church [that] came of age during the years of heightened racism" in the post-Reconstruction South.[21] The church was not only a place of worship but also a place of community organizing and information sharing. During the Black populist movement, from the 1880s to 1900, churches offered key support in initiatives to organize Blacks around voting and farming issues.[22] Black populism represented a widespread movement across the Black South, focusing on economic and political rights to improve the lives of the Black and mostly rural population of the South. One of its most celebrated and stalwart leaders was Oliver Cromwell, a Black Mississippian. Cromwell was killed in 1889 by white supremacists, but his bold leadership and his expectation that Blacks should and would have better lives in the South represented the spirit that carried many Black southerners in the worst of post-Reconstruction times.[23]

When one considers that "upwards of 92 percent of adult African Americans were landless" in the two post-Reconstruction decades, it is not unremarkable that the Cistrunks entered into landownership in the very year that marked the first southern Black migration.[24] The greater percentages of Blacks who did not leave the South at the close of Reconstruction found themselves trapped in the emerging world of sharecropping that was issued in "when confiscated land had been placed back into the hands of wealthier white southerners following the Civil War."[25] This transformed white plantocracy could no longer depend on chattel slavery as an institution, but this was replaced with the lien system that virtually chained Black farmers to plantation lords once again—this time through an institution of debt that white planters and merchants controlled.

The plan outlined by Shadrick and Hillman to purchase their land in 1879 appears to have been well-calculated. Having started out as tenant farmers themselves, the brothers farmed, bought farming supplies and livestock over the first post-emancipation decade, and managed to purchase their land through a loan. Rather than entering into a loan or indenture agreement with a local planter or white businessman, the brothers bought their land from Mobile & Ohio RR Co. through the Farmers' Loan and Trust Company.[26] Purchasing railroad land rather than buying from a local planter and securing the loan through a national rather than local company or individual spared them from yet another economic tie to the untrustworthy and unscrupulous whims of white locals who held economic power. By 1879 when the brothers purchased their tracts in the Bottom, the Farmers' Loan and Trust Company "was the trustee for 47 of the 128 railroad mortgages in which trust companies were appointed as trustees."[27] Farmers' was the "registrar and transfer agent," and their services built stockholder confidence.[28] The company prospered by maintaining mortgage activity and transactions that left stockholders feeling little risk of their investments being lost to fraud or dishonesty. That is not to say that the company did not find itself in legal contests and the subject of accusations, but Black borrowers, such as Hillman and Shadrick, were at least free of the personality whims that were integral to small-town transactions between Blacks and local white planters and businessmen.[29]

Black Mississippians found themselves for generations engulfed in a social infrastructure designed specifically to deny their rights to access these key elements in ways that could offer opportunities for economic stability or prosperity. The promise of the forty acres and a mule for the newly emancipated had dissipated even before the 1877 compromise, leaving Blacks to understand that farming land that they owned would not be their destiny as free people in the South. The Cistrunks were determined farmers, but like the body of Black southerners they understood that farming and landownership for Blacks were only pieces of the larger infrastructure necessary for long-standing security for Blacks. They thus saw education and voting rights as integral to improving the lives of Black southerners. It is not clear that the Cistrunks were ever open participants in politics or ever cast a ballot, but they embraced the ballot as a means to equal rights. The staunch rejection by white leadership and complicity of the white population against Black suffrage was made profoundly evident in the proposal and enactment of the 1890 poll tax, a legislative weapon that proved to be "most effectual" in barring Blacks from voting.[30] The combination of tenant farming and sharecropping and the requirement to pay a poll tax left few Blacks able to muster the fee required to cast a vote. While one might register to vote or remain on the voting roster, the final clearance required payment of the tax, so even if they were listed on tax rolls, in practice, Blacks were effectively denied this constitutional right.

At the dawn of the new century Mississippi law would require that the names of registrants whose poll taxes were unpaid be published in local newspapers. In Noxubee County, the *Macon Beacon* published the list each year beginning in 1900 after passage that year of the law that called for "publication of names of poll tax delinquents."[31] In a 1912 article, "Who May Vote in Mississippi," the details of the state's voting law were outlined for readers. This included a reminder that the $2.00 poll tax had to be paid, and if in arrears, the past two delinquent years had to be paid for clearance to vote.[32] This requirement alone was a hindrance for most would-be Black voters even if they remained registered voters in spite of threats and retaliation from whites. Cistrunks were regularly among those names published for delinquent poll taxes. In 1901, the year after passage of the 1900 law, the oldest brother, John, is among those listed.[33] In subsequent years the first freeborn generations of Cistrunks would also be stifled by poll taxes. Throughout the first decades of the new century Shadrick's son, Noah (b. 1882), and John's grandsons Dossie (b. 1885) and Elisha (b. 1883) would appear on Noxubee County's delinquent poll tax lists.[34] That the Cistrunks continued to appear on the published list of those in arrears on poll taxes reveals Mississippi's ongoing refusal to honor the right of Blacks to vote, and as was noted in the *Macon Beacon* in a May 19, 1911, article, the poll tax had accomplished its intended purpose.[35] In his complaint about whites who were allowed to vote despite being delinquent on their poll taxes, the columnist points out that this was an unintended consequence of a tax enacted so that "over 100,000 negroes in the State would default, thus disfranchising themselves." While great numbers of poor whites who were unable to pay their poll taxes were also denied the vote, the intended result of the tax had been achieved. The right of Blacks had been nullified, thus bringing "tranquility and prosperity" to the white populace.[36]

The continued presence of Cistrunks on the delinquent poll tax lists may easily be seen as a sign of defeat, and especially through the lens of whites who were expressly intent to deny them this right. Through the lens of the Cistrunks who would maintain their names on the voting rolls, their names speak defiance. What columnist, L. P. S. misses in his 1911 assertion that just because a man is registered to vote "does not necessarily mean that he is a qualified elector" is the symbolic power of having one's name called—that is, listed. Appearing on the delinquent list suggests itself an assumption of the right to vote, a recognition even, of the persons you are attempting to erase. The right to vote may be denied, but the right is nevertheless asserted. The appearance of a listed name suggests that barring the delinquent fee, the named person is a qualified elector. Moreover, out of a legacy where enslavers attempted to erase Blacks from the landscape by not naming them on official records, the Cistrunks are part of the record of Mississippi's voting history, even as Mississippi denied them the right to vote. Their names on those lists tell us that they were forced to endure this discrimination, but they were not accepting it. This defiance clearly sprang from the memory of the Reconstruction era when Blacks were able to and did energetically embrace this new symbol of their free status. Blacks had seen the right to vote as a key element of racial uplift during Reconstruction. Given their high population numbers in Mississippi, the rollback of this short-lived right of citizenry was a blow to the political power that Blacks would have otherwise mustered in the decades following emancipation.

Despite the disillusionment issued in by post-Reconstruction politics, there were certainly still moments of personal triumph and joy. By 1880 Francis was in her mid-50s and no longer carrying the weight of responsibility for six children. Perhaps she had the privilege of enjoying the role of grandmother. By year 1880 the birth of their daughter Annie (b. 1870) increased John and Chany's count to three children—all daughters; Lucretia and Alfred Dobbins were parents of son and daughter, Warren (b. 1871) and Emma (b. 1876); and Shadrick and Susan were parents of one child, Maria (b. 1878). From the youngest to the oldest, Francis's grandchildren would have spent from a year to more than a decade under her influence. With her sons leading the family's farming endeavors and her daughter married to an independent farmer, Francis was free of the pressures that come with being the provider. Living in the household of her son Shadrick and near the families of her other children, it must have been the most secure and forward-looking moment of her life. She was now living with the certainty that her children and grandchildren were free and that for the generations ahead, they too would live as free persons.

The final recorded appearance of Francis is the 1880 Census in the household of son Shadrick and his wife, Susan.[37] As with most of the nation's census records for 1890, Mississippi's enumerations were destroyed in the 1921 Commerce Department fire. It is therefore not clear whether Francis was alive in 1890; however, that she is not listed on the 1900 Census suggests that she died between 1880 and 1900, between the age of 52 and 70. In that near twenty-year period her adult children who remained in Noxubee had begun to set roots that looked promising for themselves and their posterity. By 1880, Willis and his wife, Hopea, had left Noxubee County. They appear to have moved to Jackson, MS, but Willis may have died soon after the birth of their son, Robert, in 1881.[38] There is no evidence that Willis, Hopea, or Robert ever returned or maintained contact with their family that remained in Noxubee. Robert Sistrunk's 1952 death certificate names his mother, Hopea, while showing "unknown" for his father. The record informant—his wife, Viola

Sistrunk—appears to have had little if any knowledge of Robert's father, Willis. This suggests that Robert was young when he lost his father to death or some other cause. After his 1880 enumeration in the 1880 Census in Noxubee, Willis does not appear again in the Census for Mississippi or in Tennessee where his son would later live.

With Willis's departure and the death of her son, Robert, Francis spent her last years in the circle of her Noxubee four: John, Hillman, Shadrick, Lucretia. By the close of the century, this circle expanded with additional births of grandchildren and great-grandchildren. Shadrick and Susan now had three biological children—Maria (b. 1878), Noah (b. 1882), and Sophia (b. 1882)—and Susan's biological relative Aggie Landrum (b. 1872).[39] John's daughters would become mothers by the mid-1880s, marking a new phase of his and Chany's lives as grandparents of three. Grandsons Elisha (b. 1883) and Dossie (b. 1885) and granddaughter Renee Holmes (b. 1883) would be living with John and Chany by 1900 and would remain close to their grandfather's family circle throughout their lives.[40] John and Chany's daughter Annie was the only one of their three children to marry. She married Bony Holmes in 1882, and gave birth to daughter, Renee, in the following year.[41] Francis's only daughter, Lucretia, was mother of two by the time of the 1880 Census. She and husband, Alfred, are recorded with son, Warren age 9, and 4-year-old daughter, Emma. If Francis lived at least three years after the 1880 Census, the birth of her first great-grandchild, Elisha, would have marked her as matriarch of a four-generation kinship circle: all free. Formed during and after the Civil War, this bonded unit would have been improbable in the enslaving society of the prewar South. Despite Mississippi's post-Reconstruction rebirth of white supremacist rule, Francis Cistrunk had come to know before her death a sense of security and joy with the family that she had brought through one of the worst human atrocities on record. She represented the generations of enslaved Blacks who lived when death may have seemed more inviting, who brought life into the world when killing may have seemed more practical, and who passed on a belief in Black humanity and perseverance that brought families like the Cistrunks to their four-generation collective in the twilight of the nineteenth century.

Reflecting on the legacy of enslavement that had shaped the first four decades of her life, Francis must have marveled at her own family's energy and optimism and that of their community. While there are no written accounts from the generation of emancipated Cistrunks to tell their experiences and perceptions of this period, by simply tracing their transactions throughout decades of trust deeds from the 1870s into the early years of the twentieth century, an informative and dynamic narrative emerges. These deeds show the Cistrunks as farmers and reveals the annual financial anxiety that certainly hovered over their lives. The family borrowed yearly to cover the costs of preparing and bringing crops to harvest. Most emphatically these deeds capture the herculean resolve summoned by Hillman and Shadrick to not only purchase their own land but to hold it in their name until death. In some years this meant not only attending to their own land but leasing other land to farm as well. In 1879, the year that Shadrick and Hillman would enter into a trust to purchase their land, they would also sign deeds of trust to secure funds for raising crops on land they rented.[42] They would continue this practice of cultivating their own land while lease farming. This is much like households today with family members working multiple jobs to meet household expenses and to work toward financial security. The brothers worked this strategy to both pay the mortgages on the land they had purchased and to bring in sufficient income to cover the expenses of maintaining their households.

Executing trust deeds in 1879, John, Hillman, and Shadrick borrowed $100 each to secure supplies and necessities for planting and bringing their crops to harvest.[43] These trust deeds were secured through promissory notes that guaranteed transfer of the crops harvested during the season as well as livestock and other assets to the trustee in the event of default. These were high stakes contracts for farmers who had little cash reserves and whose livelihoods were tied to the livestock and farming assets they owned. To lose these assets could leave one no other recourse except sharecropping, which was in most instances considered the worst of options. Sharecroppers lived on and farmed land they didn't own. To meet the fundamental costs of food and shelter, they borrowed against the estimated worth of the crops they would harvest for the landowner while being bound to the accounting ledgers maintained by the landowner who determined their debt and their income. It was well-known that this system was a new iteration of slaving: Those who worked had no power in the negotiation and no oversight of the accounting. Just as in the antebellum era, the legal and law enforcement systems stood ready to authorize and enforce the practices. Like Blacks throughout Noxubee County, the state of Mississippi, and the US South at large, the Cistrunks lived this battle.

Hillman's loan amount in 1879 may have been the result of debt that mounted from an 1877 trust deed he executed with his brother John.[44] In this contract, Hillman was the lender to John, for $101.25. If John did not fully repay this debt, it may have resulted in the need for Hillman to later borrow in excess of what he needed for his own farming needs. Trust deeds from years 1879 to 1881 showing John and Hillman sharing half interest in a grey horse mule suggest that Hillman's half interest may have been a partial payment from John on the 1877 debt to Hillman.[45] That John may have had an ongoing problem with repaying loans is underscored in trust deeds for years 1880 and 1881. Unable to fully repay the $125 he borrowed in an 1880 trust deed, John executed a trust deed in the subsequent year for $250 to cover the balance from 1880 plus the amount he was borrowing for year 1881.[46] In the 1880 trust deed John's collateral is not uncommon among deeds executed by his Black farming peers during this period. He commits his half interest in the grey horse mule, along with two cows, two calves, his entire crop of corn, cotton fodder, and other produce that he may raise on both properties that he leases. The ante is magnified, however, in 1881, as he must borrow to cover past debt and money needed for the present year. In this agreement the collateral increases to two mules, three cows, three calves and their increase, three bull yearlings, and all cotton, corn, and produce he farmed on any lands.

Hillman and Shadrick fared better than John in these start-up years. Their execution of trust deeds throughout the 1880s highlight Hillman and Shadrick's early and ongoing determination to secure their properties in their own names, free of a mortgage. Through the last decades of the century, they settled into what seems a constant and manageable financial regimen to cover expenses for each year's crop. Their loans during this period were as little as $51 and $150 on the higher end. The terms of these trust deeds required the borrower to offer chattel as collateral. This meant that in addition to their harvested crops that always included cotton and corn, they would also stake all other crops they raised along with livestock such as horses, mules, cows, calves, and steers. In many years the terms were so definitive and burdensome that in addition to cows and their calves being specified, cows and "their increase" were also stipulated.[47] The stakes grew over the years as well. In 1877 Shadrick borrowed $68.32 and his collateral was "one gray mare mule and two bales cotton raised on the AH Marrs place."[48] In 1886 he would execute a deed of trust, borrowing $85. In this contract Shadrick would stake three cows and their increase, two calves, one bull, one mule, and his "entire cotton crop, cotton seed, corn fodder and all other products of agriculture to be grown by myself my family and employees on the place on which I reside or on any other land that I may cultivate or have cultivated the present year."[49] Contracts like these left the lender in a win-win situation and the borrower in a survive-or-lose-all predicament. If Shadrick were unable to repay the $85 loan, he, his family, and anyone else working with him would effectively realize no revenue for their months of labor. This was revenue needed to fund their households until the next growing season. This unimaginable pressure constituted the norm for all parties. It was a system that allowed little room for a bad crop year or personal calamities. There was no safety net, no golden parachute. There was the limited autonomy of farming as a landowner; and then there was sharecropping.

In this world of high stakes, limited options, and extortionist lending practices, the Cistrunks and their community had to forge a living, a life, and a

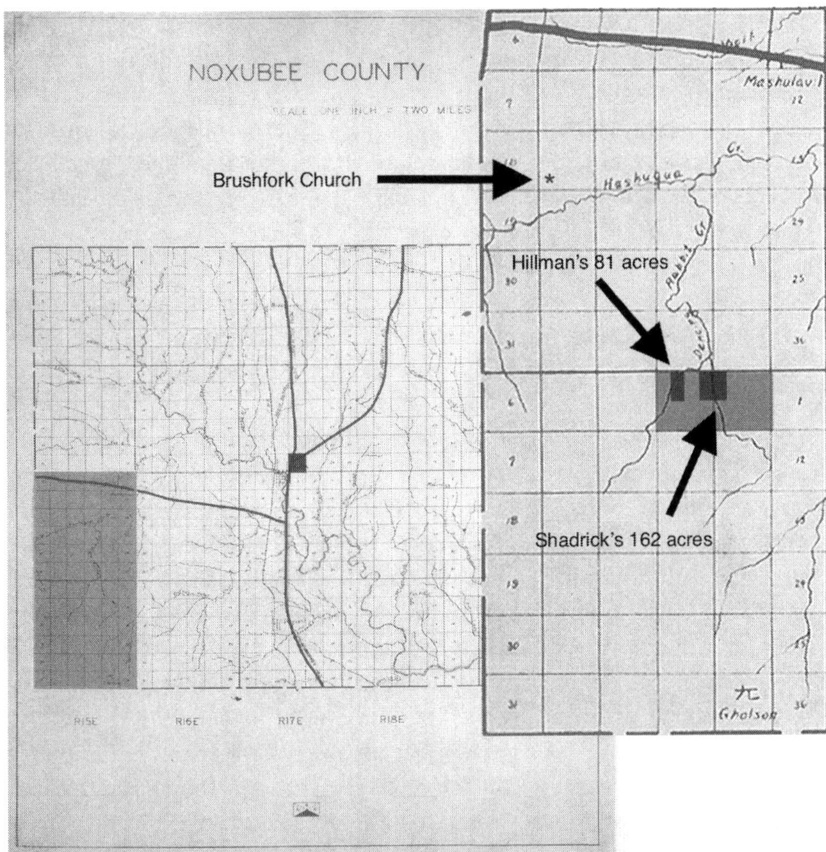

*Map of Noxubee County showing the lots owned by brothers Hillman and
Shadrick. Courtesy of the Archives and Records Services Division, Mississippi
Department of Archives and History.*

vision for a more promising tomorrow. They did this by working together
and offering support where they could. Hillman's loan to John in 1877 suggests that from the start, this ethos of collaboration and industry defined their
journey as freed people. The proximity of their lands contributed to their
ability to maintain family collaboration. The 1880 Census shows Hillman, Lucretia, and Shadrick and their households listed on the same page in sequen-
tial order.[50] Oldest sibling, John, and his household appear five entries before
Hillman, on the previous page.[51] On the western boundary, Shadrick's eighty-
one acres in Section 3, Township13, Range 15 met the eastern boundary of
Hillman's property, also located in that same grid. Shadrick owned an additional eighty-one acres in Section 2, adjacent to the eastern border of his land

in Section 3. The brothers' adjacent properties were purchased in 1879, at a price of $121.83 for Shadrick and Hillman paying $162.44. The 1879 deed of trust for these contracts do not appear to have been maintained in the court archives; however, when the deed loans are fully paid in 1900, the original purchasing price is noted.[52] Why Hillman's land commanded the higher price is not clear. Though tributaries of Dancing Rabbit Creek seem to have flowed in part across both properties, water accessibility and volume may have influenced the difference in prices.[53]

The Cistrunks collaborated both within their own family and with members of their community. Again, yearly trust deeds offer insight into the ethos of community and cooperation. In 1881 Shadrick cosigned with Leboo Coleman, who appears to have been a neighboring farmer.[54] The two are coborrowers for a $125 loan that is guaranteed through the promise of their entire crop of cotton, corn, and other agricultural products that they and their families would grow that season. Leboo stakes his crops as does Shadrick, but Shadrick offers the additional livestock collateral. No other livestock are offered other than Shadrick's mule, named Rody, and his cows, Beulah and Sophie, that appear on trustee deeds that he executes alone.[55] In 1883 Hillman and brother-in-law Alfred Dobbins are connected on separate trustee deeds where each offers their half of a mutually owned Tennessee wagon as collateral.[56] In a 1909 trust deed cosigned by Hillman, his wife, Harriet, and their neighbor Martha Lloyd for a loan of $315.00 (deed of trust with E. F. Nunn & Co), we see again an example of the collective economics of southern Black communities. In this contract we find a rare occasion where Hillman offers his land—all eighty-one acres—as collateral for a loan.[57] That he and Harriet would have entered into a contract with Martha, staking their land—the one major asset that they owned outright—suggests a relationship that had developed over years. The Lloyd and Cistrunk families appear on the same pages for the 1880 and 1900 Census reports.[58] The 1880 record shows 48-year-old Joe Lloyd, his wife, Hester, and their family. Twenty years later the 1900 Census suggests that Joe and Hester have died, and the Lloyd family is now headed by 37-year-old Martha. Martha and her five children, ages 11 months to 17 years, are listed directly below Hillman. Martha is not listed in the Lloyd household in the 1880 Census, but she may have been overlooked by the enumerator or living elsewhere at the time of the Census. As the Freedmen's records reveal, it was not uncommon after the Civil War for adolescent and teenage Blacks to be remanded to servitude in white households until they reached adulthood. Joe Lloyd was a farmer, and while he may not have owned his own land, he may have owned chattel assets that Martha could leverage in a trust deed. This would explain her role as coborrower on the 1909 trust deed.

White supremacy in the South depended on maintaining Blacks in poverty, and landlessness was central to the equation: "Black landownership . . . threatened the control of both land and labor which formed the foundations of the plantation economy."[59] As Black landowners, Shadrick and Susan understood that their landownership was always under threat, and that any hope for a future in independent farming for their family required the commitment of all. The inclusion of their 27-year-old son, Noah, as witness on the 1908 trust deed for a $170 loan illustrates their understanding of the necessity to educate Noah in the financial aspects of farming as a business, and this would have additionally signaled to Noah that he was an integral part of the family business collective.[60] Noah entered adulthood as part of a family farming unit determined to hold on to their land—the reins to their future. He had spent his formative years witnessing his father and uncles living stressful but financially autonomous lives. It was probably this image of self-determined, self-assured men that set the model for Noah that he would pass on to his children. Perhaps it is this deep level of self-respect and resistance that informed what I have been told was one of Noah's repeated maxims to his children: "If your head ain't itching, don't scratch it." Noah's son, Bunnie Cistrunk, who was a young boy of only 10 years when his father died in 1937, told me that Noah's words stayed with him throughout his childhood and into adulthood. Noah was shaped by those who raised him and, it is therefore more likely than not, that the straight and stern self-assuredness he demanded of his children was conveyed to him from his parents and elders.

While Shadrick and Hillman had served as models for Noah when he signed as witness on his parents' 1908 trust deed, there was one cautionary tale that loomed. While Noah was an infant when his uncle John met with financial misfortune, the lingering memory for his father, Shadrick, and uncle Hillman must have left the family pensive at knowing how the potential for financial ruin lurked and could unravel with lightning speed. After the financial hurdle that John faced in 1880 and 1881, his name does not appear on trust deeds in subsequent years, suggesting that he lost all or most of his chattel assets. With no livestock and no substantial farming assets, John would have had to resort to sharecropping. He was probably spared this fate, however, because of the more secure circumstances of his brothers, Hillman and Shadrick, and his sister, Lucretia, and her husband, Alfred. With his siblings as landowners and lease farmers, John could work under their contracts and not resort to sharecropping to secure food and shelter.

The industry and solidarity of the formerly enslaved Cistrunks is underscored in the records of their financial transactions and commitment to finding self-sufficiency through farming. Their adaptability, like those in their community, was most evident in their ability to stay alive in a culture where the Thirteenth Amendment may have been law, but the 1857 Dred Scott ruling was still the custom: Blacks effectively "had no rights which the white man was bound to respect."[61] Throughout the late nineteenth-century South, Blacks held a deep respect for and faith in education and the necessity for literacy. The first-generation freed Cistrunks were ensuring that their children would be educated, but they too felt compelled to be literate. By 1880 Hillman, Shadrick, and Lucretia could read and write, and in the 1900 Census, John was designated as able to read.[62] Ironically, however, throughout the decades of trust deeds signed by the Cistrunks, their names were always entered by the person penning the contract, and they were required to sign their "mark," that is an *X*. Clearly, this was one of the many embedded insults designed to maintain ongoing stereotypes of Blacks as the inferiors of whites. Perhaps this was the defining impetus for the departure of Margaret Murray (Washington), one of Noxubee's most celebrated Black figures. Today in Macon, Noxubee's county seat, a landmark stands in recognition of Margaret Murray, who was born in Macon in 1861 and educated there in the years after the war. She left Macon as a teenager, and after attending Fisk University, accepted a position at Tuskegee Institute and later became the third wife of Booker T. Washington. Murray left Noxubee, but she is an important figure symbolizing the primacy that Blacks placed on literacy and education even in the face of severe economic and political repression.[63]

Whites may have imposed their supremacist discourse in public-facing encounters, but Blacks had their own churches, schools, and social clubs where they were able to promote racial uplift. Churches were places of worship, sources of support in the communities, and they were also physical structures that Blacks built to outwardly express their solidarity and pride. Today, old iron church bells are one example of that expression still found in some churches dating back to post-emancipation era Noxubee. While their present-day structures are not the original buildings of the earliest church worshippers, Brushfork Baptist Church (established pre-1890, rebuilt circa 1992) and Second Baptist M.B. Church (established 1867, rebuilt 1990) are among local churches that still display the church bells from the old church architecture. Blacks in Noxubee introduced these bells into their churches in the latter decades of the nineteenth century. The bells were a transformation of a pre-emancipation tradition of calling out, or "hollering," the news of a death. Prohibited from freely traveling across the countryside, enslaved people employed "hollers" and other methods as workarounds for communication. Word of newly deceased members of the community would be announced and spread by a chain of hollers.[64] The constraints of movement were less severe in the postbellum era, and the hollers were not as vital a communication tool as they had been. While not a necessity for communication among the freed people,

Brushfork Baptist Church and bell

the church bells served as a symbol or reminder of the legacy of the hollers. They would have reminded the earliest congregations of the rituals they observed as enslaved people to show respect and to honor the dead. The church bells were not a necessity for church worship; for generations, enslaved African Americans had practiced their spirituality without them. By the closing decade of the nineteenth century, however, the bells hoisted out front for public viewing symbolized the church's resilience. Not only were these Black churches standing decades into postwar racist aggression, but some, like Brushfork, celebrated their endurance by adorning their exterior with an object that spoke to their financial capacity and will.

No known records remain that would confirm Shadrick and Susan's household as members of Brushfork, but as discussed earlier, the dedication of their son, Noah, suggests that this was probably his church home from a young age. Noah's second-youngest son, Bunnie, along with other Cistrunk descendants convey their first- and secondhand knowledge of Noah's membership. In the twenty years that Noah lived in Winston County, on Sundays he crossed the county line into Noxubee, returning to Brushfork to attend service and carry out his duties as deacon. Similarly, while no known records exist to confirm that Shadrick and Noah were Prince Hall Masons, family accounts that Noah's oldest son, Carl, was a Mason leave the possibility worth considering. Founded by Prince Hall in 1784, Prince Hall Masons were located primarily in

Photograph (hung in foyer entrance of the newer church location on Hwy 14) of old Brushfork Baptist Church. The bell was located inside the church steeple.

Ruins of old Brushfork Baptist Church

The bell at Second Baptist M.B. Church

the North during the antebellum era. This African American branch of free-masonry was introduced throughout the South in the aftermath of the Civil War, and the first Mississippi lodge was organized in 1867 in Vicksburg.[65]

Although lodges have no church affiliations, Prince Hall Masons have historically been tied to Black churches. It is likely therefore that among Prince Hall Masons in Noxubee, membership would have included worshipers from Brushfork Baptist Church. Membership into Prince Hall Masons is extended through invitation and priority is awarded candidates who have family member affiliates. Though separate from the church, Prince Hall Masons have a tradition of active service in their churches, and from the time of their founding they advocated for Black solidarity and uplift. Remembering two of my uncles who were Prince Hall Masons, I recall their commitment to church and to the advancement of Black people in their communities. Children of Carl recall that he was a Prince Hall Mason and Carl's sister, Arah, was an Eastern Star, which is the women's affiliate organization of the Prince Hall Masons. Carl's membership may have been facilitated through that of his father and grandfather, who may have been Masons themselves, or in close alliance with them. Prince Hall Masons are known as a tight-knit collective that operates as a family or kinship group, working often behind the scenes to support efforts or advance interests of their Black communities. Again, given their active family and community alliances, Hillman and Shadrick may very well have been members of a Noxubee lodge. Even in Mississippi, freemasonry allowed for a blurring of the strict publicly drawn racial lines. This is exemplified in an account an elder family member shared of his experience as a Prince Hall Mason in 1940s Mississippi. He explained that despite the pervasive racial intimidation that whites executed against Blacks, he encountered white freemasons of other orders who would sometimes, in private, share important aid and advice. This network proved helpful in shaping his decisions while still in Mississippi, including his decision to migrate north in search of his dream to become a journeyman electrician. It is this story that I recall when considering the conciliatory reception of Hillman by H. S. Halbert, an official who interviewed him in 1895 to confirm the location of a historic site marking the official settling of Mississippi. Accompanied by two white locals who were well-informed on the history of the county and guided by written records and accounts, Halbert visited the grounds to locate and confirm the site where the 1830 Treaty of Dancing Rabbit Creek had been signed. In his report, Halbert summarized his findings as follows: "On the 29th of October last, I visited the treaty-ground in company with Mr. J. A. Jernigan, of Noxubee County. The ground is on the farm of a respectable old negro, named Hillman Sistrunk, who conducted us to the locality described by Mr. Shields, and who also told us that this was the place that he had always heard the old settlers speak of as the treaty ground."[66]

Halbert, despite being accompanied by two white locals, quotes Hillman to affirm his conclusion, which underscores one of those rare moments that a white southerner would show deference to a Black man—particularly in a public document. Whether this extraordinary encounter was informed by connections that any of the parties may have had to freemasonry is uncertain, but not unlikely. Hillman, Halbert and/or other parties who may have introduced them may have been operating through the network of freemasonry. Halbert acknowledged Hillman as an authoritative source, and Hillman certainly did not miss the implication of such acknowledgment: A white authority had publicly recognized him as landowner on the site of the state's birth. Halbert and the state of Mississippi established in official government records that Hillman's land marked the grounds where the 1830 Treaty of Dancing Rabbit Creek had been signed. Halbert's account reveals Hillman's pride in being the possessor of this property, and it also reveals his assumption of the role of historian. He had not been in Mississippi or born at the time of the treaty, but Hillman understood the historical importance of that 1830 event, and he logged it in his memory. Remarkably, two decades following this exceptional moment, Hillman would be dispossessed of his land. Today, a painting of the treaty hangs in the Macon City post office and a state historical signpost reveals the nearby location of the treaty site where a fragment of the land has been remanded to the original inhabitants, the Choctaw, as a sacred burial ground. This place that marks the home and history of the Choctaw, who had been displaced, also marks the beginnings for a family freed from a legacy of displacement and forced migration. Hillman may have never reflected on the paradoxical histories of displacement between the Choctaw and his family that were tied to this land. That he and his family expected to settle in and establish this new place as home is reflected not only in his assumption as owner of the land but also as voice of its history. It is ironic that the contemporary public narratives of this key historical piece of land

Highway marker noting site where the Treaty of Dancing Rabbit Creek was signed

Treaty site now a Choctaw memorial ground

From a painting depicting the signing of the Treaty of Dancing Rabbit Creek, which hangs in the Macon post office

carry no mention of the "respectable old negro" who during his life, assumed stewardship of the land and its history.

THE DEATH OF FRANCIS AND THE HORIZON OF A NEW CENTURY

Francis's absence on the 1900 Census confirms that she had died sometime before the new century. Matriarch of a kinship collective propelled by the promise of familial permanency that seemed beyond imagination prior to the Civil War, she had lived a remarkable journey. She set her family's stakes in Noxubee, the Mississippi county and community that they had known little more than a year before the close of the war. After being forcibly moved across county and state lines from childhood, the emancipated Francis chose to stand firmly upon the ground where she had entered into freedom to plant the seeds for a new legacy. From childhood, her life had been marked by loss and separation, by the physical and mental violation that enslaved women constantly faced, and by the prospect that she and her posterity would never know freedom. Francis was the product of generations of enslaved people who had no immediate hope of freedom for themselves, but who had eyed the future, knowing that their generations would not always be enslaved. She was informed by an ethos that centered enslaved people in the confirmation of their humanity, readying them for the time of deliverance. Enslaved people were not guided by the vision of eternal captivity. They believed that freedom would come, and when it did, they would enter into a new realm with the force and expectation that fuels the human spirit. Francis died encircled by four of her children and two new generations of Cistrunks, all living and working together, anticipating the brighter future ahead.

The Cistrunks's optimism at the turn of the century became tempered by rocky financial times over the first decades of the new century. The struggles were wearying on their finances and their health. By spring of 1920 the three brothers, John, Shadrick, and Hillman had died. I have found no death certificate for John or Shadrick, but it appears they both died sometime between enumeration of the 1900 and 1910 Census reports. Shadrick died in late 1909 or perhaps early 1910, evidenced by the record of Susan on the 1910 Census listed as widow. Hillman died in March 1920, a decade after Shadrick's death.[67] Shadrick and Hillman would be dispossessed of their land in the closing months of their lives. The last standing of Francis's six offspring would be daughter, Lucretia, who had seen her share of hardships as well. As the younger of the four children who settled in Noxubee County, it is not surprising that her brothers would precede her in death. Her younger age had not however rendered her life less filled with loss and struggle. The new century opened for Lucretia in the shadow of two losses beyond her mother's death. Between the years 1880 and 1900, she lost her first husband, Alfred, in 1889, and only a few years afterward, before the close of the century, their older child, Warren, died.[68] Lucretia did not remain widowed forever. Six years after Alfred Dobbin's death she married Hyram McDaniel, a farm laborer, five years her junior, who had resided in the Dobbins's household years earlier.[69] Having married the widowed Lucretia, Hyram was designated head of household on the 1900 Census with Lucretia's and Alfred's daughter, Emma Fleming, and her two young children shown as residing in the household as well. As had been the case in 1880 when Dobbins was head of household, the 1900 Census shows the property as owned. Lucretia would be the only living child of Francis when the 1920 Census for Noxubee County was enumerated, and she was shown as head of household and her land as owned.[70]

John Cistrunk's household was the hardest hit by deaths in the last two decades of the nineteenth century. By 1900 his three daughters had died, and he and wife Chany were the guardians of their two orphaned grandsons, 16-year-old Elisha and 14-year-old Dossie, and one granddaughter, 16-year-old Renee Holmes.[71] In December 1882, John and Chany's 12-year-old daughter Annie married 20-year-old Bony Holmes, a "student" who appeared on the 1880 Census living in John's household. The marriage may not have been a voluntary choice for either, in particular Bony, who might have consented under the threat of criminal charges. The birth of Bony and Annie's child

Renee in June 1883, six months after their marriage, suggests that Annie was pregnant at the time of their marriage. If this was the case, Bony could have faced charges for engaging in sexual relations with a minor. Bony and Annie do not seem to have remained married for long, and the records leave unanswered questions about Bony's role as father to Renee. When Renee appears on the 1900 Census in in the household of her grandparents, John and Chany, her father Bony is shown in a separate household. Bony is recorded as head of household, listed with his wife of 16 years, Alabama, and their seven children, ages 4–16. If this record is correct, this was Bony's second wife whom he would have married a year after Renee's birth. Annie is not listed in her parent's household which suggest that she may have died shortly after giving birth to Renee. It is difficult to discern whether Bony Holmes married Annie as a favor to the Cistrunks or whether he had taken advantage of their minor child. There is no evidence of open hostility or disagreement between Bony and the Cistunks, that is, none that appears in court records. Bony remained in the community, seemingly naming three of his children—John, Annie, and Charity—after members of the Cistrunk household.[72] Whether Renee was Bony's biological child is uncertain, but of his own accord or perhaps under pressure from his new wife, he left Renee to be raised by John and Chany after Annie's death.

By the year 1900 the grandchildren in John and Chany's household were old enough to help work in the home and in the field, offering some relief. Depending on how long the children had been orphaned, however, John and Chany may have spent more years having to provide for them than having them as helping hands in the family's farming pursuits. Chany would have missed having the children's mothers present to help care for them as she managed the household. In 1900, at ages 56 and 54 respectively, John and Chany had already raised their three daughters but found themselves in a second cycle of child rearing. This would have offered them little opportunity to lighten the heavy stress that came with not only providing for self, but for dependent grandchildren. With the decades of labor and financial commitment required to keep them fed, clothed, and sheltered, there would have been little room for monetary indulgences or relief from household demands. For John and Chany this may have felt like a grind with little promise of better circumstances. Perhaps it was witnessing these conditions that inspired their grandson Elisha's later foray into illegal whisky production. In 1913, the *Macon Beacon* reported that Elisha, who it appears was also known as "the Mashulaville Tiger," had been returned to Noxubee from Indianola, MS, to face charges of "retailing." Business must have been good if he in fact paid the $50 for each of the three convictions.[73] In its most devastating and despairing form, poverty can inspire extremes of risky behaviors. In the Prohibition Bible

Belt South, a Black man running whisky was certainly daring. Elisha seems to have been a risk taker, but it is unclear how the fifty-day jail sentence may have tempered his activity. Elisha survived the experience, as evidenced in subsequent Census and deed records in Noxubee County, and remarkably by 1920 he would appear on the Census as a landowner.[74]

With their mother gone, sons, Hillman and Shadrick, continued the effort she led at the end of the Civil War. They entered the new century with a triumph that seemed a sign of future prosperity and confirmation that their roots were being firmly planted in Noxubee County. In 1900 the brothers fulfilled their loan obligations.[75] This meant that the deeds were conveyed to them, showing them as landowners outright, free of any encumbrances. This was a major accomplishment, but it may have been as well a target on their backs. Black landownership was a threat to whites, and Black entrepreneurs and independent farmers were ready targets for whites who deemed them not only "uppity," but also a threat to white rule. The answer to what many whites saw as visible threats was visible retaliation, and lynching was the most formidable of white responses to Blacks who inspired notions of Black prosperity and racial equality. This was most notably and widely publicized in the lectures and writings of Mississippi native Ida B. Wells whose anti-lynching campaign was so impactful that it forced her into exile from Mississippi.[76] In her most noted publication, *The Red Record* (1895), Wells documents the history of lynching in the thirty-year aftermath of the Civil War. She contends that in the postwar era where Blacks were no longer legal property, and their death did not then amount to a financial loss for a white person, freedom meant that "the Negro was not only whipped and scourged; he was killed."[77] Wells argued further that "the statistics as gathered and preserved by white men, and which have not been questioned, show that during these years more than ten thousand Negroes have been killed in cold blood, without the formality of judicial trial and legal execution."[78] An 1896 newspaper article summarizing the shooting of a Black farmhand in Noxubee County reveals the ease with which whites could execute life-threatening violence against Blacks with no concern for scrutiny or retribution. Conveying only the summary of events from the perspective of Mr. Joe Lee, the white shooter, the article explains that after encountering "trouble with one of his hands about getting in the crop," Lee shot the "negro" after he had "made an attack on him."[79] It was believed that the unnamed "negro" would survive if blood poison did not set in, but there was no concern articulated by Lee or the unnamed author of the article about penalty for shooting the Black farm laborer. The Civil War was thirty years in the country's past by this time, but the encounter described by Lee illustrates that slavery had been resurrected out of the ashes of the war into a new edition of the earlier form.

The Cistrunks themselves appear to have been spared the loss of family to this mode of violence, but lynching was a looming weapon in the arsenal of white supremacist terrorism. They would have been aware of the threat and the need to operate cautiously. Blacks who owned land or had successful business ventures knew that to flaunt their achievements was to flirt with death. Lynching was clearly a looming threat to such insolence, but financial sabotage at the hands of whites was also a well-known tactic. How well the Cistrunks treaded these trepid waters is not certain. Whether they raised the ire of local whites is not clear, but if one considers Noah's maxim to his sons, "If your head ain't itching, don't scratch it," the Cistrunks had inherited an unmistakable disdain for cowering to whites. If the Cistrunks were refusing to follow fundamental protocol, that is, common performances such as looking downward when addressed by a white person, shuffling the body in a show of uncertainty when addressed by or in the company of a white person, or scratching the head in a show of confusion to signal one's limited intelligence, then they would have been navigating life under the radar of white displeasure. They would have been targets.

Despite a racial climate that was never without disquietude, the bright future foreshadowed by Shadrick and Hillman's ownership deeds seemed manifested for Shadrick through the expansion of his family. He and wife, Susan, would witness the marriage of their firstborn, Maria, in 1893 to Isaac Grimmett, son of Mike and Eveline Grimmett, a Black landowning family in their Noxubee community.[80] Within a few years Maria and Isaac grew their household with the birth of two children, Will (b. 1896) and Lillie (b. 1898), presenting Shadrick and Susan with their first grandchildren. In 1900 daughter Sophie still resided in her parents' household, but a year later she too married a member of the Grimmett household, 19-year-old Will Grimmett, younger brother of Mary's husband, Isaac.[81] The sisters seemed to be following their cousin Warren Dobbins with their attraction to the Grimmetts: In 1890 Warren had married Mary Grimmett, older sister of Isaac and Will. Shadrick and Susan's only son, Noah, looked to a different household in 1900 when at age 18 he married 16-year-old Lula Hudson. The couple had not been married a year when they were enumerated on the Census that year. They would have children in rather rapid succession: Carl in 1901, and daughter, Lula, in 1902.[82] Lula Hudson's parents, Nathan and Cresy, were landowners as well, so she too had spent her childhood in a household where Black economic autonomy was celebrated.[83]

Like his father, Shadrick, Noah appears on the 1900 Census as a landowner.[84] This was a promising sign for the first-generation freeborn landowner in the family. Two years later he is among those listed in the *Macon Beacon* for delinquent poll taxes in the Hashquua District.[85] Noah's regular appearance on delinquent poll tax lists suggests that he insisted on being recognized as a legal voter even though he would not be able to exercise that right. As a young man, he was perhaps flexing his muscles, not fully aware yet that the laws worked concomitantly with the economic and social order to obstruct Black freedom. If Noah read the brief article on the same page of that day's issue of the *Beacon* reporting the fate of the African Methodist Church near Cedar Creek, perhaps his self-assuredness was somewhat shaken. While noting that the congregation had declared their intent to repair the building, the paper reported that with the building in need of repair and having not been in use for years, it was condemned and then blown down. The burden for the church is clearly noted in the article's concluding words: "now if they want a church, they must rebuild, if the lot is not sold."[86] The tone of those final words in the article suggests an emphatic indifference to what the Black church members valued and held as sacred. More alarming was the threatening undertone; that is, at their discretion or will, whites could declare the property of Blacks worthless and as easily then destroy it and announce the act publicly as if for the sport of it. Despite these harsh realities in 1902, there were elements of Noah's life that inspired hope. He was a 22-year-old Black man farming under the mentorship of his father and uncles, heading his own household, and residing on property he owned.

The optimism of Noah's early years of adulthood was interrupted, however, in short order when his wife, Lula, barely, if at all, out of her teen years, died sometime between 1902 and 1904.[87] Within two years of Lula's death, Noah married Luella Hunt (1904), and while they were married more than thirty years and had fourteen children, the optimistic lens of the young Noah in 1900 was severely blurred by the end of the century's first decade. The financial fate of his parents likely informed the change of fortunes for Noah and family after 1910. The cataclysmic turn of fortunes for the family was made public in February 1911 with a trustee's sale announcement that Shadrick and Susan Cistrunk's land would be presented for public auction to cover their unpaid debt.[88] In the following month the *Beacon* would list Shadrick Cistrunk among property owners whose land was slated for public sale due to delinquent taxes.[89] It is ironic that the debt that precipitated the 1911 auctions may have stemmed from the January 1908 deed of trust executed by Shadrick and Susan, with their son Noah as witness.[90] In this contract, Shadrick and Susan borrowed $170, staking not only all crops they and employees would cultivate for that year, but the couple additionally staked their 162 acres as collateral. The lender, Merchants and Farmers Bank, added a ten percent per annum penalty if the loan was not paid by the January 1909 due date. The more severe terms of the trust deed may have stemmed from the 1907 recession that was marked by a run on banks. Set off by risky investments of leading

New York trust banks, the ensuing recession was felt across the nation where bank deposits were being emptied as people feared that their banks may default. The resultant rise in interest rates trickled down to the rural South. Considering Shadrick borrowed from a bank instead of the usual local lenders suggests that the local lenders may have themselves been short on cash to loan. With banks holding less cash because of the panic, they not only increased interest rates, but some could and did demand more collateral in loan transactions. Shadrick and Susan had staked their land as collateral at least three times prior to the 1908 trust deed, including a 1901 trust deed for more than twice the loan amount of the 1908 deed.[91] Fortune had played in their favor in those previous transactions where they met their loan obligations and staved off the loss not only of their chattel assets but their land as well.

In the next year, Shadrick and Susan followed the 1908 trust deed with an almost identical contract. The 1909 trust deed was executed with the same lender and same terms of the previous year, but this time for a loan amount of $315, with the loan payment due in January 1910.[92] It is not clear whether the 1909 trust deed enfolded unpaid debt from the 1908 contract, thus explaining the near double loan amount in the new contract. If this was not the case, Shadrick had perhaps been emboldened by the success of meeting the 1908 obligation, deciding then that he could manage a larger loan. The execution of a larger loan could have as well been fueled by any one or combination of factors: a desire to increase his crop production to increase his income, a need for new farming tools or livestock, or even the need or desire for personal home goods. It is likely as well that Shadrick and Susan folded Noah's farming expenses into the sum they would borrow. Rather than have Noah stake his land or assets, the parents may have concluded that they, rather than their son and his family, should assume the risk. Whatever their rationale, Shadrick and Susan again staked all 162 acres in the 1909 trust deed. This time, however, fortune did not treat them favorably. They did not meet the January 1910 payment deadline, and four months after this loan default, Susan Cistrunk was enumerated on the Census as a widow, living with daughter Sophie, her husband, Lem Nichols, and 10-year-old daughter, Mariah, in Tallahatchie County, 140 miles northwest of her Noxubee County home.[93]

It is not clear what happened between January 1909, when Shadrick signed that year's trust deed, and a year later when the loan went into default. Shadrick was 61 years old in 1909 and while that is not an age of looming death by twenty-first-century standards for developed nations, those 61 years had been hard on both his body and mind. Just as medical studies today reveal the debilitating health effects of racism on African Americans, this was no less the case for enslaved and post-emancipated generations. Shadrick's son, Noah (1881–1937), would not live past the age of 60. While Noah's first son,

Carl (1901–1979), would live to age 78, his senior years were spent struggling through the severities of diabetes and its complications—including the amputation of both legs. Carl's only son, Edgar (1924–1979) would die before age 60 from decades of complications stemming from tuberculosis. It is plausible that prolonged years of enduring racial terrorism and the racist economics of farming while Black in the US South had worn heavily on Shadrick. He may have been severely ill when he signed the 1909 trust deed, but given the family's financial dependence on their yearly crop harvests, he likely saw no other option than to proceed as he had for decades.

The life cycle of farming dictated that each year money was borrowed on the hope that the harvests that year would cover the debt incurred to finance supplies, seeds, and labor. That Shadrick and his family had maintained ownership of their land and their chattel assets two decades from post-Reconstruction into the new century, suggests that despite the hardships, they had been successful. Each year they covered their debts, they remained independent farmers, avoiding the entrapment of sharecropping, which by the new century had clearly emerged as a new iteration of plantation slavery. With bills paid, shelter secured, and mouths fed, there were years when the Cistrunks had some room for a few comforts or luxuries. This would have included things like nice clothes for church or social affairs, having portraits taken, owning a wagon, purchasing a timepiece, placing curtains in the windows of their home, or owning dining extras such as tablecloths and napkins. How much of the extras the Cistrunks enjoyed is indeterminable, but Shad's wagon, even though homemade, shows that he enjoyed an independence of mobility. The family's connectedness to church, and one with longevity, would have informed not only their own interest in appearing on Sundays in their finest wear but also their investment and pride in their worship home. Brushfork Baptist Church had bought their land outright in 1890, and the congregation built its own structure, dressed the church with an iron bell outside, and maintained a graveyard on the church grounds. While no pictures of Shadrick or Noah have survived in the family, at one time there were pictures in the possession of Noah's wife Luella verifying that the first-generation freed Cistrunks had invested in photographs to capture evidence of their presence and achievements. The surviving photograph of Noah's son, Carl, and relative Will Grimmett provides a window into the extras that marked the Cistrunks's commemoration of their successes. While the picture is an image of Carl as a young man, I have not been able to confirm that the person beside him in the picture is his cousin or his uncle—both named Will Grimmett. The photo of Carl and Will standing outdoors with a wooded field as backdrop, captures them dressed for a special occasion. It may have simply been the aftermath of a Sunday church service or something less routine, but Carl in a suit and Will in dress clothes appear pleased and proud. They have a look of ease and optimism that seems to speak an expectation for a future of possibilities and opportunities. The watch chain draped across the front of Carl's trousers indicate that there was money, even if on rare occasions, for such an extra.

Shadrick's death and Susan's move to Tallahatchie County signaled an impending turn in the legacy they would leave their children in Noxubee County. Unlike her father, Sophie's second husband was a sawmill laborer, and the family rented, rather than owned, their residence. Her marriage to Will Grimmett appears to have been brief. The marriage license is dated 1902, but the 1910 Census shows that she and Lem Nichols had been married for 4 years.[94] Her daughter, Mariah, is not shown as Lem's stepdaughter, but if she is 10 years old as noted in the 1910 census, Grimmett was probably her father. It is not clear whether Grimmett died or whether he and Sophie divorced, but Sophie's removal from Noxubee would eventually lead to nearly three decades during which she and her Cistrunk relatives would not be in communication. Lem's employment in a sawmill reflects the dynamic of increasing corporate and large landholding entities that were engulfing small farms throughout Mississippi, pushing Black laborers into the sawmill plants or into tenancy and sharecropping farming. These trends also fueled the early twentieth-century Black migration when Blacks in significant numbers left the rural South, seeking out southern cities and cities beyond the South, with hopes of opportunities for more substantive and secure incomes. When the Cistrunks reunited with Sophie in early 1940s Jackson, MS, she had married again and was settled in with her husband as cooperator of their small grocery store. Sophie had been determined to find a way in the world beyond the grinding uncertainty of rural farm life. According to her great-nephew, Bunnie Cistrunk, as a young woman Sophie had enjoyed traveling and was not content to simply assume the role of homemaker, being restricted to those boundaries. According to Bunnie, at the time of Sophie's departure from Noxubee she left on strained terms with her sister-in-law, Luella, who had at one time been Sophie's regular companion. As Noah and Luella's household expanded, Luella had little time for visiting, traveling, or socializing, and her concentrated focus on household affairs left no time for leisure escapades with her childhood friend and sister-in-law. The two would lose contact until Carl Cistrunk's family in Jackson discovered Sophie by chance as they stopped into her store to purchase goods on their way home from school. With the discovery of their father's aunt decades after her departure from Noxubee, the Cistrunk teens set the pathway for Sophie and Luella's reunion and mending of their splintered relationship. This was more than three decades after the family's loss of Shadrick and their dream of independent farming in the county that had been their first stance as free people.

Carl Cistrunk and (cousin/uncle?) Will Grimmett

Though Black landowning farmers were always small in numbers, the numbers dwindled over the twentieth century, with Black farmers losing "upwards of 90% of their land from 1910 to 1997."[95] In 2021, the percentage of Black farmers in the nation was reported to have dwindled from 14% in 1920 to 1.4%.[96] The fate of the first-generation freed and landowning Cistrunks is rooted in this history of land disenfranchisement. From early on, like farmers across the country, Black farmers depended on loans for their operations, but they systematically had to pay higher costs for those loans, and when crises hit farming industries, unlike their white counterparts, Black farmers saw little if any support from the federal government. Shadrick and Susan, and later their son Noah were among the numbers of those Black farmers whose lands were lost during that near century expanse. In government and other official data, their losses are registered simply as numbers; however, when we enter into the lives of those individuals and families that constitute the data, we understand more clearly the profound historical cost to Black families and communities in the South. Made more detrimental than the political and bodily violence against Black southerners, the failure to meaningfully compensate Blacks at the end of the Civil War—that broken promise of "40 acres and a mule"—paved the way for a continuation of the forced migration and displacement that enslaved Blacks had faced in the antebellum era.

With Susan Cistrunk's move to Tallahatchie County in 1910, Noah and family were the last of Shadrick's line in Noxubee County. Sophie had left by 1910, and the Census that year, showing Isaac Grimmett widowed and living with his children in neighboring Kemper County, MS, reveals that Maria had died between census years 1900 and 1910.[97] While the 1910 Census shows his wife Luella and household in Noxubee, Noah was not enumerated on that year's census. Luella is recorded as the head of household with her three biological children—Evelyn, Lorenzo, and Bessie (fathered by Noah), and two stepchildren—Carl and Lula (Noah and Lula's children). Luella is listed as laborer and even though Noah is absent, the property is still shown as owned. Noah's absence from his Noxubee residence may seem perplexing, but it would not have been highly unusual. With the boom of the timber companies, Noah, like his uncle-in-law, Lem, in Tallahatchie County, was likely exploring employment beyond farming. Noah's son, Bunnie, remembers being told that in Noah's early years he had worked as a fireman for a manufacturing company. His absence from the family roll in the 1910 Census may represent the period that he sought employment in industry. As revealed by his name listed in the April 1910 Delinquent Poll Tax publication, Noah may have been away from the household, but he was clearly not disconnected from his county of residence.[98] Financially, Noah was trying to make ends meet and searching for a way out of the vicious cycle of uncertainty that was inherent in farming. As his family rapidly expanded, Noah would return to full-time farming, however. Even with its uncertainty, farming was a more reliable profession for a man looking at yearly increases in mouths to feed. And while the century's second decade opened with loss—Shadrick's loss of his land and the deaths of both Shadrick and John—in 1910 Noah still owned his land. His father's siblings—Lucretia and Hillman—still owned theirs.[99]

Like his brother Shadrick, Hillman would suffer severe financial consequences from the high stakes trust deed he executed in 1909.[100] In this cosignatory agreement with their neighbor for a $315 loan, Hillman and his wife would not only leverage the usual horse and mule, several cows and calves, and all crops grown and harvested during that year, but they included as collateral the 2-year-old Studebaker wagon, all six head of cattle and their increase, and most alarmingly, their eighty-one acres. If he failed to repay this loan, the 60-plus-year-old Hillman and wife, Harriet, risked becoming homeless and being forced into the impoverishing cycle of sharecropping. Why Martha Lloyd entered into the trust deed with the Cistrunks is not clear. There does not appear to be a direct blood relation between Martha Lloyd and the Cistrunks; nevertheless, Hillman and Harriet felt close enough to enter into a loan with Martha, staking their greatest material security. Martha Lloyd appears on the 1900 Census in the entry directly below Hillman and Harriet as widowed head of household with five children ages toddler to 17 years old.[101] Before his death, Martha's husband may have had a farming partnership with the Cistrunks. With her husband gone, Martha was perhaps residing on Hillman and Harriet's land. Her position as coborrower may have stemmed from farming supplies or livestock that she included as part of the collateral staked for the transaction. Census reports from 1880 and 1900 show Cistrunk and Lloyd families as neighbors, and in the Mississippi Enumeration of Educable Children, 1908–1957, in Noxubee County Hillman, Shadrick, Noah, and neighbor Martha, are recorded registering children for school.[102] The Cistrunk and Lloyd families appear to have known each other from as far back as the post-Reconstruction era and they seemed to have shared a close personal and work relationship. With Martha and family living on Hillman's land, the personal relationship was likely more tightly yoked by their mutual dependency on Hillman's financial success. If Hillman and Harriet lost their land, Martha Lloyd and her family would have to seek out a new home and a new farming alliance.

The year 1909 would end with Hillman unable to repay his loan, and for the first time in his adult life, he was at risk of losing all his financial assets. The new decade entered with Hillman and Harriet in a battle for their lives—to lose their assets at their age would be devastating not only for the loss of all they had worked for over decades, but with their health waning, they would not have the physical constitution to labor as they had in the early post-emancipation decades. At this time, he and Lucretia were the only two surviving from their family of seven that had been led by Francis. The four siblings—John, Hillman, Shadrick, and Lucretia—had weathered the storms and enjoyed the bright days of many post-emancipation years in Noxubee County. Lucretia still owned her land but like her brother John, she found herself in her grandparenting years, providing emotional and financial support for an adult daughter and her children. By 1910, the surviving post-emancipation generation of Cistrunks consisted of Hillman and Lucretia and economic and social struggles were getting more difficult. Like so many rural places in the South, Noxubee's lure was its roads that pointed elsewhere. Within a decade after Shadrick's death, his and Susan's two living children, Noah and Sophie, and their children would migrate from Noxubee. John's grandson Dossie would eventually leave as well, but grandson Elisha would remain. Though some departed, generations from Elisha's line of descent are the Cistrunks found today in Noxubee County.

Chapter 4

HILLMAN

A Man's Story Bookended by Women

It is our duty to bury our dead
  Anna Cistrunk

Long may you live
Long may you tarry
Court who you may
But mind who you marry
  Anna Cistrunk to Wessie M Cistrunk 1948

With the post-Reconstruction era of white rule firmly in place throughout late nineteenth-century Mississippi, Noxubee County welcomed in the century with a new jail. Built in 1907 at the emergence of the so-called modern age, this county jail was constructed with a hangman's gallows visibly placed in the interior of the jail. That the gallows were not placed and displayed outside for open viewing was perhaps in the mind of county leaders evidence that they were in step with the civilized world. The sheriff and his family resided on the first floor of the jail oddly in plain view of the gallows' hatch. This seems to reflect the ease with which white southerners could straddle the line between savagery and performances of gentility. While there are no official accounts of hangings in the jail, a local Black man Cy Connor was hung within the first year of the jail's opening. In August 1907, Connor was arrested and found guilty of the brutal murder of his wife, Elizabeth, who he had accused of infidelity.[1] Elizabeth was found with her head nearly severed from her body from the blow of an axe. While there were reportedly no eyewitnesses to the crime, the local newspaper declared him guilty, asserting that "the circumstantial evidence is so strong that it leaves little doubt that he was the murderer."[2] During an interview on September 14, a month after his arrest and a week before he was scheduled for execution, Connor reportedly forecasted his death by hanging, describing it as taking place on the courthouse yard.[3]

While the jury was convinced of Connor's guilt, he never confessed; however, before his execution he repeatedly told the story of arriving home and finding his wife with a man named Jake. According to Connor who had clearly slipped into dementia by the time of his September interview, his wife and the man named Jake remained in his company even as he was in jail. Connor reported further that both Jake and Elizabeth admitted that he had done right, and that Elizabeth had forgiven him.[4] Deeming Connor "a horrible example to a portion of his race," the reporter asserted that "there is nothing serious about Connor in the way of a white man's seriousness."[5] In May 2021, I visited the former jail that is today a library. The library tour guide explained that the official story maintains that the hangman's gallows inside the jail was never used. The guide did add, however, that in contrast to the official record, many local Blacks express skepticism of this claim, with some maintaining that Connor was the first to depart the world by way of the gallows in the newly built jail in 1907. The story of Connor's execution surviving in two different versions in two different communities is perhaps a reflection of the uncertainty of Connor's guilt. The September 14, 1907, interview depicts Connor as insane, which he may have been. This, however, does not preclude some elements of truth that may have been communicated in his account.

Connor's presumed hallucinatory account of encountering his wife and a man named Jake on the day of her murder may have some elements of truth. If triggered by the trauma of his wife's violent death, Connor's deranged mental state would explain the disjointed nature of his story. If we add to his mental state the reality of a culture and a legal system that gave no weight to Black testimony or rights and, further, readily allowed the sexual and physical violation of Black women, Connor's account demands a closer read. If as Connor maintains, he found his wife and another man in his home engaging in sexual intercourse, his rage may have driven him to murder her, and his fall into insanity may have ensued. This would fit the finding of the jury, with the exception of a third-party present, namely the man named Jake. If, as Connor insists, a man named Jake was present, Jake may have witnessed Connor's act or Jake may have himself been the murderer. If Jake was there and escaped, then Connor was the likely suspect, and there would have been little inclination on the part of a white jury to consider that Connor was telling the truth. If Jake was a white man, Connor would have had even less recourse for justice through the legal system of Mississippi. The tale that Connor reportedly recites throughout his incarceration—that his wife and a man named Jake remain with him and have exonerated him, that angels took him for a preview of heaven where he was warmly received while his wife was noticeably absent, suggests that Connor may have killed his wife out of rage and then fell into a psychosis that allowed him to imagine that he was guilt-free. Just as possible, however, is that Connor was not guilty but that he knew there was no means to tell the events as they occurred, especially if he was already presumed guilty and if the guilty party was someone white. The factor that renders the truth of the story indiscernible for Blacks was the absence of an eyewitness and the all-white jury that decided the case. Connor was arrested in August and executed the next month. The crime had been committed in the Black community, but Blacks were excluded from the legal and judicial process that decided the case. In an era and a region where Blacks had been indiscriminately lynched with no to little legal recourse, Blacks in Noxubee in 1907 could not trust the verdict of an all-white jury and the story they would pass along to successive generations would include doubt over the verdict in Connor's case.

Ultimately whether Connor was executed on the grounds outside or the gallows inside the jail is not the overarching point of significance: It was the very placement of a hangman's gallows in the jailhouse where the sheriff lived with his family in the city of Macon, the county seat, that sent a clear message to the Black community. Lynching had become a hallmark statement of white supremacy and just as the noose symbolized this power outside the halls of justice, the gallows, a central fixture within this jailhouse, would have echoed this assertion of white rule to all aware of its presence. While lynching may not have been a practice in the jail itself, the gallows inside the jail reflected for Blacks the power that the law bestowed upon whites. Blacks held over in the jail knew that they had to tread carefully, for all was aligned to justify their killing should the impulse strike those holding legal power. The ingrained casualness of it all reflects the tenor of the time. The chilling tone evoked from that image is present today, even with the 1984 transformation of the jail to a library.

When John Cistrunk's grandson was held over in jail in 1913 for bootlegging, it was at this jail facility—where Cy Connor had been tried and executed in 1907—that Elisha Cistrunk was detained. Sometime in mid-July 1913, "Deputy Sheriff Sam Clark went to Indianola and returned . . . with a negro named Elijah Cistrunk who was indicted for his "large scale" illegal operation."[6] The following month, "Elisha Cistrunk, the Mashulaville tiger . . . plead guilty to retailing, was fined $50 and 50 days in one case and $50 each in two other case."[7] Whether Elisha served that fifty days in the local Noxubee jail or was handed over for prison labor in the state's notorious Parchment Prison, the experience would have left an imprint in his psyche. Opening in 1901, Parchment Prison replaced the state's notorious convict leasing system, only to become a twentieth-century enslavement camp under the guise of criminal justice policy.[8] Blacks convicted of state crimes in Mississippi were remanded to Parchment where they labored in the fields much like those enslaved in

Noxubee County Library
(former jail, 1907–1980s)

the antebellum South. It became in the minds of Black southerners early on and into the present a nightmarish symbol of the torture and exploitation into which they could be thrown in any unpleasant encounter with a white person or white law. At some point in his life before age 40, Elisha lost his sight in one eye.[9] While this loss may have been the result of a farming or home accident, it may have as well resulted from a violent encounter with law officers or fellow inmates during his incarcerated period.

Six years after 35-year-old Elisha was captured and conveyed to the Noxubee County Jail, his 76-year-old great-uncle (his grandfather's brother), Hillman, was arrested by local authorities and jailed. With his arrest in December 1919, Hillman would never return to the land and the home that had been his for forty years. When I visited Noxubee County for the first time in summer 2021 and was given a tour of the 1907 jail that was converted to library, I did not imagine at the time that the structure would intersect the story of Hillman and his last months of life. I did not imagine as well that the courthouse, which was a key archival resource for this project, would also prove a structure, an institution, that played a major hand in Hillman's fate in the last months of his life. The records held in the courthouse reveal the pathway to what seemed a promising future for the first-generation Cistrunk landowners, and ironically the events that reversed their fortunes, ultimately leading to the dispersion of their Noxubee descendants. The story culminates into a more deeply catastrophic narrative than the David versus Goliath trope that initially framed the narrative outcome I expected. Knowing early on that the story would end with the first-generation Cistrunks unable to pass on landownership to their descendants, I anticipated that this outcome was the direct result of embedded practices to undermine Black prosperity and citizenry in the South. Family, community lore, and Mississippi's history of racial intimidation served as foundation for my initial monolithic framing. While the Cistrunks's story clearly underscores this historical reality, Hillman's fate serves as a resounding reminder of the problem with limiting minoritized subjects to simplistic and singular characterizations. While in the throes of resisting discrimination themselves, victimized people can and do engineer and perpetrate wrongs against others who are subjected to systemic or institutionalized injustice. The lure of material gain, no matter how small, can inspire acts of inhumanity in individuals across population groups. In short, Hillman's fate was a crushing reminder that as with all populations of humanity, even those operating out of a more communal ethos, there are individuals who act in the interest of self-gain and in ways that are destructive to their communities at large and to individuals and families in their communities. Sometimes, the betrayal occurs within a family or kinship nucleus, and, in such cases, can create division and disconnect that resonate for generations.

IN THE ABSENCE OF HIS BROTHERS

Unlike Shadrick, Hillman would survive his high-risk loan of 1909, but it would take him years and a creative contract with his great-nephew, Dossie, in 1910 to come out with his acres still under Cistrunk ownership. Hillman would hold onto his land, but the cosigned deed of 1909 with neighbor, Martha Lloyd, appears to have put him in financial stress that followed him into the last decade of his life. Hillman's enlistment of Dossie to help pay off the $366 debt to E. F. Nunn in 1909, while on one hand seems to bring the aid he needed, would, on the other hand, become an axis of contention that would ultimately create a deep family rift. Evidence that Hillman survived the near financial destruction from that loan survives on the document itself, which shows a marginal note inscribed in 1913 with the signature of the county clerk confirming that the debt was cleared.[10]

After the strain of his 1909 debt, Hillman realized that at age 63 and in failing health, he no longer had the stamina to farm at the intensity needed to bring annual crops to harvest. The crisis in this moment was of course the reality that while farming required the assumption of debt for operation, it was his household livelihood. As Hillman expressed in the 1910 contract executed with Dossie, he was aging, tired, and in failing health.[11] He and Harriet, his wife and peer in age who had been with him throughout more than three decades of post-emancipation farming, had no children. There was no direct descendant to assume ownership of and to work the acres they had worked and sacrificed to own. They had, however, helped raise their great-nephew, Dossie, after his grandparents, John and Chany died. It was thus Dossie to whom they turned in 1910 to help them save their land and their assets. His older brother, 26-year-old Elisha, was now head of his household—married with two children—but Dossie had not yet ventured out on his own. At age 23, he was living with Hillman and Harriet when the three entered into a legal agreement presumed to be mutually beneficial for all three.[12] The gravity of the circumstances and all that was at risk can be best-appreciated through hearing the anxiety that seems to come to life through the words in the contract that are narrated in the first-person voice of Hillman:

> In consideration of my age and failing health and off a certain indebtedness due E. F. Nunn and CO/ of three hundred and sixty-six dollars secured by a trust deed on my property I hereby agree to give my nephew Doss Cistrunk one third interest in all my property consisting of all land now owned by me, also one third interest in my stock and increase consisting of
>
> one black horse named Roosevelt-

> One dark bay mare mule named Kate
> One cow named Jezebel
> One cow named Dolly Madison
> Also wagon, buggy or other personal property we may accumulate[13]

In payment for the one-third allotment of Hillman and Harriet's eighty-one acres and other assets, Dossie agreed to cultivate the land and pay off the $366 owed to Nunn & Co. The debt was noted as cleared in 1913, which suggests that Dossie honored in full his part of the 1910 contract with Hillman and Harriet. Dossie was young when he signed the agreement, and it may have been an overwhelming commitment for a 23-year-old. Whether his older brother or his great-aunt, Lucretia, offered help is not knowable through court records. It is, however, conceivable that with Hillman and Harriet aging and in poor health, Lucretia and Elisha may have assisted financially and, in the case of Elisha, that help may have been in cultivating the land. If we consider that in 1913, the same year the loan was cleared, Elisha was arrested and convicted of running a still, it is not unlikely that Elisha may have provided financial help to his brother and Hillman through revenue from his illicit operation. At age 23 Dossie was charged with rescuing his aging great-uncle from a magnitude of debt beyond his youthful experience and comprehension, and with Hillman's debilitating health, the probability that Elisha assisted is high. For all three—Elisha, Dossie, and Hillman, the $366 debt was significant for their circumstances. This amount in year 2021 dollars is more than $10,000. The debt of $366 in 1910 was a longshot even with the three working together. Elisha was married with a family that relied on his financial support; Hillman was physically unable to work at the level needed to cultivate and harvest the needed crop; and Dossie came with no financial assets to contribute to the effort. If things turned financially dire between 1910 and 1913, and they likely did, Elisha's illegal enterprise would have been the source of Hillman and Dossie's financial survival.

While it was Hillman in the 1910 contract who expressed concern about his age and health, it was Harriet who succumbed to those anxiety-driven years they worked to clear the lien on their property. Harriet died sometime between the signing of the 1910 contract with Dossie and the year 1916. Her death is not marked by a death certificate record, but rather by a 1916 marriage license that was filed for 72-year-old Hillman Cistrunk and 35-year-old Patsy Cutts.[14] Two years prior to her marriage to Hillman, Patsy was in the closing chapter of a 3-year divorce saga. Her husband William Cutts filed a petition for divorce in 1911 alleging that during their seven-year marriage Patsy had entered into adulterous relationships that included a man named Allen Cotton and several unnamed others.[15] The circumstances and history behind Patsy and Hillman's marriage are not revealed in the records, but a notable foreboding sign was the groom's absence at the signing of the license. The marriage license record shows that R. A. Haggard signed for Hillman Cistrunk. Whether Hillman was physically present seems of little consequence, but even if present in body, Hillman appears to have been restricted physically and/or cognitively from signing on his own authority. Did Hillman request Haggard's assistance in signing the marriage license, or were Haggard and Patsy in collusion to orchestrate the proceeding? Whether a member of his family would have been granted the authority to sign a marriage license for him is unlikely; however, that Hillman was not accompanied by a member of his family suggests first of all that they would not have approved of this union. It is also unlikely that the court would have allowed a family member to commit him to a marriage when his capacity for consent was questionable. Why then, was Haggard permitted to sign a marriage license for an aging and ailing man who was unable to be present to sign for himself? It is likely that the R. A. Haggard, who signed for Hillman, was Robert Arthur Haggard of Noxubee County, MS, recorded in the World War I draft registration. He is shown to be a single white male, medical doctor, residing in Noxubee's Shuqualak Precinct.[16] What Haggard might have gained for his role in facilitating Patsy's marriage to Hillman is not clear, but the outcome for Hillman was predictably grave.

The year of Hillman's marriage to Patsy, an event that would change the course of his life, also marked the infancy of what has been named the Great Migration. By summer 1916, the migration wave of that year "had reached flood tide in the states of the deep South."[17] While this six-decades-long event "would become perhaps the biggest underreported story of the twentieth century," it entailed the departure of an estimated six million Black southerners from the rural South to cities across the Unites States.[18] While the ongoing social and political persecution of Blacks in the South informed their decision to escape, some historians argue that economics was the driving force: "The deadly blows to the South's economy from natural disasters during 1915 and 1916—drought and rain and the boll weevil—launched the evacuation."[19] The racist economics of farming in the South would certainly become a major impetus for a long-term Black exodus. The system was built into a structure that was arguably as well-oiled as the enslaving system of the antebellum South; it was an economy that "rested essentially on the servitude of tenantry, sharecropping, and the crop lien. To survive, the tenant or cropper needed credit . . . Year after year . . . the price he received for his crops did not even come close to paying off his debt, and he was forced to commit himself to still another year to obtain credit. It proved to be an ingenious way for whites to assure themselves of a cheap and bound labor force."[20] Who cannot imagine the impulse to escape such exploitation, especially when accompanied by the force of legal and extralegal violent force? In general, Americans have at least a vague knowledge of the historical movement of Black people out of the economic, political, and social oppression of the Jim Crow, plantation South. Few have a hard numerical understanding of this exodus or what it meant with respect to the life-changing environmental shifts for Blacks as a population group. The move from rural, land-based to urban, industrialized environments represented a great wave or shift: "Nine out of ten Black Americans still lived in the South in 1917, some three of four of them in rural sections. Half a century later, Black Americans had become primarily urban (75 percent)."[21]

The economic hardships of life in the South compelled Blacks to leave, but again "many also felt they were running for their lives."[22] White violence and political rule informed the decisions of those who left, and the refueled racial terrorism of white supremacists in the aftermath of World War I deepened the impulses of Blacks who felt compelled to free themselves from this unchecked license to intimidate and to kill.[23] Though Blacks had fought in World War I, white southern neighbors felt no compulsion to rethink their status or citizenry. In fact, seventy-eight Blacks were lynched in 1918, the year of the war's end, and "Southern newspapers editorialized ghoulishly about the fate awaiting any Afro-American veteran daring to come home uniformed, bemedaled, and striding up main street like a white man."[24] The year 1918 was particularly noteworthy as well for the arrival of a worldwide pandemic that likely emerged in the United States, and that over a stretch of two years "would kill more people than any other outbreak of disease in human history."[25] As the deaths escalated, terror and fear were spread not just by everyday people but by leaders who should have been fostering actions to mitigate the spread of the violence and the wild, uninformed streams of misinformation that could easily take root and grow. In Starkville, MS, located in Oktibbeha County—Noxubee's northwest bordering neighbor—a leading health official, Dr. M. G. Parsons, cheerfully spread fear and conspiracy around the virus.[26] Parsons was the US Health Service officer for northeastern Mississippi, but rather than communicate calm and thoughtful directions, he boldly spread rumors that the virus was an attack coming from the Germans.[27] His unfounded public claim exemplifies the fuel that escalated the fears of the public while causing resources to be diverted to quell unwarranted investigations.

In the midst of the pandemic, during the summer of 1919, racial violence across the nation intensified to such a magnitude that author and activist James Weldon Johnson would coin the term, "Red Hot Summer" to describe the violence "that ushered in the greatest period of interracial strife the nation had ever witnessed."[28] The outbreak and pervasiveness of unrest stretched from summer into the year's end with an estimated twenty-five race riots having occurred during this period.[29] With soldiers returning home and to the labor market in the aftermath of World War I, job competition heightened. Across the nation, whites increasingly saw Black laborers as threats to their livelihood, but in the war's aftermath Blacks "showed a willingness to defend themselves that they had not shown before." [30] Black resistance was met by "fascist organizations like the Ku Klux Klan," who sought to "terrorize Blacks into submission."[31] Noxubee County and its county seat, Macon, would not be excluded from this season of terror. In June 1919, the *Columbus Dispatch* reported news that in neighboring Noxubee County "race clashes at Macon" had occurred in the past few days.[32] According to the *Dispatch,* "a negro of that place who stood high in the estimation of both races before the war, returned from a few months ago and he has devoted his efforts toward the organization of the Blacks of that section, their organization providing that only a certain number of hours should be worked each day, that certain wages should be demanded, etc."[33] News of the efforts of the unnamed Black leader became known to white men of the area who promptly organized and "took the matter in charge and the negro was given a severe whipping and ordered to leave the county, which he did. This occurred on Thursday night and on Friday night several hundred white men whipped others who were implicated in the plot and they were given a few hours to leave."[34] The incident at Macon went beyond the state boundaries to at least one other news outlet. In the neighboring state of Tennessee in Memphis, the *News Scimitar* published its version of the incident, noting that via a telephone report they had received news that "a mob took three prominent negroes, one of them the principal of a school 'across the river and gave them good advice.'"[35] On the following night a Black man was "knocked down" and "'taken across the river'" after drawing a pistol on a planter.[36] Tensions had risen to such a height, and "Negroes were said to be flocking to Macon from every direction." [37] As with the *Columbus Dispatch* report, the *Scimitar* also pointed to labor demands on the part of Blacks as the source of the conflict. In both news accounts, there was no questioning of the rights of the white mobs, thereby suggesting that it was accepted custom for white mobs to violently attack Blacks who dared to challenge the labor terms and conditions forced upon them by white employers. Although neither account mentioned that Blacks had been killed, it does not mean that all had come out alive. White violence and killing of Blacks did not always go acknowledged in public records. Death tolls of Blacks in race riots and massacres were regularly underrecorded even when reported.[38] It is not unlikely that some of those who were "taken across the river" were killed. It is also not unlikely that many of those who were forced to leave, also ultimately lost possession of their land if they were landowners. This kind of violence was not uncommon among the methods of confiscating land belonging to Blacks. When Black landowners were forced to flee, their land was often seized for unpaid taxes and then sold through auction.

This clash in June 1919 in the deep Mississippi town of Macon illustrates the simmering frustrations of Black residents who were being held in economic and legal prison by institutional racism that was little more than a variation of antebellum slavery. Noxubee may have been a place seemingly far away from the bustling, burgeoning modernity of post-World War I, but its Black residents knew that there were possibilities for better living. Many left to seek those promises for improved living, but many still looked for that better world right where they were. For those, like Hillman, who had entered the twilight years of their lives, leaving was not a promising option. In the urban hubs where Blacks flocked, their employment opportunities were in sectors that required a physical capacity for hard work. Though Black professionals migrated from the South, the greater number of Blacks arriving into cities across the country were workers seeking employment opportunities in industry jobs such as "the manufacture of ammunition and of iron and steel products," work in "meat-packing industries . . . automobile and truck production . . . and the manufacture of electrical products."[39] Even if Hillman would have considered leaving, he was no longer in a state to command the physical strength or energy required to work in these kinds of industries. Migration was calling Blacks away from their southern roots, but not everyone was leaving. Hillman still had family in Noxubee and nearby Winston County. His one surviving sibling, Lucretia, still resided nearby. His nephew Noah, and grand-nephews Elisha and Dossie, and their families were among those who even with the Red Hot Summer of 1919 had not fled for the promised land of the North.

As the tumultuous year of 1919 entered into the final month of December, Patsy Cistrunk petitioned the Noxubee County Chancery Court to issue a writ of lunacy for Hillman Cistrunk, her husband of three years. Signed by Patsy on December 4, the document declared Hillman insane and "at large" in the county with "his relations and friends having neglected or refused to place him in an asylum."[40] Entered with Patsy's petition was a deposition by a local physician, T. C. Alford of Mashulaville, certifying that "Negro Hillman Sistrunk residing near Mashulaville is insane and being at times violent it is absolutely necessary to confine him to an institution for safekeeping."[41] Alford states that he has treated Hillman for several weeks and is "thoroughly convinced of his unbalanced mental state."[42]

Hillman's marriage to Patsy ends as it began—with the stroke of a pen in the hands of a white medical doctor and the stamp of approval from white courthouse authorities. In 1916 physician, R. A. Haggard signed in Hillman's stead on the license binding him in matrimony to Patsy. Haggard did not iden-tify himself as a doctor on the marriage document, but his presence and his signature signaled his validation of the marriage contract and implied that he was merely carrying out Hillman's will. Of course, implied in Haggard's signature was that Hillman, though unable to sign or to appear himself, was mentally fit to enter into marriage of his own accord. Later in 1919 when physician T. C. Alford signed a document freeing Patsy of Hillman, this time ironically the supposition would be that Hillman was now incapable of ra-tional decision-making. Within four days of Patsy's court filing for a writ of lunacy, a jury trial was convened, and on December 10, 1919, Hillman was declared insane and in need of confinement. The Noxubee County sheriff was then ordered to "arrest the said lunatic forth with and place him in one of the insane hospitals of the State of Mississippi for the care and treatment of luna-tics and insane persons, if there be a vacancy, and if not, confine him in the County Jail until there be room in one of said hospitals."[43] In the following month, Hillman would appear on the 1920 Census as an inmate in the Missis-sippi State Insane Hospital in Jackson. On March 7 of that year, two months after being enumerated on this census, Hillman died in the facility and was buried there on the asylum grounds.[44]

More than 10,000 of the 35,000 patients admitted during the asylum's eighty-year history died on the premises, and it is estimated that more than 7,000 were buried on the institution's ground.[45] Hillman is among those. Con-struction on the grounds of the University of Mississippi Medical Center com-plex in 2012 revealed that the location marked for the planned expansion is the site of the old asylum cemetery.[46] When its doors opened to patients in 1855, The Mississippi State Hospital, then called the Mississippi State Lunatic Asylum, was restricted to white patients, not admitting Blacks until after the Civil War.[47] Although Blacks were not admitted until more than a decade after the asylum opened, records show that "between 1912 and 1935, most who died there were 'Black.'"[48] When the asylum closed its doors at the original loca-tion in 1935, the buildings were later destroyed to make room for expansion of the University of Mississippi Medical Center. Since the 1935 relocation from its original Hinds County site to the nearby city of Whitfield in Rankin County, the asylum has been referred to as Whitfield by generations of Mis-sissippi natives. Among Black Mississippians, Whitfield has lived in lore as a haunting place. I recall throughout my childhood references to Whitfield as a place you should fear. Adults referenced it regularly as the threat of where you might land if you behaved badly or irrationally. It was painted as the place of no return. Not until I learned of Hillman's fate did I come to under-stand that this lore was born out of real-life experiences and histories.

According to the death certificate, Hillman's length of stay in the asylum was two months and nineteen days. If he was arrested on the day the jury decreed him insane, he spent at least one week in the Noxubee County Jail before his delivery to the asylum in the latter part of December. The sheriff may have had to cross county lines into Winston County to capture Hillman. This is perhaps why the death certificate shows Winston as his county of residence. At the time he was captured, his nephew Noah was a resident in Winston County.[49] Noah may have been harboring Hillman during the period of the court proceedings. Given Patsy's intention to have him committed, Hillman would have been easily captured if he remained at his Noxubee County home with her. Although others may have offered him refuge, for a 76-year-old struggling with poor health, Hillman must have felt disoriented and angry. If Hillman was subject to violent behavior as T. C. Alford claimed in his deposition, the stay in the county jail was likely nightmarish.

The swiftness of the court proceeding and the absence of any testimony or deposition from other family members suggests that the insanity verdict was as good as done before the case was heard. With only two documents submitted and no testimony to the contrary, all was in place to lead the jury to a determination of insanity. Once Hillman was in the hands of law enforcement authorities there was no recourse for his family. Notably absent in the court records of his case is his sister, Lucretia. Living in close proximity to Hillman, she would perhaps have had insight on the state of his mental and physical health, but there is no testimony on record from her. If Lucretia were willing to corroborate Patsy's assessment of Hillman as insane, it seems that the court would have sought a deposition from her. This would have strengthened their case. If she disputed Patsy's account, however, her testimony would have added an element of dissention that the court could easily avoid. To dispute Patsy would have meant that Lucretia was also disputing the assessment of the white doctor who had declared Hillman insane. In Jim Crow Mississippi the easy answer to the dissent of Lucretia or any other member of Hillman's family or community would have been a refusal to include their statement on the record. In general, an African American who would posit public or legal testimony against a white person or contradict their story, would also have reconciled themselves to the likelihood of violence or other forms of retaliation at the hands of whites.

With Hillman declared insane, Patsy held the legal right to manage and possess his assets and affairs, and in the event of his death, she would be recognized as his beneficiary. In less than three months after Hillman was conveyed to the asylum, Patsy would be able to assert her claim as heir. The short period between Hillman's arrival and his death at the asylum suggests that he arrived in grave physical health. The record maintains that the cause of death was nephritis. Whether Hillman entered the hospital with this condition is not clear. He may have suffered with nephritis due to an ongoing illness such as high blood pressure, or it may have set in from an infection introduced during his time in the asylum. No matter the cause of the nephritis that was recorded as cause of death, Hillman entered the asylum at an advanced age and in poor health. Patsy must have expected that Hillman's time at the asylum would not be long.

After Hillman's death in March 1920, Patsy's claim as widow and inheritor of his property was called into question by Dossie. In November of that year Dossie filed a lawsuit, "Dossie Cistrunk, Complainant—Versus Patsy Cistrunk-Lucretia McDonald, Defendants," demanding his right to one third of his late great-uncle's land and assets.[50] Dossie argued that the terms of the 1910 contract he executed with Hillman and Harriet entitled him to the percentage of Hillman's assets prescribed in that agreement. Dossie was responding to what appears to have been swift action by Patsy to claim Hillman's assets after his death. With the exception of the half of Hillman's land claimed by Lucretia, Patsy took immediate "possession of all said real and personal property," disregarding Dossie's claim. Dossie not only petitioned the court for his one-third of Hillman's assets that Patsy refused to turn over, but he additionally disputed his great-aunt's claim to one half of Hillman's eighty-one acres. According to Dossie, both Patsy and Lucretia were collecting rent from the land. Given that the two women do not appear to have challenged the other's claim, they were likely in collaboration or at the least in a standoff. While they may have disputed each other's claim, they may have seen it as more prudent to only have one legal challenge to address. They both benefitted by denying Dossie's claim. In the meantime, with Dossie dispossessed, they were both able to collect rent from the half of the property they claimed. While the case would not be resolved for several years, the Noxubee County land roll for 1921–1922 foretold that Dossie had already fallen victim to the age-old maxim that possession is nine-tenths of the law. Hillman's eighty-one acres was now divided with half of the lot (E ½ of E ½ of Nw ¼ Sec 3, Township 13, Range 15) still in his name, and the other half (W ½ of E ½ of Nw ¼ Sec 3, Township 13, Range 15) now in Lucretia's name.

The case was not resolved until 1924, but not by a trial judgment. It appears that Patsy set the course for the case to languish and for the eventual conveyance of Hillman's property to a new owner for a pittance of its value. In February 1921, three months after Dossie's petition, Patsy executed a trust deed with R. L. Anderson, staking as collateral half the property that was still in Hillman's name for a $40 loan at six percent.[51] At an estimated value of $37 per acre for farmland in Noxubee County in 1920, the value of half Hillman's eighty-one acres would have been nearly $1,500.[52] A month after Patsy's trust deed with Anderson the *Macon Beacon* published a "citation notice" for Lucretia McDonald, then a resident of Birmingham, AL, to appear before the Noxubee chancery court to "plead, answer, or demur to the Bill of Partition in said cause" where she was a codefendant.[53] By the May 1921 hearing, Patsy's trust deed with Anderson, a white man, had clearly heightened and complicated the dispute. Anderson now had claim to the land that was still recorded in Hillman's name.[54] With Anderson now holding interest in half the property, what remained was the half in dispute by Lucretia and Dossie. The extant case docket shows no record of legal deliberations after May 1921. The case languished until October 1924 when a "decree dismissing cause" was entered. The case was dismissed with the explanation that it was "a stale cause, no action having been had therein, as is shown by the general chancery, since the 6 day of May 1921."[55] The decree does not address the matter of the 1921 trust deed that Patsy had executed, but she appears to have defaulted on the loan. In 1926 the land that had remained on record in Hillman's name was now recorded as owned by R. L. Anderson.[56] Of note is that the other half that had remained in Lucretia's name throughout the court case now showed Anderson as owner. In 1926 when Anderson appears officially on the record as owner of the land that had formerly belonged to Hillman, the *Macon Beacon* reported that a number of business entities were bringing a suit against the county assessor, charging that he had overestimated the value of timber.[57] Anderson was not listed, but E. F. Nunn was among the group that included Brooksville Lumber Company and the Sumter Lumber Company, which reportedly owned "60,000 acres of timber land, much of which is in virgin timber."[58] Both Nunn and Anderson were prominent businessmen in the Shuqualak District.[59] Nunn had held the lien against Hillman's land in the 1909 trust deed that severely weakened him financially, and Nunn and Anderson held joint liens against Shadrick in trustee deeds from 1881–1887. The influence of the business entities in the 1926 case against Noxubee County is revealed in the *Beacon's* report that was clearly sympathetic to them: "The litigation from a standpoint of revenue is very important to the county, and the general feeling in regard to the suit is one of fairness no one desiring that the lumber companies should be excessively taxed."[60] When I consider stories I have heard from elderly relatives of the aggressive takeover of lands from Black farmers in this area in the early 1900s, particularly in the interest of the timber industry, the *Beacon's* call for fairness in the interest of these companies does not sound particularly convincing. In the last decade of his life, Hillman's fate was in large part juggled between two highly powerful commercial white men in the county who were connected to the powerful timber industry of the region. His experience is one snapshot of a larger montage of land losses for Blacks in Mississippi and the South.

How Anderson came into ownership of the western half of Hillman's property is not clear. Hillman was gone and the land he had labored to keep and to pass on to an heir was lost. Records in the court docket show no indication that Lucretia appeared before the court on May 6, 1921. She may have died before this date. An undocumented date of death posted on Ancestry.com shows 1921 as her death year. I have found no death certificate for Lucretia, but with death certificate registration begun in the nation in the first decades of the twentieth century, many deaths, especially deaths of African Americans, went unrecorded in the first years of this registration. If alive, Lucretia would have been 75 years old when the 1930 Census was enumerated. She does not appear on the Mississippi or Alabama Census in that year, suggesting that she died sometime earlier. Hillman's and Lucretia's deaths brought a close to Francis Sistrunk's first generation of Noxubee Cistrunks. The first generation free and landowning Cistrunks had been part of a small but distinct group of emancipated Blacks. Emerging out of enslavement with little to no assets to begin, they built small independent farming enterprises that provided for them and their families. Their landownership provided a place that they could work and call home, but their lands also offered opportunities for landless Blacks to farm with fellow Black farmers who owned land. Black landowners who rented living units on their land could also offer some in their communities an escape from the abusive rental arrangements often imposed by white planters and businessmen. As Blacks became increasingly dispossessed of their lands and farms, these former landowners suffered financially and became renters themselves. Those who were already landless in their communities suffered as well under the losses of Black landowners. Hillman and Shadrick's loss of land represented a trickle-down financial loss beyond just their own families, and in their own family the loss fueled migration that would become generational.

By 1920, families from Shadrick and Susan's line of descent had died or left Noxubee. Noah and his family were lease farmers and later sharecroppers after their move to Winston County, but his children and grandchildren would migrate to cities across the United States. Sophie had departed in 1910, and the oldest daughter, Maria, had died by then. Her children would be raised by their father, Isaac Grimmett, in adjacent Kemper County. Families from Lucretia's line of descent left Noxubee by 1920 as well. In 1910 Lucretia and granddaughter, Bertha Dobbins, were living in Attala County, MS, which borders Winston County's western line (1910 Census). She and Bertha were enumerated in Noxubee on the 1920 Census, but again Lucretia is reportedly in

Birmingham in 1921 and Bertha is not on the 1930 Census in Noxubee. Lucretia's daughter, Emma Dobbins, and her two sons appear in Lucretia's household on the 1900 Census, but they do not appear to be living in Noxubee by the time of the 1910 Census. After 1920 it was Elisha, grandson of John, who would remain in Noxubee and raise his family there. Although his father had not owned land, Elisha had emerged in 1920 as the last Noxubee Cistrunk remaining as landowning farmer in the place that Francis had determined would be home for the start of her family's legacy as freed people.[61] Many of his descendants would leave Noxubee, but those who have remained represent a generational connection to the place and history of a Black Mississippi family led into freedom and a transformed identity by a matriarch, Francis, whose name and story was almost lost. Just as Sophie adopted the name Francis in her later years to keep the memory of her grandmother alive, I hope that in the twenty-first century, her descendants—in blood and in spirit—will say her name and tell her story. Her story is our story.

CODA

Reflections on Methodology

In the film documentary, *Examined Life,* Cornel West argues that the art of "riding the dissonance" is not only foundational to the birth of the blues, but that the dexterity of this musical genre reflects more generally how Blacks see and engage the western-dominated world in which they must operate.[1] West maintains that in contrast to an Anglocentric American ethos that imagines a world progressing with deliberateness toward order and wholeness, African American art and ways of knowing emerged out of and through the world of catastrophe and chaos anchored in racism. His analogy underscores a challenge I wrestled with early in this project as I initially imagined the work as simply biography. But West reminds us that the violence and trauma experienced by Blacks in the Americas has informed Black epistemology and life. Therefore, while white-derived conventions of narrating historical accounts serve a white monolithic origins story, these methods and interpretations do not suffice for narratives of America's history from the perspective of Black experience and interpretation. In many cases we have to return to the very documents that have anchored white-centered histories, but we must read them through different lens and different codes. The American story of Francis and her children emerges out of the terror of the Middle Passage and generational enslavement that disrupted Black social and familial systems and traditions, introducing the lens of catastrophe and chaos that West finds in the blues. The world of Francis and her Cistrunk lineage sheds light on the congruency of southern and Black as identity—but this view emerges only through a challenge to conventional western-informed principles of history, biography, and genealogy.

SUBJECTS, METHODOLOGIES, HISTORIES, AND LIFE NARRATIVES

In general, the survival of history as an academic discipline has been predicated on assertions that it is established out of a repository of facts and accounts of the past, presumably formed from truthful, unbiased sources and interpretations. However, for those misrepresented or not represented at all in national narratives, history is a force and a process regarded with suspicion.

This point is illustrated in the centuries of US history making that has excluded interpretations of accounts and events through the lens of African Americans and their descendants. As revealed in the ongoing cries of white nationalists in the immediate post-Obama era through that of the forty-fifth president of the United States, the prevailing narrative of US history continues to convey the message that this is a white-constructed and white-intentioned nation. At the very least, then, the need persists for a historiography that takes us beyond a white-centered, white-derived intellectual lens, adding to or balancing the nation's narrative through histories of the so-called marginalized. This must go further than merely dropping the name of some non-white entities here and there to give a nod to inclusion. It is not enough, for example, to simply mention that a Black man, Crispus Attucks, was first to die in the colonists' war against Britain. History must do the work of building out the narrative of this man, including his place in the eighteenth-century society that drew him into a conflict of white interests. Images abound in history books that show Attucks taking the fatal blow for the colonists' freedom, but these same texts tell us little to nothing about Attucks and the society of Blacks in colonial Massachusetts. We are offered no understanding of their hopes and expectations or their views of the economy, politics, and social world in which they lived. Silencing Attucks and his Black colonial contemporaries obscures the multidimensional history of race and US nation building, specifically buoying a monolithic version that privileges and projects an Anglocentric narrative of national origins and evolution.

As Natasha Trethewey demonstrates in her Pulitzer Prize winning work, *Native Guard,* we cannot rely on conventional Anglo-Americentric history to narrate the story of African Americans and their part in the building of the nation. Through a mix of biography, history, and poetry *Native Guard* expands our understanding of the Civil War and the active role played by Black soldiers. In this work Trethewey takes us beyond the narrative of conventional history that has publicly subjugated Black voices through its memorials and monuments—both physical and narrative—to the dominant myth of the Confederate lost cause. She imagines and articulates the history of the Civil War through the vision and experience of the Louisiana Native Guard, a long-silenced presence in a war that marked one of the nation's deadliest conflicts. Trethewey's collection of poems ruptures the tightly knit narratives of the South's lost cause and the North's sacrificial cause, illustrating historian Elsa Barkley Brown's reminder that history is "everybody talking at once, multiple rhythms being played simultaneously."[2] The United States has long maintained a two-faced narrative of its internal war: The southern version has been the story of the South's noble fight against northern aggression that threatened its sovereignty; and for the North, the narrative paints the picture of a sacrificial body of whites risking and giving their lives for the freedom of the Black enslaved in the nation's South. In both versions, whites are the heroes, the seers, the voices that constitute the official records, and Blacks are the unspoken figures in the backdrop of these glistening narratives of Anglo-American heroism.

In the absence of what western historiography deems "firsthand" sources, Saidiya Hartman warns that the historical narrator may very well be "straining against the limits of the archive" as they attempt to give voice to the enslaved. [3] Hartman illustrates this point by recalling her desire to tell the story of two enslaved girls murdered aboard a slaving ship in 1792 and her reckoning with the impossibility of telling their story beyond the white shipmates' accounts found in the archives. She sees her inability to center the two enslaved girls beyond the white narrators as illustrative of the ongoing challenge for these projects, given the predominance of white-voiced archives. The result according to Hartman is that "the history of Black counter-historical projects is one of failure, precisely because these accounts have never been able to install themselves as history, but rather are insurgent, disruptive narratives that are marginalized and derailed before they ever gain footing."[4] If we accept self-serving western constructed conventions of historiography, there is perhaps little room to envision pathways to hear history beyond white-derived constructions. Arguably, we must consider as well the danger of accepting or seeing oneself as silenced because the victors refuse to hear. Such submission would have rendered numerous African American accounts lost. Consider, for example, Thomas Jefferson's sexual exploitation of Sally Hemings or the white terrorist campaigns of Rosewood and Black Wall Street. Despite the erasure of these stories and voices in white-authored histories, they lived in oral accounts throughout African American communities. While it is more challenging to reconstruct or uncover accounts of the enslaved long-deceased, most of whom left no surviving material records of their lives, these stories can be narrated through more critical methods and analysis and more nuanced valuations of what constitutes archives.

In her preface to *Wayward Lives, Beautiful Experiments,* Saidiya Hartman explains that in this work that narrates the lives of everyday urban Black women through their eyes, she was challenged like all historians who would tell the stories of marginalized people and populations. To tell these stories the historian must "grapple with the power and authority of the archive and the limits it sets on what can be known, [and] whose perspective matters"[5] In this "counternarrative" Hartman engages "a vast range of archival materials," narrating through "a style which places the voice of narrator and character in inseparable relation."[6] Hartman's bold melding of historian and subject persons may certainly invoke reservations on the part of historical scholars who wrestle with western-imposed edits on what constitutes "pure" history, but for those whose work is seated in an ethos of interdisciplinarity, Hartman's method allows for a more meaningful and comprehensive understanding of the past. Hartman's insistence on reading artifacts of conventional repositories through the lens of Black and female positionalities provides a pathway to see otherwise discounted Black people for their key impact in Black resistance and culture. Black people and communities have their historical tropes of the heroic and the daring, and Hartman challenges scholars to seat these into academic explorations of Black history and culture. Though Hartman's focus is the city, I found her work a call for research across periods and locations. The world of Black urban women that she introduces to readers was a reminder to me that the stories and voices of Black women, like Francis Sistrunk in the antebellum and early twentieth-century rural South, must be told as well.

The expanse of institutional archives that house records of early white histories in the United States significantly outnumber the repositories of bound narratives or accounts of the enslaved, particularly those articulated in their own voices. For contemporary researchers, then, diverse sites of memory must be mined to hear either the voices of enslaved people or to create reliable approximations. With the exponential growth of database collections of historical records and documents, access is more readily available and in greater numbers than imaginable just decades ago. For example, online resource compilations of early newspapers, government records, property records, and transatlantic slaving records are known resources for scholars across many disciplines. Massive projects such as the online database, "Enslaved: Peoples of the Historic Slave Trade," launched in 2020, portend a new era of history and biography of the enslaved.[7] This repository represents the type of mass digital archiving and organizing that will lead us into the lives and worlds of the masses of less-documented peoples of the slaving Atlantic world.

While the expansion of information available through online databases will change the course of narrations of the enslaved, the beginning is still most often, the oral—that is stories passed down through families and communities. To date, Alex Haley's 1976 novel, *Roots,* remains the most well-known narrative of generational transatlantic enslavement, and Haley's internationally known novel and television documentary of his family's history began with the oral accounts of his enslaved ancestors conveyed to Haley by his grandmother. Haley's grandmother imparted stories of enslavement that had been told to her from those who had experienced it firsthand. Through his grandmother, he was very near those original voices, and *Roots* captured and conveyed the story of US slavery through their lens. A work of fiction based on history, *Roots* was nevertheless criticized for its failure to remain consistent with historical "facts," and what some deemed a one-sided view of slavery. That Haley's was not a historical work and that his larger aim was to counter the prevailing one-sided white voice of US slavery and historiography continues to be ignored. While Haley fueled the ire of some scholars, his novel arguably offered a model for understanding the history and impact of slavery through the ethos of the enslaved. Before *Roots,* Haley's contemporary, Margaret Walker, published *Jubilee* (1966), a historical novel of slavery and the Civil War, based on stories Walker's grandmother had told of her enslaved foreparents. Walker, like Haley afterward, narrates her story through the backdrop of historical and archival sources. Whereas *Jubilee* focuses on the period leading up to and through the Civil War, *Roots* covers an expanse of generations, time, and movement that ultimately centers Africa as origins. It is perhaps this element of Haley's novel that informed its overshadowing of *Jubilee,* the work from which according to Walker Haley borrowed.

Haley and Walker's novels are reminders that orality and folklore have been central to preserving African American histories of experience and ways of knowing. Maintained for the most part free of white-imposed voices and interpretations, these Black histories have been disregarded in academia as unvalidated, undocumented, and biased. When setting out then to narrate an "authoritative" history that privileges oral and folk sources, but just as works such as *Roots* and *Jubilee* will inevitably utilize materials of conventional research, how does one avoid slipping back into white-anchored frameworks of interpretation that these sources invite? Not unlike most works that explore the lives of the enslaved, writing a biography of Francis Sistrunk and her offspring required the employment of conventional tools. This includes the common range of conventional archival sources such as census reports, birth and death certificates, marriage licenses, deeds, tax records, military records, wills and estate records, litigation records, and newspaper publications. Given the centrality of slavery in the study, documents such as slave schedules, slave sales, slave transportation records, and Freedmen's Bureau records were accessed. While these conventional resources were used, most were accessed through emerging or unconventional means. This includes digitized government and library databases as well as more layman's digital repositories such as Ancestry.com, 23andMe, and FamilySearch.org. The online networks also opened the sourcing reach to individual and organizational genealogy databases and narratives that though sometimes inaccurate, served as useful clues in the ongoing search for people, documents, and narratives. An unconventional resource in this project included the expansive and expanding DNA databases compiled by companies focusing on ancestry and medical information encoded in genetic composition. Advances in DNA research have resulted in a bank of information that has opened new pathways for interdisciplinary scholarship. In this study of Francis Sistrunk and her Cistrunk heirs, DNA information emerged as a narrative itself, both answering and posing questions as it was layered with other textual sources.[8] The use of DNA information in this work speaks to Katherine McKittrick's reflections on how "engaging interdisciplinarity and forging relational knowledges" can facilitate research and teaching that disrupts colonial frameworks of anti-Blackness.[9] McKittrick reminds us, however, that interdisciplinary work that engages science to critically interrogate race and racism, must operate with the understanding that "the logic of race is anchored to a monumental biocentric narrative that is invested in replicating scientific racism even in critique."[10] It was with both enthusiasm and caution then that I employed DNA information to corroborate other sources and open gateways to otherwise unknown information, helping to bring the life and voice of Francis in closer range to us today.

SAMPLING AS METHODOLOGY: EARLY MODELS

In Christina Sharpe's study that explores "the archives of the everyday of Black immanent and imminent death," she underscores the immediacy of the challenge for Black academics, who "Despite knowing otherwise . . . are often disciplined into thinking through and along lines that reinscribe our own annihilation."[11] Sharpe argues further that breaking the academy's intellectual tradition of Black erasure and denigration "requires new modes and methods of research and teaching; new ways of entering and leaving the archives of slavery."[12] This notion that we can arrive at new and liberating knowledge through the experiential narratives of everyday Blacks captures the foundation of this study of Francis Sistrunk and her lineage. Additionally, this work's connection to Sharpe's intellectual premise lies in the conviction that academic research in race and the American South must extend beyond Anglocentric practices and ideologies. An early challenge in imagining this project in its final form was to chart out a critical, coherent, and cohesive methodology to corral the range of sources amassed into a critical unity. The diverse range of sources and the not-so-common subject focus called for critical reading/ rereading and interpreting/reinterpreting to flesh out voices and faces that have been significantly obscured and silenced. An answer to the need for an alternative theoretical axis for this work came ironically through a rereading of William Wells Brown's nineteenth-century novel, *Clotel,* and the contemporary criticism that derides Brown and the novel as model example of plagiarism. First published in 1853, *Clotel* is the first published novel by an African American. It is a fictionalized narrative of Sally Hemings, the real-life enslaved half-sibling of Thomas Jefferson's wife. After the death of his wife,

Jefferson would compel the adolescent Hemings into a sexual arrangement out of which Hemings gave birth to enslaved children fathered by him, their enslaver.

Semesters of assigning *Clotel* in my literature courses inspires numerous lively classroom discussions on plagiarism, sampling, and the matter of originality or authenticity in creative works. In classroom reflections on scholarship criticizing Brown for his inclusion of numerous unacknowledged textual sources in *Clotel*,[13] I ask students to consider the obvious similarity between Brown's creative craft and that of the contemporary musical technique called sampling.[14] In the 1980s and 1990s the rising popularity of sampling in hip-hop and rap music introduced an era of increased copyright disputes and litigations. Decades past the birth of this musical and cultural movement, we have now settled into an acceptance of musical productions in which artists incorporate fragments from other works into their own to create compositions that the artistic borrowers then market as their own original works. Of course in today's music world the guiding premise regarding reuse or sampling of others' works is the requirement that the borrowing artist must acknowledge and pay the original artist for the privilege of reuse.

The appropriateness of sampling as an approach to telling the story of Francis Sistrunk rests in its cultural devolution as theory and act—or theory in action. Sampling offers no overtures to objectivity, no pretense to a clinical-like process. It is fueled by intent and does not seek to veil this. My choice to anchor and describe the theory and method of my project as sampling might be likened to Henry Louis Gates's election of the term "signifying" over "satire" to explore African American oral practice. Sampling is a dynamic and deliberately subversive act, that is grounded in African American culture and oral tradition. To free Francis's narrative from the bondage of a master narrative calls for a method and theory that reflects African American resistance through language and language practices. Sampling does this.

With the highly publicized debates on unauthorized reuse of artists' music, the public has become conditioned or trained to think of art as property. Whereas music has been in many societies a participatory and improvisational experience, under the authority of western capitalism and the growing integration of technology and music, it has been transformed into a commodity, an asset of exclusive individual ownership. Consumers may buy music for their listening enjoyment, but reuse of the music requires additional payment to the licensed owner (who may or may not be the creative artist). In this modern-day context of intellectual and artistic property and copyright, it is not surprising to find analyses or assessments of Brown's *Clotel* shaped through the lens of plagiarism or reuse principles. These analytical impulses, however, can limit our understanding of Brown's narrative strategy as it is informed through the artistic principles and practices of his era—one in which it was not unprecedented for writers to incorporate into their work ideas or excerpts from other writers. Rather than dismissing *Clotel* as inauthentic because of Brown's unauthorized reuse of materials, we might read this reuse as a subversive mechanism. *Clotel* is ostensibly a text that calls on readers to consider the damages and evil that slavery propagates. The novel, however, is more than a simple appeal to the anticipated highly empathetic nature of its readers. In fact, Brown is not pleading to his white audience, but rather chides and mocks them for their unwarranted presumptions of superiority and self-righteousness. Ironic in this regard is that early in the novel, we met the central and immoral character, President Thomas Jefferson, who in real life lifted directly (without acknowledgment) from the works of his Enlightenment idols, Hume and Kant, to buttress his assertions of Africans as innate inferior beings.[15] Through *Clotel*'s open display of Thomas Jefferson as a delinquent father, Brown in fact unveils origins of the long historical myth of the single Black mother and the absent Black father. He points the history of single Black mothers squarely at slavery and more directly at enslavers.

In addition to acknowledging that the neoclassical proclivity for imitation informs Brown's novel, it is again worth noting that Brown is not the originator or singular practitioner of literary reuse in his era. In her article focusing on Brown's use of newspapers and advertisements, Mary Ganster points out that this was an established practice in abolitionist works by the time of *Clotel*'s 1853 publication.[16] She further notes that Brown's incorporation of these extratextual sources is not simply for introduction or shock, but rather a highly stylized employment of varying forms to demonstrate the complex and multiple perspective world of slavery:

> Brown does more than merely pepper the fictional narrative with advertisements and other documents; the fictional narrative incorporates the evidence he cites into the flow of the story. Thus, fact and fiction cease to be two opposing categories and instead mutually inform one another, working together to provide a highly authenticated and multiperspectival representation of institutional slavery such as neither can do alone.[17]

Beyond analysis of Brown's work as product of nineteenth-century Anglo-American literary practices, it is important to recognize that Brown is also a product of African American oral traditions that incorporate multiplicities of narrative and artistic sources.[18] While he does not specifically call attention to the African rooted influences of Brown's reuse practices, literary historian Ezra Greenspan makes the case that Brown is an important precursor to America's contemporary cultural and artistic ethos. Greenspan maintains that Brown was "arguably the parent of our postmodern cultural concerns/

preoccupations a century before they were born. Fragmentation, alternating perspectives, sampling, multimedia, generic confusion were his signature practices."[19] Greenspan draws an important line between Brown's narrative craft and the practice of sampling more than a century after *Clotel*. What is overlooked in his assertion that Brown is the "parent" of this tradition, however, is the pre-Americas, African-originating oral practices that inform sampling as it morphed into African American oratory. The oral storytelling tradition of griots in some West African countries exemplify early origins of sampling in African diasporic peoples of the Americas. Storyteller historians of their people, griots maintain stories of origin, culture, beliefs, and heroes for many West African people. The griots of Gambia and Mali are probably the most well-known today as the descendants of a centuries-old narrative tradition. Their narratives are passed down generationally to descendants who continue stories that have been told for hundreds of years, but that evolve as new griots and different nation groups add or revise according to changes and new perspectives in the culture. The well-known, thirteenth-century West African tale, *The Epic of Son-Jara* exemplifies this narrative dynamic. Available in English-translated anthologies of world literature, this epic of the Manding people survives to date across populations of West Africa, particularly Mali and Gambia. Though the hero, Son-Jara, is central to the various versions, West African griots tell different versions that arise from griots who over time have sampled the text and other sources to compose a narrative of their own historical and cultural interpretation. *The Epic of Son-Jara* is itself a sampling of Islamic and Manding beliefs that the griots mix to construct a narrative representative of their society's fused history. The numerous populations that hold the story as their ancestral and historical legacy do not have to concern themselves with questions of plagiarism or ownership of the story. Their reuse comes out of a centuries-old practice and vision of history that is free of western-imposed assertions of textual authenticity or universality. In *Clotel*, Brown echoes this perspective: He reuses conventional sources but adds sources and perspectives of African Americans to tell a new and different tale, and his narrative flow is free of the intrusive interruptions of source citations.

My reflections on Brown and *Clotel* were not focused on the debate over plagiarism in the novel, but rather to consider how I would employ Brown's use of mixed media sources and forms as methodology/technique for narration. It is a point explored extensively in Jeffrey Sanborn's *Plagiarama: William Wells Brown and the Aesthetics of Attraction*, a full-length study that builds from Sanborn's previous work on *Clotel*. While Sanborn does not ignore the extensive inventory of reused texts embedded in *Clotel*, in *Plagiarama* he focuses on Brown's reuse of extratextual materials for dramatic, sensational, and ironic effect. Just as Sanborn, I was less interested in the growing count of reused sources in Brown's novel or the debate over authenticity tied to the charge of plagiarism. I was more intrigued with how Brown's reuse informed the novel's overriding critique of US slavery, and how Brown's use of multiple modes of narration and sources—that is, literary sampling—served as a narrative model to tell the Cistrunk story.

In an analysis of newspaper and article insertions in *Clotel,* Mary Ganster explains that Brown is not simply imitating a commonly employed practice in abolitionist writings. Ganster argues that Brown is deliberate and shrewd in his use of these extratextual sources, that he "deploys advertisements and newspaper articles strategically, juxtaposing them with and integrating them into the fictional narrative in ways that both authenticate his claims and draw attention to reified history's representational inadequacies."[20] She clarifies her use of the term "reified history" as denoting "texts whose generic and formal conventions become naturalized to the extent that they obscure the texts' underlying assumptions."[21] In the US "reified history" has been constructed through a kind of sleight of hand wherein the argumentative or analytical end/conclusion rests in the bias of a given Anglocentric worldview that is embedded into a presumed objective or universal premise/truth. Texts such as government and institutional records, newspaper publications, and legal documents are among the commonplace works etched into social consciousness as factual and free of bias. These are, however, the kinds of documents that exemplify the deep-rooted bias underlying the long-term circular power of these works to anchor generations of racial discrimination. Consider, for example, pre-emancipation census records. That enslaved people were not counted or recorded by name speaks to the cultural bias that was a gateway to numerous conclusions drawn about white and Black people. Antebellum census reports told much about those listed by name and almost nothing about those unnamed whose existence in the earliest census was simply tallied by checkmarks in boxes that denoted age group range and sex (and later by age rather than age range). The distinction between the narrative content describing the free (whites) and the enslaved (Blacks) said much about who the nation deemed worthy of acknowledging in the official record of its citizenry. The Census recorded the wealth of the enslaver but did not record the labor value of the enslaved who was the manufacturer of that wealth. The Census then "naturalized" the theft enacted by one segment of the population, that is white enslavers and the white citizen enablers of the system, stealing what should have been the wages of those enslaved Blacks they forced to work without compensation.

Conventional assertions that reified history offers a bias-free chronological account of events and people from the past to the present ignore the bias or "naturalized discourses" embedded in those presumably objective records. Ganster argues that "in the context of Brown's antislavery agenda, reified history includes the everyday assumptions of a newspaper article or advertisement that naturalize a given ideology so effectively that the absurdity, self-interest, and cruelty of the underlying ideological assumptions are invisible to many readers."[22] *Clotel* remains significant for its place in the tradition of slave narratives and the African American novel, but as Ganster argues, its significance also rests in Brown's method and creativity that operate to challenge prevailing paradigms of race and slavery in nineteenth-century America. Ganster's definition of reified history provides a critical axis upon which the case for employing sampling as methodology and ideology can be made. As an act of subversive resistance in *Clotel,* Brown's use of sampling offers a conceptual framework for transforming an otherwise array of narrative fragments into a cohesive biohistoriography. Ultimately then Brown samples numerous extratextual sources to "unmask naturalized discourses of reified history and destabilize their truth value for the reader."[23] While Brown's use of sampling serves as a tool of subversion, I employ sampling in this work as a theoretical anchor for revisiting and reinterpreting a heavily one-sided national narrative.

Conversations and debates on sampling typically rest within the perspective of musicality, especially considerations of the titles being reused in a work and the artists' transformations of the old into the new. Sampling, however, is arguably a skill employed in both music and literature, and in both genres its power arises in great part out of its radical praxis. Sampling is a process or method, but the act is rooted in a political ethos that in this regard reflects African American struggles in American society. Sampling is an interpretive or arguably reinterpretive tool; it is a medium of defiance; sampling defies dominant oppressive and denigrating discourses; sampling is a mechanism for reclaiming ownership of self and cultural ethos/self-realization; and sampling challenges the capitalistic-informed notion that knowledge, information, and art are individualized possessions. While the latter point is not a focus of this study, it speaks to how truths become authenticated or reified as history and fact. Capitalism creates a platform upon which ideas and information and their physical manifestation are transformed into commodities owned by individuals. While these owners may hold legal possession, they often are not the creators. As legal owners, individuals or entities can determine reuse, thus exercising the power over how their asset may play into "reified history." Numerous examples in literature illustrate this point. If we consider the late nineteenth-century plantation narrative, the well-known "authors" of this era, mostly white, clearly appropriated African American literary traditions and stories and then through copyright laws, came to own those stories. In contrast to sampling, this appropriation is antithetical to the radical and counterculture origins of African American sampling.

Today, Joel Chandler Harris and his late nineteenth- to early twentieth-century plantation narratives stand among the most widely published appropriations in literatures of the South. Harris, who transcribed and published African American folktales he heard throughout his youth, is to date credited as "author" of these tales. From 1880 until his death in 1908, Harris published and republished collections of these stories that were then republished decades after his death and reproduced into cinematic versions. The creators of those tales—generations of African Americans—received no revenue from the incomes of the sales in published form, and they had no artistic input on the production and presentation of those tales for public consumption and interpretation. A contemporary of Harris, African American author Charles Chesnutt published his own version of the plantation narrative tradition, subverting the simplistic and singular lens of Black folktales that were represented in works such as Harris's *Uncle Remus: His Songs and His Sayings*. On the surface, Chesnutt's collection of conjure tales (*Conjure Woman* 1899) seemed to reify the white-authored regional tales of his white contemporaries. Images such as the former slave Uncle Julius who remains on the plantation after emancipation seem to reify white-authored representations of happy, docile, simple-minded Blacks pre- and postwar South. In one of the early depictions of Julius, readers find him smacking his lips as he enjoys grapes that are legally the fruits of the new landowner, John. Julius's seeming acts of stereotyped Black simplicity and cunning, are rather assertions of his rights to the land and its fruits. Julius is on several levels a rightful inheritor.[24] Chesnutt samples African American folktales and folkways to counter the commonplace denigrating representations of southern Blacks in white literature and discourse of the era. As with the case of the African American language play called signifying, however, the subversive nature of Chesnutt's critiques rested in cultural codes to which white readers lacked access. In general, white readers of Chesnutt's era could enjoy his conjure tales and his fictional Uncle Julius as they interpreted or read the character and the stories through the reified historical lens that maintained their ordered racial world. Reified history granted Chesnutt readers the luxury of denying the power of the silenced to see and critically process their own narratives as well as those imposed through white hegemonic interpretations.

Reified history works differently in Joel Chandler Harris's appropriation of Black folktales and folkways. As "author" and "owner" of the African American folktales bound in his publication, Harris meshes the voices and narratives of the formerly enslaved with his white hegemonic narrative of the South. The result is work that furthers the narrative of an antebellum golden age of simple, indeed, happy Black slaves and their benevolent endearing white masters. With over a century of southern iconography and monuments that have reiterated a white-constructed history, African American experience and history in the antebellum South have been historically muted and disregarded. As illustrated in Harris's decades of published Uncle Remus stories, when recognized or acknowledged in white-authored texts, Black southern life is imagined and presented through the lens of the white author, reinscribing a white ethnocentric ethos.

Late nineteenth- to early twentieth-century plantation narratives illustrate a predominantly white-authored appropriation of Black folktales and culture packaged to reify a white southern version of the antebellum South. In his conjure tales Chesnutt borrows from folktales and ways of southern Blacks—that is sampling archival materials—to a contrasting end. Through the lens of Black southerners, Chesnutt's folktales present the unflattering portrait of southern whites who prospered from the stolen labor and lives of Blacks while showing little to no regard for their humanity. In this version of historical interpretation, Uncle Julius lays bare the savagery of whites themselves. Sampling the numerous oral folktales of Black southerners and their presumed inferior dialect, Chesnutt provides depictions of not so benevolent slaveowners and of Blacks who through the means that were available fought for autonomy and declared their humanity.

As Chesnutt realized in short order after the publication and acclaim of *The Conjure Tales,* the work's challenge to white reads of Blacks in the antebellum South were lost on his white audience who found his tales as enjoyable as those of his white peers. The paradox of this experience led Chesnutt to his full-length fictional work, *The Marrow of Tradition* (1901). In this novel Chesnutt samples literary conventions—most notably sentimental and realist fiction. He then integrates real history, notably the 1898 Wilmington Race Riot, and he integrates textual forms (fictionalized) such as newspapers, official documents, and legal documents. Additionally, signaling his own capacity for critical observation and interpretation, Chesnutt samples and assigns speech variations that include African American, southern white, and non-southern dialects. And in *The Marrow,* Chesnutt's message was unambiguous to white readers whose expectations had been primed by his earlier conjure tales. At its core *The Marrow* was a story laying bare the historic and systematic violence of white southerners against Blacks. Chesnutt had sampled an array of archival resources recognizable to his white audience, and he brought them to a conclusion—a reading of themselves—that countered their own reified history and the concomitant self-affirmation that defined their existence.

The Marrow jaded Chesnutt's primary audience of white readers, and drew the published disdain of the likes of William Dean Howells, the celebrated critic who had a year earlier lavished Chesnutt with praise.[25] With its overt and direct charge of white, southern, racialized violence the novel was a striking contrast to the subtle critique of American racism in his conjure tales. Chesnutt could not sustain a financial livelihood as author with the few African Americans who bought his books; therefore, with white critics and readers who considered *The Marrow* an attack on whites, the novel effectively ended Chesnutt's literary career. With its lengthier and more direct messaging, *The Marrow* echoes works by Chesnutt's contemporaries, Pauline Hopkins and Frances Harper—in particular Harper's *Iola Leroy* (1892) and Hopkins's *Contending Forces* (1900), *Winona* (1901–1902), *Hagar's Daughter* (1901–1902), and *Of One Blood* (1902–1903). Harper and Hopkins's novels return to the pre-Civil War era, revisiting the world of the plantation South through interpretations of its Black inhabitants. Both authors sample a variety of dialects, written and oral folk histories, and Black folkways and ideals to illustrate the limited and misleading perspective of nostalgic narratives of a golden-age antebellum South. Hopkins's fiction is of particular interest with respect to the matter of sampling in the works. As with her authorial model and predecessor, William Wells Brown, Hopkins samples liberally in her fiction—most notably in *Winona, Hagar's Daughter,* and *Of One Blood*.[26] Her fiction has thus become the subject of scholarly contemplations on the meanings and significance of her numerous unacknowledged reuses of texts and documents. Ironically, in *Hagar's Daughter,* Hopkins extracts from and reuses characters and episodes from Brown's *Clotel*. Unlike Brown's *Clotel,* however, *Hagar's Daughter* leaves readers with more than a targeted white villain (Thomas Jefferson) or critique of the damage suffered by a certain class of enslaved (mulatto and near white). While Hopkins certainly infuses *Hagar's Daughter* with similar buffoonish Black characters as those in *Clotel,* the point of departure is that she concludes with an affirmation of Black culture and ways of knowing. While the dialect of the southern Blacks may lead readers to see them as mere local color or sideline amusement, it is the Blacks throughout who either know the secrets, or as in the case of the novel's secondary heroine, Venus, have the intellectual prowess to solve the mystery and unveil the secrets. In *Hagar's Daughter* sampling is a narrative mechanism for revisiting reified or white-centered historical accounts of the South and its people. Employing this mechanism through a mix of genres such as sentimental, detective, and slave narrative, Hopkins overturns hegemonic misrepresentations of events and people. In this more nuanced representation of history, she also demonstrates that the Black lens is a necessary one to more fully see and understand the South and the experiences of its Black citizenry.

SAMPLING: NARRATING THE CISTRUNK STORY

The story of Francis and her children from antebellum to post–World War I America is not unlike the fictionalized nineteenth-century works of Brown, Chesnutt, Harper, and Hopkins with their emphasis on forced migrations and family separations that were endemic in the antebellum South. Just as these early fictionalized narratives, *Francis* is built from sourcing and resourcing a wide body of archives and artifacts. The shift, however, is from creative fiction to speculative historiography. Just like my nineteenth-century predecessors, I sampled sources to tell a story whose end and whose subjects I had imagined from the imprinted codes and cultural nuances of my Black epistemological orientation. Having been taught Black modes and codes of survival in white spaces—both physical and ideological—I began reading Francis, her children, their family, and communities through this lens. I began knowing before the documents confirmed, that my enslaved and emancipated ancestors knew the art of living Black in anti-Black spaces. I knew that they knew and that those before them knew, and I knew that my own presence and understanding confirmed this legacy. Just as Brown sampled an array of documents to tell an alternative story of the young girl that Thomas Jefferson enslaved and sexually violated, I set out to utilize the archives to tell a narrative version that gives voice to my ancestors, to tell the story of our southern history.

The conception of sampling as methodology in this work is informed as well by scholar Henry Louis Gates's seminal work in African American literary criticism. In *The Signifying Monkey* (1988) Gates explores the African origins of African American oral traditions that carry over into the literary, especially the legacy of the signifying monkey who can maintain self-realization even under the weight of a seemingly mightier foe. Gates's parallel of the practice of close reading in western criticism to what "the Yoruba call *Didafa* (literally 'reading the signs')" arguably captures the heart of creation and interpretation in sampling.[27] The indeterminacy of reading meaning or signs that is embodied in the Yoruba mythical figure, Esu, becomes central to African American oral tradition, specifically the signifying monkey whose articulations in double meaning leave the audience, especially those unable to read the signs, unsure of the meaning behind the words.[28] Like signifying, Sampling is a dynamic and deliberately subversive act, that is grounded in African American cultural and oral tradition. The sampling narrator is a mirror of the signifying monkey, who is as Gates explains, "the figure of the text of the Afro-American speaking subject, whose manipulations of the figurative and the literal both wreak havoc upon and inscribe order."[29] The sampling narrator/ narration is an iteration of that trickster manipulator of new world Africana, that speaks Black resistance and resilience. We have only to read via the multitude of Black cultural signs, expressions, and epistemologies—oral and written—to hear voices of the enslaved that speak beyond America's so-called master narratives.

Extending across genealogical and geographical boundaries, *Francis* is a biohistoriography that breaks from Anglocentric discourses that have bound us to repeating loops of a social death myth of Black life and family. As with most genealogical searches for African Americans, my search that began with a known ancestor—Noah Cistrunk—necessitated a search for those who had enslaved his parents and ancestors. The sampling began to broaden in ways reminiscent of the array of texts sampled by Brown in his fictionalized account of Sally Hemings. To tell his story of Sally Hemings—even as fiction—Brown had to return to the story of her enslaver, Jefferson. Brown sampled the conventional history of Jefferson and his family, but he told the story through the lens of the enslaved. His narrator intervenes throughout the narrative to instruct readers on the meaning of the facts he has set before them. He shows a picture of slavery and enslavers painted through the eyes of those they enslaved and persecuted. While he presented his readers with texts that they would have considered reliable or authoritative, Brown rooted the very presumption of the story in a narrative of Jefferson that was told, preserved, and affirmed as authoritative primarily by African Americans. Even though there was mention during his life and long after that Jefferson fathered enslaved children, official histories of Jefferson were silent or dismissive of this fact. In his fictionalized account of Hemings and Jefferson, Brown begins by affirming this as fact, and all that unfolds in the fiction emanates from this. Similarly, the story of Francis that I tell is rooted in the vision of a Black southern legacy of grit, industry, determination, and wisdom that anchored African Americans through and beyond enslavement. Black survival did not happen by chance, and the histories preserved and retold by my own and other Black families affirmed for me that I was rediscovering and retelling a story of Black fortitude—of a people acting with deliberateness and an eye to the future.

It is ironic that today many texts that historically silenced the enslaved foreparents of African Americans have come to serve as part of the integral repository bringing to light their voices, their experiences, and sometimes their names. Such was the case in bringing Francis Sistrunk to the forefront of what began as a search for the lineage of her grandson, Noah Cistrunk. To meet Noah's foreparents I had to discover the names and stories of their white enslavers, and to face the reality that in some cases the enslaver was a biological link in the ancestral narrative. Noah Cistrunk's descendants have kept his name and legacy alive, but the family narrative has focused on his life, centering him as the family's origin figure. With this focus and Noah's birthplace in Mississippi, few family accounts from the late twentieth century to the present considered the nativity of his parents and foreparents. That Noah's father, Shadrick, entered the state as a forced, enslaved, migrant has not been part of the contemporary family narrative or that Mississippi had only been a state for two decades prior to Shadrick's arrival.

It was the search through standard archival records that brought Shadrick S/Cistrunk into clearer focus and then pointed the narrative to his mother, Francis, the nineteenth-century matriarch who headed the household as they were forced to cross into Mississippi. In finding Francis, the story of Noah became a much richer and broader narrative, not just of a family, but of a kinship collective. Francis headed her family of five children as they were forced to migrate to Neshoba County, MS, with their enslaver, Jacob Sistrunk Jr. and his family. The expanse of sampled texts that overlap to narrate Francis's story and legacy moves beyond the reified "facts" of white-centered history. It is a story that moves beyond simplistic depictions of a generational voiceless, lifeless, and agentless Black presence in the white-ruled South to unearth a dynamic account of Black southern life and experience—pre and post emancipation. *Francis* complicates long-standing reductionist discourses of "single Black mothers," "absent fathers," and Black families in crisis, revealing instead that despite centuries of American slaving, the enslaved found ways to create and preserve systems of family, kinship groups, and community. Central to this legacy of resilience were countless enslaved Black women, who like Francis, "spoke" their resistance through signifying narratives—manifested in action and language—that even when not conveyed from them directly, can be mined from numerous surviving artifacts and sources. Francis tells us that enslaved Black mothers left a legacy of resistance and transformation that when revisited, demands new narratives of the Black South.

The patterns and pathways of forced movements of African Americans across the pre-Civil War South can probably never be fully traced, but by mapping out individual genealogical narratives we can create overlapping or interlacing narratives that bring us to more comprehensive histories. The story of Francis and her family is one such layer. Modeling nineteenth- and early twentieth-century Black literary sampling, *Finding Francis* reuses, reissues, and repackages a range of conventional and innovative sources to retell, reaffirm, and reinscribe the story of the Black South. The outcome is a historiographical narrative, a family's epic of everyday extraordinary Black life.

Appendix

Line of Descent: Francis Sistrunk to Carl Cistrunk

Line of Descent from Heinrich Süsstrünk to Jacob Sistrunk Jr.

Line of Descent from Shirley Whatley to Daniel Whatley

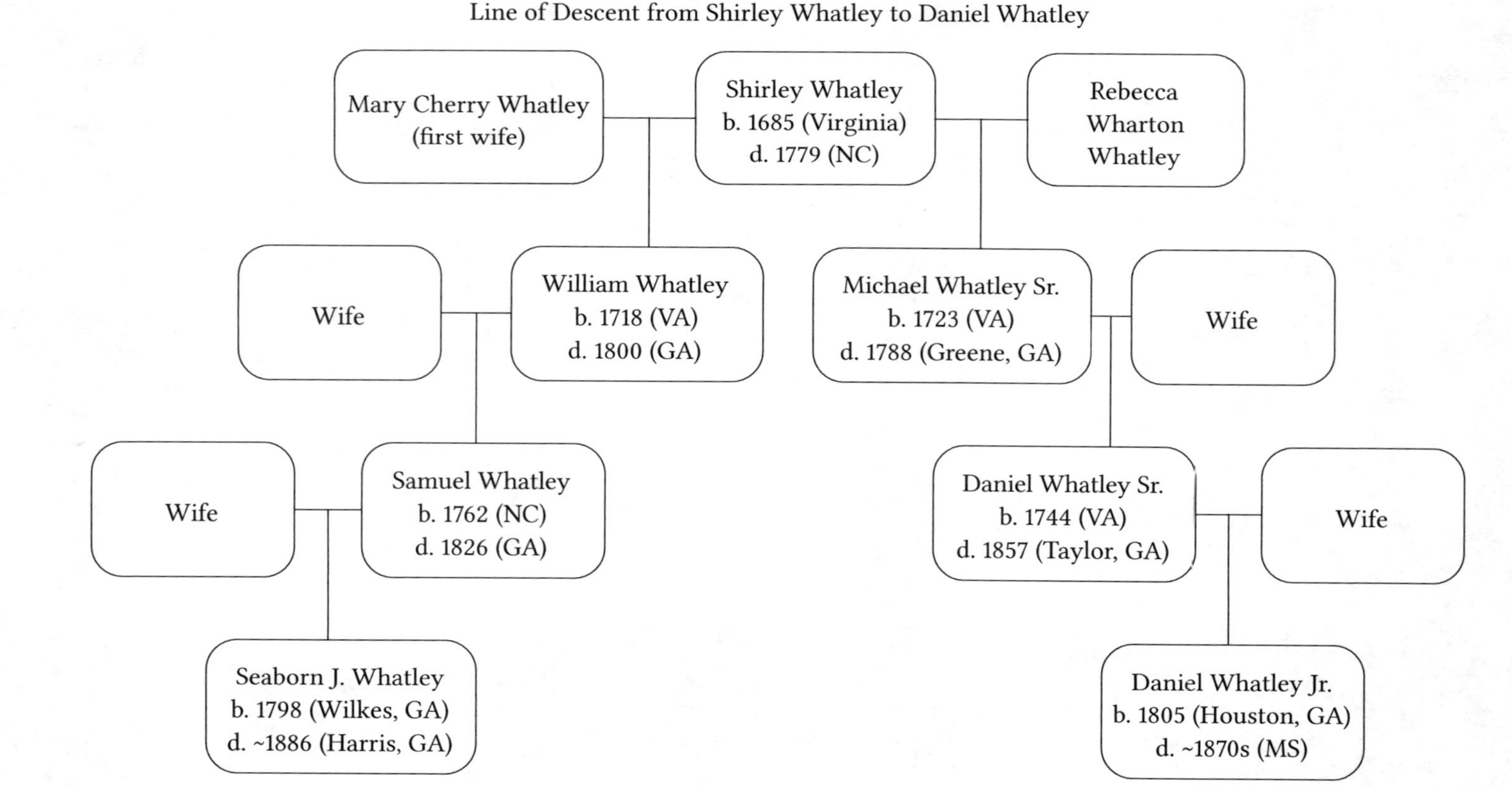

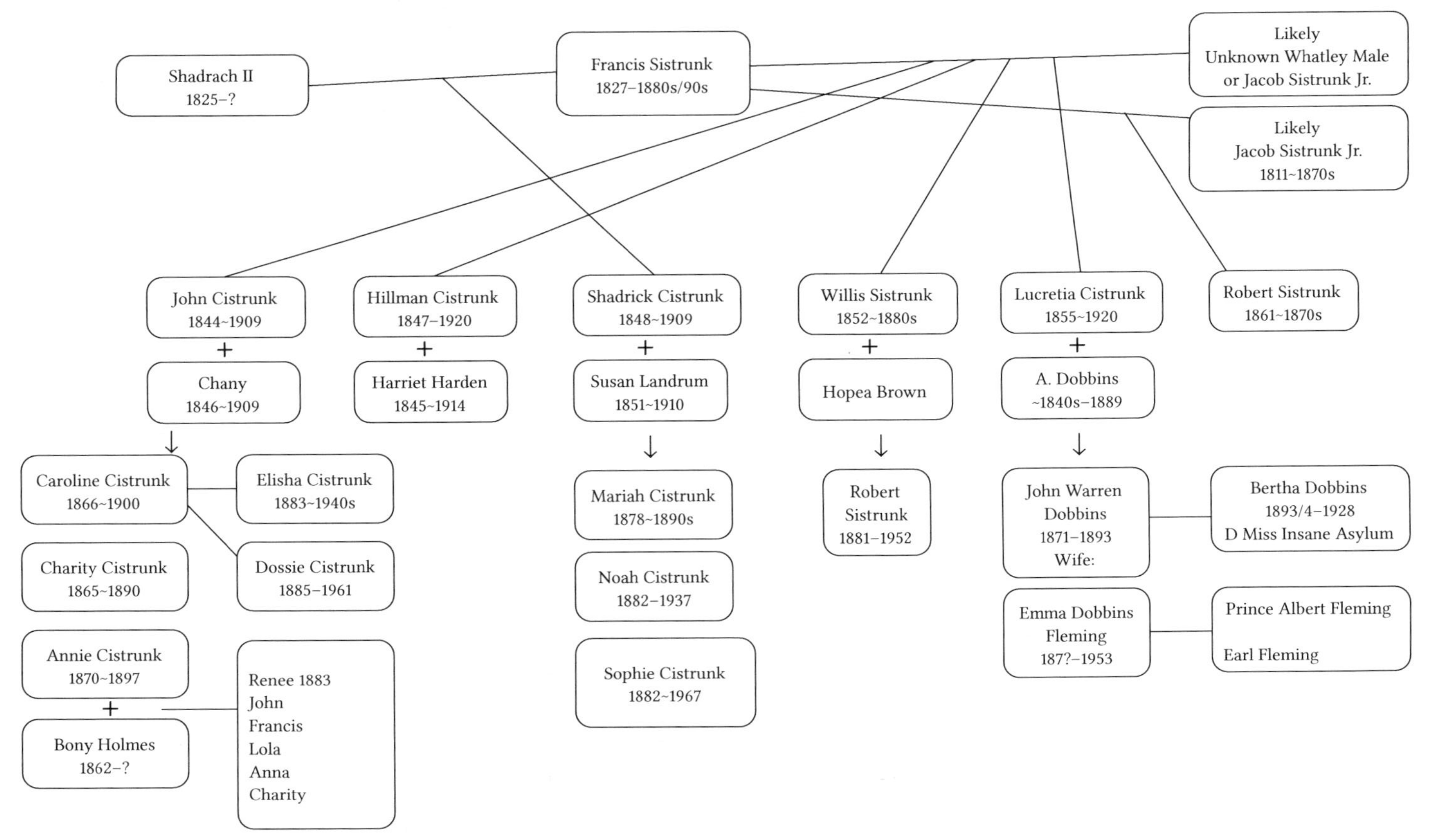

Shadrach II
1825~?
Francis Sistrunk
1827~1880s/90s
Likely
Unknown Whatley Male
or Jacob Sistrunk Jr.
Likely
Jacob Sistrunk Jr.
1811~1870s
John Cistrunk
1844~1909
+
Chany
1846~1909
Hillman Cistrunk
1847~1920
+
Harriet Harden
1845~1914
Shadrick Cistrunk
1848~1909
+
Susan Landrum
1851~1910
Willis Sistrunk
1852~1880s
+
Hopea Brown
Lucretia Cistrunk
1855~1920
+
A. Dobbins
~1840s~1889
Robert Sistrunk
1861~1870s
Caroline Cistrunk
1866~1900
Elisha Cistrunk
1883~1940s
Dossie Cistrunk
1885~1961
Charity Cistrunk
1865~1890
Annie Cistrunk
1870~1897
+
Bony Holmes
1862~?
Renee 1883
John
Francis
Lola
Anna
Charity
Mariah Cistrunk
1878~1890s
Noah Cistrunk
1882~1937
Sophie Cistrunk
1882~1967
Robert
Sistrunk
1881~1952
John Warren
Dobbins
1871~1893
Wife:
Emma Dobbins
Fleming
187?~1953
Bertha Dobbins
1893/4~1928
D Miss Insane Asylum
Prince Albert Fleming
Earl Fleming

Notes

INTRODUCTION

1. Francis and her children spell their last name with an *S* as their Sistrunk enslavers. Francis will maintain this spelling throughout her life, but her sons John, Hillman, and Shadrick will change the spelling to Cistrunk in the early post-emancipation years. The transition to this spelling will appear on some documents as Scistrunk, but the spelling with the *C* is, with a few exceptions, established at the turn of the century (Ninth Census, Noxubee County, MS, 30). On the 1870 Census, Francis spelled her last name with an *S*, while her children John, Hillman, Shadrick, and Lucretia would shift to the spelling that starts with *C*. The last census record showing Francis indicates that she maintained the Sistrunk spelling (Tenth Census, Noxubee County, MS, 25). Not long after the 1870 Census, records show that the four children began to shift to the Cistrunk spelling.

2. Miles, *All That She Carried*, 30.

3. Hartman, "A Note on Method," in *Wayward Lives, Beautiful Experiments*, xiv.

4. See US Census 1900, 1910, and 1940. The 1900 Census lists Sophie in Noxubee County in the household of her parents, showing her name as Sopha Cistrunk. She is listed in the 1910 Census in Tallahatchie County, married to Lem Nichols, with their 10-year-old daughter and Sophie's mother, Susan. Upon her death in 1967, however, the funeral program shows her name as Francis E. Marsh, daughter of Shedrick and Susan Cistrunk. She and husband Frosh Marsh are listed on the 1940 Census in Jackson, MS.

5. See US Census 1870 and 1880.

6. Publications by descendants of Heinrich Süsstrunk include Sistrunk, *The Sistrunk Families*. Sistrunk, *A Walk Through Caney: The Sistrunk Family*. Lefvendahl, *Oliver-Sistrunk Families: Orangeburg Area, South Carolina*.

7. Jones, "An End," 3.

8. Jones, 5.

9. White, *Ar'n't I a Woman?*, 153.

10. White, 153.

11. Jones, "An End," 7.

12. See Gomez, *Exchanging Our Country Marks*, chap. 7, "Talking Half African," for an in-depth examination of the processes of historical conveyances of African origins throughout antebellum America.

13. Gomez, 180.

14. Gomez, 177.

15. Lindsay, *Biography*, 1.

16. Miller, "A Historical Appreciation," 44.

17. Kendi, "Hopefulness."

18. Kendi, "Hopefulness."

19. West, Elizabeth, "Community and Naming," 426. Some portions of chapters 2, 3, and 6 were drawn from Elizabeth West's "Community and Naming.

CHAPTER 1: FRANCIS IN GEORGIA

1. Ninth Census, Noxubee County, MS, 30; Tenth Census, Noxubee County, MS, 25.

2. Sharpe, *In the Wake,* 126.

3. See Michael Gomez's *Exchanging Our Country Marks,* 22–23, 293–95, for an overview of Black population growth in colonial and antebellum US and Georgia.

4. Sixth Census, Marion County, GA, 58.

5. Betty Wood, "Slavery in Colonial Georgia,"

6. Library of Congress, "Establishing the Georgia Colony."

7. Georgia US Property Tax Digests, 1799–1806, Lincoln County, GA, Captain Parks District, 16. John, Richard, Gasper, and George Sistrunk are all listed on the same page.

8. Watson, *Slave Importation,* 10.

9. Watson, 10.

10. Watson, 37.

11. Watson, 42.

12. Watson, 37.

13. Sixth Census, Marion County, GA, 58.

14. US Census Bureau, Slave Schedules, 1850, Dowdells District, Harris County, GA, 1.

15. US Census Bureau, Slave Schedules, 1860, Township 11, Range 13, Neshoba County, MS, 5.

16. Tenth Census, Noxubee County, MS, 25. The 1870 Census that lists Francis as 65 years old is out of the range of the other census reports and is apparently incorrect. If Francis was 65 years old in 1870, she would have been 35 years old at the time of the 1840 Census, and she would have thus been listed in the 24- to 35-year-old age category. She is listed in 1840 in the 10- to 24-year-old age range and appears to have no children. It is unlikely that she would have reached age 35 with no children. Given the other reports suggest her birth year was in the 1822 to 1830 range, the age reported in 1870 suggests that an 1805 birth year is the only outlier. The 1880 Census that lists her as 58 years old follows the age progression range suggested in the 1840, 1850, and 1860 reports. If Francis was born in 1805, she would have been 75 years old in 1880. It is unlikely that at 75 she would have been listed as 58 years old. The 1870 Census reporting her age is thus clearly an error.

17. Fifth Census, Elbert County, GA, 126; Sixth Census, Elbert County, GA, 174.

18. Jacobs, *Incidents in the Life of a Slave Girl,* 27.

19. Jacobs, 27.

20. Jacobs 28.

21. See Sixth Census, Elbert County, GA, 174; Seventh Census, Clarke County, GA, 20, which show that Jeptha V. Harris moved from Elbert County to Clarke County between 1840 and 1850.

22. Fifth Census, Harris County, GA, 184; Fifth Census, Muscogee County, GA, 284.

23. Watson, *Slave Importation,* 10.

24. Ninth Census, Noxubee County, MS, 30; Tenth Census, Noxubee County, MS, 240.

25. Tenth Census, Noxubee County, MS, 25; Twelfth Census, Noxubee County, MS, 9.

26. Tenth Census, Noxubee County, MS, 25.

27. Twelfth Census, Noxubee County, MS, 18.

28. Thirteenth Census, Noxubee County, MS, 20; Fourteenth Census, Noxubee County, MS, 9. Thirteenth Census, Attala County, MS, 10A.

29. Fourteenth Census, Noxubee County, MS, 9.

30. Sixth Census, Marion County, GA, 58.

31. Wilson, *Our Nig*, 17.

32. The term *mulatto* is used here and elsewhere in this book considering its explicit use in the records and texts that are referenced.

33. US Census Bureau, Slave Schedules, 1860, Township 11, Range 13, Neshoba County, MS, 5.

34. This Black cultural ontology and epistemology has been explored in hallmark scholarship dating back to the ethnographic work of Zora Neale Hurston to present-day studies of the African diaspora. See Zora Neale Hurston, *Mules and Men* (1935) and *Tell My Horse* (1938); Lorenzo Dow Turner, *Africanisms in the Gullah Dialect* (1949); The Georgia Writers' Project, *Drums and Shadows* (1940); Lawrence Levine, *Black Culture and Black Consciousness* (1977); Joseph Holloway, *Africanism in African American Culture*; and Michael Gomez, *Exchanging Our Country Marks* (1998).

35. Moynihan, "The Negro Family," 16–17.

36. Jones, "An End," 7.

37. Kolchin, *American Slavery*, 138–39.

38. Kolchin, 141.

39. Wilson, *Our Nig*, 10; US Census Bureau, Slave Schedules, 1860, Township 11, Range 13, Neshoba County, MS, 5.

40. Sixth Census, Marion County, GA, 58.

41. White, *Ar'n't I a Woman?*, 128.

42. White, 133.

43. See Emily West and Erin Shearer, "Fertility Control" for more detailed consideration of labor in Black enslaved women's communities.

44. White, *Ar'n't I a Woman?*, 122–26.

45. Tenth Census, Noxubee County, MS, 25.

46. Sixth Census, Marion County, GA, 58.

47. White, *Ar'n't I a Woman?*, 97–98.

48. Bay, "Love, Sex, Slavery," 194.

49. Tenth Census, Noxubee County, MS, 25; Twelfth Census, Noxubee County, MS, 18. Both the 1880 and 1900 Census corroborate John Cistrunk's birth year as 1844.

50. *Deeds and Mortgages*, Marion County, GA, book A, 327.

51. Sistrunk, Sistrunk, and Sistrunk, *The Sistrunk Families*, 126, 135.

52. Both Jacob and John Sistrunk can be found in the Georgia, US Property Tax Digests, 1793–1892, for Lincoln County, GA, 1818, p. 12.

53. Sistrunk, Sistrunk, and Sistrunk, *The Sistrunk Families*, 135; *Deeds and Mortgages, 1796–1909* (Lincoln County, GA), 296–97.

54. See Deed transfer Jacob Sistrunk Sr. to John Floyd, 348–49.

55. Fifth Census, Marion County, GA, 139; Sixth Census, Marion County, GA, 57.

56. Sixth Census, Marion County, GA, 57.

57. Sistrunk, Sistrunk, and Sistrunk, *The Sistrunk Families*, 137.

58. Sistrunk, Sistrunk, and Sistrunk, *The Sistrunk Families*, 137.

59. Rousseau, "Jacksonian Monetary Policy,."

60. Sistrunk, Sistrunk, and Sistrunk, *The Sistrunk Families*, 137.

61. Scott, "The Troubled World."

62. Probate Records, Inventories, Appraisements, Sales, Returns, Vouchers, Marion County, GA, book A, 56.

63. *Deeds and Mortgages,* Marion County, GA, book A, 327

64. Watson, *Slave Importation*, 34.

65. Watson, 34.

66. See 1860 Slave Schedule, Houston County, GA.

67. Sistrunk, Sistrunk, and Sistrunk, *The Sistrunk Families*, 84.

68. Mitchell, *A New History*, 134.

69. See Thomas Sistrunk, *A Walk Through Caney*, 26.

70. Sixth Census, Marion County, GA, 58.

71. DNA tests for B. Cistrunk were administered in 2018 and 2017 through the genetic testing companies, African Ancestry, Inc. and 23andMe. Both results show that B. Cistrunk's paternal line originates from West Africa. Given B. Cistrunk's descendancy from Noah Cistrunk, who was the son of Shadrick Cistrunk, the results confirm that Shadrick Cistrunk was Black through his male descent line. Through additional DNA tests taken by descendants of Carl Cistrunk, including those taken by the author of this work (Elizabeth West), family descendancy from the line of Shedrick Cistrunk and his paternal lineage is corroborated.

72. Through my own DNA match (determined through AncestryDNA tests) with a descendent of an enslaved man Andrew Dowdell of Harris County, GA, the genetic connection of Shedrick Cistrunk to a Black enslaved father around 1848 is further corroborated.

73. Eighth Census, Harris County, GA, 11; Watson, *Slave Importation,* 56.

74. See Watson, *Slave Importation.* Noteworthy here is that two additional Shadracks are registered as entering the state of Georgia for years 1818–1847. Early in this project, I deduced that the Shadrick reported in Samuel Oliver's 1831 affidavit was likely Shadrick Cistrunk. This premature conclusion was based on the familial relationship between Oliver and the Georgia Sistrunks. However, as the present study shows, the sampled documents to date make the strongest case for Shadrack Dowdell as Shadrick's father.

75. Watson, *Slave Importation,* 56.

76. Watson, 56.

77. Fourth Census, Captain Tomlinson's District, Putnam County, GA, 4.

78. Non-Population Schedule for Agriculture (1850), Harris County, GA, 1.

79. Seventh Census, Harris County, GA, 62.

80. US Census Bureau, Slave Schedules, 1850, Dowdells District, Harris County, GA, 1–2.

81. Sistrunk, Sistrunk, and Sistrunk, *The Sistrunk Families*, 139.

82. US Census Bureau, Slave Schedules, 1850, Dowdells District, Harris County, GA, 1.

83. Barfield, *History of Harris County*, 629.

84. Gomez, 27

85. Barfield, *History of Harris County*, 627.

86. Barfield, 628.

87. Barfield, 628.

88. Ninth Census, Sumter County, GA, 44. On this census, Henry and Silas are still among children living in the household of their parents—Shadrack and Lucinda. Son Joe, 24 years old, is listed as head of his own household below entries for Shadrack and his household. Shadrack is reportedly 45 years old, suggesting a birth year of 1825.

89. Freedmen's Bureau, Americus, GA, roll 40, Register of Patients August–November 1868. The entry for Shadrack spells his surname Dowdle instead of Dowdell. He seems to be suffering from an intestinal disorder.

90. Sistrunk, Sistrunk, and Sistrunk, *The Sistrunk Families*, 125.

91. Jacobs, *Incidents in the Life*, 55.

92. Ninth Census, Sumter County, GA, 44. The 1870 Census shows that Shadrack and Lucinda had children born in the years before and after the birth of Francis and Shadrack's son, Shadrick.

93. Hurston, *Jonah's Gourdvine*, 19.

94. Sistrunk, Sistrunk, and Sistrunk, *The Sistrunk Families*, 193.

95. A special note of thanks to graduate research assistant Joshua Jackson, who brought to my attention Jacob Jr.'s Civil War records.

96. Jacob Sistrunk, Company F, 40th Mississippi Infantry and Company I, 1st Mississippi State Troops, Confederate, Compiled service records of Confederate soldiers who served in organizations from the State of Mississippi, 1862–1864.

97. Seventh Census, Chambers County, AL, 292.

98. Sixth Census, Marion County, GA, 58.

99. Probate Records, Inventories, Appraisements, Sales, Returns, Vouchers, Marion County, GA, book A, 56.

100. Seventh Census, Harris County, GA, 62.

101. US Census Bureau, Slave Schedules, 1860, Township 11, Range 11, Neshoba County, MS, 15.

102. Seventh Census, Troup County, GA, 101; Eighth Census, Troup County, GA, 164.

103. See Whatley, *Whatley Family Reunion*, 1–9, and "Shirley Whatley Family Tree."

104. Daniel Whatley's purchase of enslaved person Jo in 1799, and Michael Whatley Sr.'s will filed in 1788 places the family in Greene County, GA, as early as 1788.

105. See 1840 Census showing John, Willis, and William in Macon County, GA; Daniel Jr. in Marion County, GA, and Daniel Sr. in Houston County, GA.

106. See Michael Whatley Sr.'s will.

107. Daniel Whatley Sr.'s purchase of enslaved person Jo.

108. Michael Whatley v. Daniel Whatley.

109. See 1840 and 1860 Census and Slave Schedule for Harris County, GA.

110. Ninth Census, Noxubee County, MS, 30.

111. US Census Bureau, Slave Schedules, 1860, Township 11, Range 13, Neshoba County, MS, 5.

112. See the will of Michael Sr. and the "Shirley Whatley Family Tree" for the recurrence of names John, Willis, and Frances throughout generations of seventeenth-, eighteenth-, and nineteenth-century descendants.

113. See "Nathan Holcomb Family Tree" to Michael Whatley Greene, GA, "Chapman Family Tree" to Matilda in Greene Co to Robert Alton in Wilkes, and "Nicholas Family Tree" William Wesley Whatley 1778 Augusta.

114. Sistrunk, Sistrunk, and Sistrunk, *The Sistrunk Families*, provide a comprehensive record of the migration of Sistrunk descendants from the lineage of the immigrant Heinrich.

115. Sistrunk, Sistrunk, and Sistrunk, *The Sistrunk Families*, 191.

116. Brown, "Social Death," 1239.

CHAPTER 2: NESHOBA TO NOXUBEE

1. Seventh Census, 368.

2. US Population in 1860, 270.

3. Mitchell, A New History of Mississippi, 134, 136.

4. Eighth Census, Neshoba County, MS, 11.

5. 1850 Non-Population Schedule for Agriculture, Harris County, GA, 1; Eighth Census, Neshoba County, MS, 11.

6. Sistrunk, Sistrunk, and Sistrunk, *The Sistrunk Families*, 193.

7. Sistrunk, *A Walk Through Caney*, 28.

8. County Tax Rolls, box 3945, Neshoba County, MS, 1860, personal roll, 25.

9. US Census Bureau, Slave Schedules, 1860, Township 11, Range 13, Neshoba County, MS, 4–5.

10. US Census Bureau, Slave Schedules, 1860, Township 11, Range 13, Neshoba County, MS, 4.

11. US Census Bureau, Slave Schedules, 1860, Township 11, Range 13, Neshoba County, MS, 5.

12. Mitchell, *A New History of Mississippi*, 160, 183.

13. Mitchell, 183.

14. Compiled Service Records of Confederate Soldiers, Jacob Sistrunk, Company F, 40th Mississippi Infantry, Confederate, 1862.

15. Sistrunk, *A Walk Through Caney*, 37–38.

16. County Tax Rolls, box 3931, Noxubee County, MS, 1864, personal roll, 5.

17. Hooks, "Representations of Whiteness," 167–68.

18. Compiled Service Records of Confederate Soldier, Jacob Sistrunk, Company F, 40th Mississippi Infantry, Confederate, 1862.

19. Compiled Service Records of Confederate Soldiers, Jacob Sistrunk, Company I, 1st Mississippi State Troops, Confederate, 1864.

20. Compiled Service Records of Confederate Soldiers, Jacob Sistrunk, Company F, 40 Mississippi Infantry, Confederate, 1863.

21. County Tax Rolls, box 3931, Noxubee County, MS, 1864, personal roll, 5.

22. Sistrunk, *A Walk Through Caney*, 30.

23. Sistrunk, 30.

24. County Tax Rolls, box 3931, Noxubee County, MS, 1864, personal roll, 5.

25. County Tax Rolls, box 3946, Noxubee County, MS, 1867, personal roll, 26.

26. Ninth Census, Noxubee County, MS, 22. See also Chapter 2 of this book, p. 38 for discussion of evidence confirming that the John Sistrunk enumerated on the 1870 Census in Noxubee County, MS, is actually Jacob Sistrunk.

27. 1850 Non-Population Schedule for Agriculture, Harris County, GA, 1.

28. See Jessica B. Harris's *High on the Hog* for a detailed history of African American cuisine.

29. County Tax Rolls, box 3931, Noxubee County, MS, 1864, personal roll, 5.

30. Ninth Census, Noxubee County, MS, 29–31.

31. Tenth Census, Noxubee County, MS, 24.

32. West and Shearer, "Fertility Control, Shared Nurturing," 1013.

33. West and Shearer, "Fertility Control, Shared Nurturing," 1013

34. Ninth Census, Americus County, GA, 44.

35. Some well-known literary texts that focus on colorism in African American culture include Chesnutt's "The Wife of His Youth" (1899), Fauset's *Plum Bun* (1928), Hurston's *Jonah's Gourdvine* (1934), and Morrison's *God Bless the Child* (2015).

36. Mitchell, *A New History of Mississippi,* 191.

37. Ninth Census, Noxubee County, MS, 30.

38. See, for example, Mississippi, Freedmen's Bureau Field Office Records, 1865–1872, roll 30, misc. records, "Macon Indentures of Apprentice," image 41, which shows the indenture contract of 5-year-old David whose mother, Malinda, was reported as dead. In 1865, David was contracted to Louis Gest for fifteen years.

39. Mississippi Freedmen's Bureau Field Office Records, 1865–1872, roll 30, misc. records, "Macon Indentures of Apprentice," image 41.

40. Mississippi Freedmen's Bureau Field Office Records, 1865–72, roll 30, misc. records "Macon Indentures of Apprentice," images 38–119.

41. Mississippi Freedmen's Bureau Field Office Records, 1865–72, roll 30, misc. records, "Macon Indentures of Apprentice," images 38–119.

42. US, Freedmen's Bureau, Records of the Assistant Commissioner, 1865–1872, roll 50, labor contracts of freedmen. Jacob signs as a witness on an 1867 contract between planter James Dorroh and freedman James Anderson and free woman of color Louiza Johnston.

43. Mississippi, Freedmen's Bureau Field Office Records, 1865–1872, roll 30, target 1, Register of Complaints, images 8 and 15.

44. Mississippi, Freedmen's Bureau Field Office Records, 1865–1872, roll 30, target 1, Register of Complaints, image 32.

45. Douglass, *Narrative of the Life,* 96.

46. Mississippi, Freedmen's Bureau Field Office Records, 1865–72, roll 30, target 1, Register of Complaints, image 32.

47. Shalby, "What's the Difference Between"; and Mann, "Cultural Visualization," 2–4.

48. Coates, *Between the World and Me,* 103.

49. Laymon, *Heavy,* 48.

50. Mississippi, Freedmen's Bureau Field Office Records, 1865–72, roll 30, target 1, Register of Complaints, image 35.

51. See Hale and Matt, "Intersection of Race and Rape," for a more extensive discussion of the history of the legal system and the rape of Black women.

52. Brown, "What Has Happened Here?" 304.

53. Population of the US in 1860, 270.

54. Mitchell, *A New History of Mississippi,* 188.

55. Mitchell 188.

56. Franklin, 24.

57. "The Late Riot at Macon," *Memphis Public Ledger,* 25 August 1869, 3.

58. "The Late Riot at Macon," 3.

59. "The Late Riot at Macon," 3.

60. "The Late Riot at Macon," 3.

61. Crummell, "Attitude toward the Negro," 296.

62. Mitchell, *A New History of Mississippi,* 193.

63. Mississippi, Freedmen's Bureau Report of Persons and Articles Hired, July 1867–Jan 1868, roll 29, images 10 and 12.

64. Mitchell, *A New History of Mississippi,* 192.

65. For details on hush harbors see Albert Raboteau's *Slave Religion* (1978), Michael Gomez's "Turning Down the Pot," in *Exchanging Our Country Marks* (1998), Paul Harvey's *Through the Storm* (2017).

66. Gomez, *Exchanging Our Country Marks,* 274.

67. In an August 2020 conversation with Noah Cistrunk's grandson Noah Cistrunk, he reiterated the account I have heard from family members, Bunnie Cistrunk and Mae Cistrunk Harrington, that his grandfather Noah had been a longtime member and deacon of Brushfork Baptist Church.

68. Deed Records, Noxubee County, MS, vol. 36, 356.

69. History of Brushfork Church. Copy of this church record was shared by Ms. Jeanette Parks, secretary of Brushfork Church.

70. History of Brushfork Church

71. Mitchell, *A New History of Mississippi,* 206.

72. Deed Records, Noxubee County, MS, vol. 6, 231.

73. Deed Records, Noxubee County, MS, vol. 67, 345–347.

74. Kolchin, *American Slavery,* 233.

75. Ninth Census, Noxubee County, MS, 30.

76. Marriage Records, Noxubee County, MS, vol. 1, 416.

77. Deed Records, Noxubee County, MS, vol. 8, 227.

78. Tenth Census, Noxubee County, MS, 24.

79. Deed Records, Noxubee County, 1877, book 8, 231.

80. Marriage Records, Noxubee County, MS, vol. 1, 367.

81. Marriage Records, Noxubee County, MS, vol. 1, 434.

82. Marriage Records, Noxubee County, MS, vol. 1, 416.

83. Marriage Records, Noxubee County, MS, vol. 4, 216.

84. Ninth Census, Noxubee County, MS, 30.

85. Tenth Census, Noxubee County, MS, 25. This Census shows Shadrick as head of household, with wife, Susan Landrum Cistrunk, their 2-year-old child Maria, and Susan's minor relative, 8-year-old Aggie Landrom, perhaps her daughter.

CHAPTER 3: POST-RECONSTRUCTION AND A NEW CENTURY

1. Fishel and Quarles, *The Black American,* 280.

2. Deed Records, Noxubee County, MS, 1879, book 11, 338 and book 13, 23.

3. Ninth Census, Noxubee County, MS, 22.

4. Tenth Census, Noxubee County, MS, 24; Sistrunk, *A Walk Through Caney,* p. 31 and 41.

5. Tenth Census, Noxubee County, MS, 24.

6. Tenth Census, Noxubee County, MS, 24.

7. Bolton, "Farmers Without Land," https://mshistorynow.mdah.state.ms.us/articles/228/farmers-without-land-the-plight-of-white-tenant-farmers-and-sharecroppers. Bolton notes that "By 1900, 36 percent of all white farmers in Mississippi were either tenant farmers or sharecroppers (by comparison, 85 percent of all Black farmers in 1900 did not own the land they farmed)."

8. Bolton.

9. Deed Records, Noxubee County, MS, 1877, book 8, 231; 1880, book 15, 73; 1881, book 18, 39.

10. Twelfth Census, Noxubee County, MS, 18.

11. Twelfth Census, Noxubee County, MS, 18.

12. Thirteenth Census, Noxubee County, MS, 7.

13. Marriage Records, Noxubee County, MS, 367.

14. Ninth Census, Noxubee County, MS, 22; Tenth Census, Noxubee County, MS, 24.

15. In Noxubee County Educable Children 1900 report, Shadrick (Shed) Cistrunk is the parent registering 17-year-old daughter, Sophy. In 1908, Hillman Cistrunk is listed as parent registering 8-year-old Martha, 10-year-old Rebecca, and 12-year-old John. In this same 1908 entry Hillman's great-nephew Noah is listed as parent registering his children, 6-year-old Carl, 12-year-old Lula, 10-year-old Noah, and 8-year-old John. In 1908 Shadrick (Shed) is shown as parent registering 10-year-old Shed and 8-year-old John. In 1885 a parent Cistrunk (probably John) registers five children: Boyd (7), Charlie (17), Katherine (15), Annie (20), and Emma (5).

16. History of Brushfork Church. Copy of this church record and information on Ethel Mosley was shared by Ms. Jeanette Parks—Ms. Mosley's daughter and present secretary of Brushfork Church.

17. History of Brushfork Church.

18. Higginbotham, *Righteous Discontent*, 1.

19. Ali, *In the Lion's Mouth*, 25.

20. Ali, 24.

21. Higginbotham, *Righteous Discontent*, 4.

22. Ali, *In the Lion's Mouth*, 24–26.

23. Ali, 67.

24. Ali, 18–19.

25. Ali, 17.

26. Deed Records, Noxubee County, 1900, p. 345 for Hillman and p. 347–48 for Shadrick.

27. Hansen, "The Farmers' Loan," in *Institutions, Entrepreneurs, and American*, 70.

28. Hansen, 70.

29. Hansen notes that Farmers' was involved in forty-seven Supreme Court, 204 federal appeals, and 400 state-level court cases from 1822 to 1929, when it merged with National City Bank (1).

30. Kirwan, *Revolt of the Rednecks*, 75.

31. Power, "Mississippi Matters," 1.

32. "Who May Vote in Mississippi," *Macon Beacon*, 4.

33. "Delinquent Poll Tax List," *Macon Beacon*, 1.

34. See *Macon Beacon*, "Delinquent Poll Tax List" in the following issues: December 6, 1902, 3; April 29, 1910, 4; May 6, 1910, 4; May 3, 1912, 3; September 17, 1914, 8; April 30, 1915, 8.

35. L. P. S., "The Mississippi Senatorial Campaign," 2.

36. L. P. S., 2.

37. Tenth Census, Noxubee County, MS, 24.

38. US Social Security records show Robert Sistrunk born 1881 in Jackson, MS, to parents, Willis and Hopea. The 1952 death certificate shows 1883 as his birth year and that he had resided in Memphis, TN. His mother's surname is recorded as Williams, suggesting that she had either divorced Willis or been widowed by his death.

39. See 1880 Census showing daughter Maria who may have died by 1900 as she no longer appears on the Census. Aggie Landrum is shown as 8 years old living in the home of Shadrick and Susan. Her relation is not shown, but she shares Susan's maiden surname, thereby underscoring relation to Susan. See 1900 Census showing daughter Sophia in the household of Shadrick and Susan. The 1900 Census shows Noah as head of household at the age of 18 (born in 1881).

40. Twelfth Census, Noxubee County, MS, 18.

41. See Mississippi Marriages, Bonie Holmes and Annie Cistrunk, 27 December 1882, Noxubee County, MS.

42. Deed Records, Noxubee County, MS, 1898, book 67, p. 345 and 347. The 1898 deed transfers from Mobile & Ohio R&R to Hillman and Shadrick marking their debts paid and clear ownership show 1879 as the date upon which the contracts were entered.

43. Deed Records, Noxubee County, MS, 1879–1881, book 11, 338; deed records, Noxubee County, MS, 1879–1881, book 13, 23.

44. Deed Records, Noxubee County, MS, 1877, book 8, 231.

45. Deed Records, Noxubee County, MS, 1879–1881, book 11, p. 338 and 379.

46. Deed Records, Noxubee County, MS, 1880, book 15, 73; and 1881, book 18, 39.

47. See Deed Records, Noxubee County, MS, 1882, book 19, 193, and book 25, 28.

48. Deed Records, Noxubee County, MS, 1877, book 8, 227.

49. Deed Records, Noxubee County, MS, 1886, book 27, 352.

50. Tenth Census, Noxubee County, MS, 24.

51. Tenth Census, Noxubee County, MS, 25.

52. Deed Records, Noxubee County, MS, book 67, 345–47.

53. See 1883 Assessments of Lands in Noxubee County Tax Records for record showing boundaries of Shadrick's 162 acres.

54. Deed Records, Noxubee County, MS, 1881, book 18, 108.

55. See for example Deeds of Trust for Shadrick in any of the following years: 1877, 1879, 1882, 1883, and 1884.

56. Deed Records, Noxubee County, MS, book 21, 246–47.

57. Deed Records, Noxubee County, MS, book 95, 203.

58. Tenth Census, Noxubee County, MS, 24 and Twelfth Census, Noxubee County, MS, 18.

59. Williams, "Articulating Agrarian Racism," 15.

60. Deed Records, Noxubee County, MS, 1908, book 90, 208.

61. See Dred Scott v. Sanford, 60 US 393 (1856)

62. Tenth Census, Noxubee County, MS, 24–5; Twelfth Census, Noxubee County, MS, 18.

63. More in-depth history of Margaret Murray Washington can be found in the 2021 biography, *Margaret Murray Washington: The Life and Times of a Career Clubwoman*, by Sheena Harris.

64. This history was conveyed to me by local resident James Bridges. 14 May 2021. Macon, MS.

65. Nan Prince, "Artifacts: First African American Masons in State," *A Sense of Place* (blog), Mississippi Department of Archives and History, 4 September 2013, https://www .mdah.ms.gov/senseofplace/2013/09/04/artifacts-first-african-american-masons-in -state/.

66. Halbert, "Treaty of Dancing Rabbit Creek," 542.

67. Death Certificates, Mississippi Asylum Cemetery Records, Mississippi Department of Archives and History, series 2148, vol. 16, 19.

68. The 1900 Census reports that Lucretia had given birth to two children, and only one was still living at the time of the Census.

69. See 1889 Obituary for Alfred Dobbins. *Southwestern Christian Advocate*. Hyram McDaniel appears as farmhand on the Tenth Census, Noxubee County, MS, p. 25, living in household of Alfred and Lucretia Dobbins. See also Twelfth Census, Noxubee County, MS, p. 18, which shows McDaniel married to Lucretia and listed as head of household. See also Marriage Records, Noxubee County, MS, Creasy Dobbins to Hiram McDaniel, 1895.

70. Fourteenth Census, Noxubee County, MS, Enumeration District 92, 9.

71. Twelfth Census, Noxubee County, MS, 18.

72. Twelfth Census, Noxubee County, MS, Enumeration District 70, 8.

73. "Elisha Cistrunk." *Macon Beacon,* 1.

74. Thirteenth Census, Noxubee County, MS, 12; Fourteenth Census, Noxubee County, MS, 2, and Fifteenth Census, Noxubee County, MS, 1. Deed Records, Noxubee County, MS, 1925, book 165, 53.

75. Deed Records, Noxubee County, MS, book 67, 345–47.

76. See Kevin K. Gaines, *Uplifting the Race*, 85–86.

77. Wells, *The Red Record*, 4.

78. Wells, 4.

79. "Mr. Joe Lee," *Macon Beacon,* 3.

80. Marriage Records, Noxubee County, MS, Maria Cistrunk to Isaac Grimmel, 1893; Tenth and Twelfth Census, Noxubee County, MS

81. Marriage Records, Noxubee County, MS, Sophie Sistrunk and Will Grimmet, 1901.

82. Twelfth Census, Noxubee County, MS, and Thirteenth Census, Noxubee County, MS.

83. Twelfth Census, Noxubee County, MS, 16, and Thirteenth Census, Noxubee County, MS, 13.

84. Twelfth Census, Noxubee County, MS, Enumeration District 70, 19.

85. "Delinquent Poll Tax List," *Macon Beacon*, 29 March 29 1902, 3.

86. "Delinquent Poll Tax List," *Macon Beacon*, 29 March 29 1902, 3.

87. The Thirteenth Census shows Noah and new wife, Luella, married five years. Their marriage license shows them married in 1904. See Marriage Records, Noxubee County, MS, Luella Hunt to Noah Cistrunk, 1904.

88. "Trustee's Sale. The State of Mississippi, Noxubee County," *Macon Beacon*, 24 February 1911, 5.

89. "Sale of Land for Delinquent Taxes. The State of Mississippi, Noxubee County," *Macon Beacon*, 10 March 1911, 8.

90. Deed Records, Noxubee County, MS, 1908, book 90, 208.

91. Deed Records, Noxubee County, MS, 1887, 1891, and 1901. Both Shadrick and Susan signed on the 1887 and 1901 deeds.

92. Deed Records, Noxubee County, MS, 1909, book 95, 203.

93. Thirteenth Census, Tallahatchie County, MS, Enumeration District 75, 7.

94. Marriage Records, Noxubee County, MS, Sophia Sistrunk to Will Grimmet, 1901, and Thirteenth Census, Tallahatchie County, MS, Enumeration District 75, MS, 7.

95. Dovich, Chamer, and Tang, "Black Farmers," sec. 1, para. 5.

96. Dovich, Chamer, and Tang, sec. 4, para. 2.

97. Twelfth Census, Noxubee County, MS, 18, and Thirteenth Census, Kemper County, MS, 8.

98. "Delinquent Poll Tax List," *Macon Beacon*, 29 April 1910.

99. Thirteenth Census, Noxubee County, MS, Enumeration District 90, 20.

100. Deed Records, Noxubee County, MS, 1909, book 90, 519.

101. Twelfth Census, Noxubee County, MS, Enumeration District 70, 18.

102. Mississippi Enumeration of Educable Children, Noxubee County, MS, 1908, 7–8.

CHAPTER 4: HILLMAN

1. "A Brutal Murder," *Macon Beacon*, 2.

2. "A Brutal Murder," 2.

3. "A Noxubee Dante," *Macon Beacon*, 3.

4. "A Noxubee Dante," 3.

5. "A Noxubee Dante," 3.

6. "Deputy Sheriff Sam Clark," *Macon Beacon*, 5.

7. "Elisha Cistrunk, the Mashulaville tiger," *Macon Beacon*, 51.

8. Mitchell, *A New History of Mississippi*, 286–87.

9. US Selective Service WWI Registration Card, Elisha Cistrunk, serial no. 990, 12 September 1918. Elisha's 1918 draft card lists him as blind in the right eye.

10. Deed Records, Noxubee County, MS, 1909, book 95, p. 203.

11. See Dossie Cistrunk v. Patsy Cistrunk and Lucretia McDonald. Hillman, Harriet, and Dossie's 1910 contract is included in these Chancery Court records.

12. See Thirteenth Census, Noxubee County, MS, 20, for a record of Dossie's age and residence.

13. Dossie Cistrunk v. Patsy Cistrunk and Lucretia McDonald.

14. Marriage Records, Noxubee County, MS, Hillman Cistrunk to Patsy Cutts, 1916.

15. William Cutts v. Patsy Cutts.

16. US Selective Service WWI Registration Card, Robert Arthur Haggard. serial no. 944, 5 June 1917.

17. Franklin, 340.

18. Wilkerson, 9.

19. Lewis, *When Harlem Was in Vogue*, 21.

20. Litwack, *Trouble in Mind*, 136.

21. Litwack, 482.

22. Carson et al., *The Struggle for Freedom*, 345.

23. Carson et al., *The Struggle for Freedom*, 345.

24. Lewis, *When Harlem Was in Vogue*, 14.

25. Barry, *The Great Influenza*, 4.

26. Barry, 343.

27. Barry, 343.

28. Franklin, *From Slavery to Freedom*, 349.

29. Franklin, 349.

30. Franklin, 350.

31. Franklin, 350.

32. "Race Trouble at Macon," *Columbus Dispatch*, 1.

33. "Race Trouble at Macon," 1.

34. "Race Trouble at Macon," 1.

35. "Race Trouble Reported," *News Scimitar*, 8.

36. "Race Trouble Reported," 8.

37. "Race Trouble Reported," 8.

38. Three well-known riots with undercounted Black causalities were the Wilmington Race Riot of 1898, the Tula Massacre of 1921, and the Rosewood Massacre of 1923.

39. "Franklin, *From Slavery to Freedom*, 340–42.

40. Application for writ de lunatico inquirendo.

41. Application for writ de lunatico inquirendo.

42. Application for writ de lunatico inquirendo.

43. Application for writ de lunatico inquirendo.

44. Mississippi Asylum Cemetery records.

45. "Welcome to Asylum Hill Project." *Asylum Hill Project*.

46. The discovery of the cemetery led to the establishment of the Asylum Hill Project, which is leading the archaeological initiative to provide greater historical context for the thousands interred here and to honorably memorialize them. asylumhillproject.org.

47. Pettus, "Asylum Hill Project."

48. Pettus, "Asylum Hill Project."

49. US Selective Service WWI Registration Card, serial no. 253. 12 September 1918. Noah's 1918 draft card lists his residence as Winston County.

50. Dossie Cistrunk v. Patsy Cistrunk and Lucretia McDonald.

51 1921. Deed of Trust.

52. See Barnard, *Farm Real Estate Values*, 54.

53. "Citation Notice," *Macon Beacon*, 4.

54. Dating back to the 1880's Shadrick Cistrunk executed several trust deeds with Nunn & Anderson. Records are not clear on whether the R. L. Anderson executing the 1921 trust deed with Patsy is the same Anderson in those 1880s contracts with Shadrick.

55. "Decree Dismissing Cause," Dossie Cistrunk v. Patsy Cistrunk and Lucretia McDonald, 1924.

56. Original Land Roll 1923; 1926–1927 Noxubee County, MS.

57. "Lumber Companies Enjoin Sheriff," *Macon Beacon*.

58. "Lumber Companies Enjoin Sheriff," *Macon Beacon*.

59. The Department of the Interior's description of the historic Shuqualak District illustrates the commercial influence of Nunn and Anderson's in the early twentieth century.

60. "Lumber Companies Enjoin Sheriff," *Macon Beacon*.

61. See Fourteenth Census, Noxubee County, MS, 20, Enumeration District 92, 21

CODA: REFLECTIONS ON METHODOLOGY

1. Taylor, *Examined Life*, 7:40–9:45.

2. Brown, "'What Has Happened Here,'" 297.

3. Hartman, "Venus in Two Acts," 11.

4. Hartman, 13.

5. Hartman, "A Note on Method," *Wayward Lives* xii.

6. Hartman, "A Note on Method," *Wayward Lives* xii.

7. Crawford, "A Massive New Database."

8. The DNA information utilized for this work was sourced from three different companies: African Ancestry, Ancestry, and 23andMe.

9. McKittrick, "Diachronic loops," 4.

10. McKittrick, "Diachronic loops," 15.

11. Sharpe, *In the Wake*, 13.

12. Sharpe, 13.

13. See Sanborn "People Will Pay," and *Plagiarama*. In "People Will Pay" Sanborn noted that the thousands of words of plagiarism found in the novel at that point would be followed by many more as scholars were hungrily in search of all that Brown had copied from other sources (65). In *Plagiarama: William Wells Brown and the Aesthetics of Attraction* (2016), one of the most recent publications on Brown and *Clotel*, Sanborn reports that the count had exceeded 200 texts from which Brown copied and inserted into *Clotel*.

14. See "A Brief History of Sampling;" "Sampling: History and Definition, Part I;" and Joe, "A Brief History of Sampling." With its current connection to the emergence of 1980s African American hip-hop culture, the birth of contemporary sampling in music is in general seen as 1980s. There is of course considerable debate on the origins of sampling that looks to its obvious pre-1980s existence. While some tie the birth of sampling to the first two commercially available digital samplers (Harry Mendell's Computer Music Melodian and Fairlight's Computer Musical Instrument in the later half of the 1970s), the practice was alive long before the birth of instrumentation designed specifically for its implementation ("A Brief History of Sampling"). Musical sampling predated the digital-era technology however as the 1960s and 1970s era of tape recording allowed for splicing and cutting pieces of works into other works ("Sampling: History and Definition Part 1"). Before the birth of technological sampling however jazz musicians from the early twentieth century sampled "little bits of melodies, hooks, licks or progressions from their peers' compositions in their live performances" ("A Brief History of Sampling"). The point here is not to debate the birth of sampling in music but to acknowledge that hip-hop does not mark the beginning of sampling as a musical technique.

15. Query 14, *Notes*.

16. Ganster, "Fact, Fiction," 431.

17. Ganster, 431.

18. See Hill and Bell, *Call and Response*. Hill and Bell offer a comprehensive look at the evolution of African American literary and musical traditions, emerging out of African traditions that survived Middle Passage. This anthology includes a history of and works from Africa that become adapted to new musical and literary forms in African American culture. In this work, for example, the editors trace transformations of traditions such as African and African American folktales, proverbs, work songs, praise songs, and prayers into forms such as spirituals, the blues, jazz, sermons, protest narratives, poetry, and the birth of African American fiction. The work shows that new artistic modes were born from borrowing and incorporating forms and content of previous traditions. The word *sampling* is not used to describe this cultural creative practice, but *sampling* is clearly a term that captures the practice.

19. Greenspan, "Ezra Greenspan."

20. Ganster, "Fact, Fiction," 431–32.

21. Ganster, 432.

22. Ganster, 432.

23. Ganster, 432.

24. See West, "Memory, Ancestors."

25. See Howells, "Mr. Charles W. Chesnutt's Stories," and "A Psychological Counter." The former received favorable reviews in 1900, whereas the 1901 review of the *latter* was negative.

26. See Yarborough, "Introduction." Yarborough writes "Although the following essays provide thoughtfully and complexly mounted analyses of Hopkins's appropriative practice, the question 'Is this or is this not plagiarism?' will not likely go away, especially given the increasing pedagogical challenges that many of us confront in teaching students how to utilize sources in a transparent and responsible fashion" (e5).

27. Gates, *The Signifying Monkey*, 11.

28. Gates, 11.

29. Gates, 42.

Bibliography

PRIMARY SOURCES

Alabama, Secretary of State. *US Census Non-population Schedules, Alabama, 1850–1880.* Montgomery, AL, Alabama Department of Archives and History. Ancestry.com.

Application for writ de lunatico inquirendo, Noxubee County, MS. Chancery Court 4332 (1919).

"Citation Notice. State of Mississippi Chancery Court of Noxubee County Dossie Cistrunk v. Patsy Cistrunk et al." *Macon Beacon* (Macon, MS), 18 March 1921. Chronicling america.com.

Columbus Dispatch (Columbus, MS). "Race Trouble at Macon." 8 June 1919.

Correspondence between Diego Glenn and the Spanish king regarding the imprisonment of 265 Germans in Havana. Translated by Patricia Coloma. 31 December 1744. Archivo de Indias, Sevilla, Spain. Box 62, folder 1.

County Tax Rolls. Box 3931. Noxubee County, MS, 1864–1887. Mississippi Department of Archives and History. FamilySearch.org.

County Tax Rolls. Box 3945. Neshoba County, MS, 1859–1884. Mississippi Department of Archives and History. FamilySearch.org.

County Tax Rolls. Box 3946. Noxubee County, MS, 1859–1886. Mississippi Department of Archives and History. FamilySearch.org.

Death certificates, Mississippi Asylum Cemetery records, Mississippi Department of Archives and History, 1912–1935. Jackson, MS. http://opac2.mdah.state.ms.us/burials2 .php.

Deed records, Noxubee County, MS, 1834–1901. Macon, MS, Noxubee County Courthouse. FamilySearch.org.

Deed transfer, Jacob Sistrunk Sr. to John Floyd of Early County, GA, District 28, p. 348–49. Film #008564259. FamilySearch.org.

Deeds and Mortgages, 1796–1909. Vols. H-I, 1812–1820. Superior Court (Lincoln County, GA) Lincolnton, GA, Lincoln County Courthouse, Family History Library.

Dossie Cistrunk v. Patsy Cistrunk and Lucretia McDonald, Noxubee County. Chancery Court 4410 (1921–1924).

Eighth Census of the United States, 1860. Records of the Bureau of the Census, Record Group 29. Washington, DC, National Archives. Ancestry.com.

Fifteenth Census of the United States, 1930. Records of the Bureau of the Census, Record Group 29. Washington, DC, National Archives. Ancestry.com.

Fifth Census of the United States, 1830. Records of the Bureau of the Census, Record Group 29. Washington, DC, National Archives. Ancestry.com.

Fourteenth Census of the United States, 1920. Records of the Bureau of the Census, Record Group 29. Washington, DC, National Archives. Ancestry.com.

Fourth Census of the United States, 1820. Records of the Bureau of the Census, Record Group 29. Washington, DC, National Archives. Ancestry.com.

Freedmen's Bureau. Records of the Assistant Commissioner, 1865–1872. Roll 50. Labor contracts of freedmen. Washington DC, National Archives and Records Administration. FamilySearch.org.

Georgia, Freedmen's Bureau Field Office Records, 1865–1872. Americus, GA, Roll 40, Register of Patients August–November 1868. Washington, DC, National Archives Records Administration. FamilySearch.org.

Georgia, US Property Tax Digests, 1793–1892. Lincoln County, GA, 1799–1806, p. 12 and 16. Morrow, GA, Georgia Archives. Ancestry.com.

Halbert, H. S. "Treaty of Dancing Rabbit Creek." In *Biennial Reports of the Departments and Benevolent and Educational Institutions, of the State of Mississippi, For the Years 1894–'95*, 542–545. Jackson, MS: Clarion Ledger Co., Printers, 1896.

L.P.S. "The Mississippi Senatorial Campaign." *Macon Beacon* (Macon, MS), 19 May 1911. Newspapers.com.

Macon Beacon (Macon, MS). "A Brutal Murder." 3 August 1907. Chroniclingamerica.com.

——. Delinquent Poll Tax List. 3 May 1912. Newspapers.com.

——. Delinquent Poll Tax List. 17 September 1914. Newspapers.com.

——. Delinquent Poll Tax List. 29 April 1910. Newspapers.com.

——. Delinquent Poll Tax List. 29 March 1902. Newspapers.com.

——. Delinquent Poll Tax List. 30 April 1915. Newspapers.com.

——. Delinquent Poll Tax List. 30 March 1901. Newspapers.com.

——. Macon Circuit. "Deputy Sheriff Sam Clark." 25 July 1913.

——. Circuit Court. "Elisha Cistrunk." 29 August 1913. Newspapers.com.

——. "Mr. Joe Lee." 31 October 1896. Newspapers.com.

——. "A Noxubee Dante." 14 September 1907. Chroniclingamerica.com.

——. "Sale of Land for Delinquent Taxes. The State of Mississippi, Noxubee County." 10 March 1911, Newspapers.com.

——. "Trustee's Sale. The State of Mississippi, Noxubee County." 24 February 1911. Newspapers.com.

——. "Who May Vote in Mississippi." 5 April 1912. Newspapers.com.

Marriage Records (1834–1952), Macon, MS. Noxubee County Courthouse, Noxubee County, MS. FamilySearch.org.

Memphis Public Ledger. (Memphis, TN). "The Late Riot at Macon." 25 August 1869. Newspapers.com.

Mississippi Asylum Cemetery Records, Certificate Number 04531. Mississippi Department of Archives and History. Online catalog.

Mississippi Enumeration of Educable Children 1850–1892; 1908–1957. "Educable Children in Mashulaville Election District." Noxubee County, MS. 1885. FamilySearch.org.

Mississippi Enumeration of Educable Children 1850–1892; 1908–1957. Noxubee County. 1908. "Race: Colored, Township 13, Range 15." FamilySearch.org.

Mississippi Enumeration of Educable Children 1850–1892; 1908–1957. "Race: Colored, Township 14, Range 15." Noxubee County, MS. 1900. FamilySearch.org.

Mississippi, Freedmen's Bureau Field Office Records, 1865–1872. Roll 30. Misc. records, "Macon Indentures of Apprentice." Washington DC, National Archives and Records Administration. FamilySearch.org.

Mississippi, Freedmen's Bureau Field Office Records, 1865–1872. Roll 30. Target 1, "Register of Complaints," Jun–Sept 1865. Washington, DC, National Archives and Records Administration. FamilySearch.org.

Mississippi, Freedmen's Bureau Report of Persons and Articles Hired, July 1867–Jan 1868. Roll 29. Washington DC, National Archives and Records Administration. Family Search.org.

Mississippi State Archives. Various records, 1820–1951. Jackson, MS, Mississippi Department of Archives and History. FamilySearch.org.

National Archives and Records Administration. Compiled service records of Confederate soldiers who served in organizations from the State of Mississippi. Folder 3. 1861–1865.

News Scimitar (Memphis, TN). "Race Trouble Reported in Macon, Miss., Vicinity." 9 June 1919.

1908 Deed of Trust Shedrick & Susan Cistrunk and Merchants Farmers Bank. State of Mississippi Trust Deed and Book 90, p. 208.

1909 Deed of Trust Shedrick & Susan Cistrunk and Merchants Farmers Bank. State of Mississippi Trust Deed and Book 90, p. 519.

1909 Deed of Trust Hillman and Harriet Cistrunk and Martha Lloyd. State of Mississippi Trust Deed Noxubee County, Book 95, p. 203.

1921 Deed of Trust Patsy Cistrunk and R. L. Anderson. State of Mississippi Trust Deed, Noxubee County, Book 132, p. 389.

Ninth Census of the United States, 1870. Records of the Bureau of the Census, Record Group 29. Washington, DC, National Archives. Ancestry.com.

Noah Nathaniel Cistrumpes [Cistrunk]. World War I Selective Service System Draft Registration Cards, 1917–1918. US Selective Service System, Washington, DC, National Archives and Records Administration.

Non-Population Census Schedules for Georgia, 1850–1890. Records of the Bureau of the Census, Record Group 29. Washington, DC, National Archives. Ancestry.com.

Population of the United States in 1860. Bureau of the Census Library, Government Printing Office, Washington, DC. 1864. https://www2.census.gov/library/publications/decennial/1860/population.

Power, J. L. "Mississippi Matters: Notes of Past and Current Events." *Macon Beacon* (Macon, MS), 14 April 1900. Newspapers.com.

Robert Arthur Haggard. World War I Selective Service System Draft Registration Cards, 1917–1918. Noxubee County, MS. US Selective Service System, Washington, DC, National Archives and Records Administration.

Seventh Census of the United States, 1850. Records of the Bureau of the Census, Record Group 29. Washington, DC, National Archives. Ancestry.com.

Seventh Census of the United States, 1850. Washington, DC: Robert Armstrong, Public Printer, 1853. https://www2.census.gov/library/publications/decennial/1850/.

Sixteenth Census of the United States, 1940. Records of the Bureau of the Census, Record Group 29. Washington, DC, National Archives. Ancestry.com.

Sixth Census of the United States, 1840. Records of the Bureau of the Census, Record Group 29. Washington, DC, National Archives. Ancestry.com.

Tenth Census of the United States, 1880. Records of the Bureau of the Census, Record Group 29. Washington, DC, National Archives. Ancestry.com.

Thirteenth Census of the United States, 1910. Records of the Bureau of the Census, Record Group 29. Washington, DC, National Archives. Ancestry.com.

Twelfth Census of the United States, 1900. Records of the Bureau of the Census, Record Group 29. Washington, DC, National Archives. Ancestry.com.

US Census Bureau. Slave Schedules, 1850. Washington, DC, National Archives. Ancestry .com.

US Census Bureau. Slave Schedules, 1860. Washington, DC, National Archives. Ancestry .com.

William Cutts v. Patsy Cutts. Noxubee County, MS. Chancery Court 3442 (1911–1941).

World War I Selective Service System Draft Registration Cards, 1917–1918. Macon, MS. 12 September 1917. US Selective Service System, Washington, DC, National Archives and Records Administration.

SECONDARY SOURCES

Ali, Omar H. *In the Lion's Mouth: Black Populism in the New South, 1886–1900.* Jackson: University of Mississippi Press, 2010.

Barfield, Louise Calhoun. *History of Harris County, Georgia, 1827–1961.* Columbus, GA: Columbus Office Supply Company, 1961.

Barnard, Charles H., and John Jones. *Farm Real Estate Values in the United States by Counties, 1850–1982.* Washington, DC: US Department of Agriculture, Economic Research Service, 1987.

Barry, John M. *The Great Influenza: The Story of the Deadliest Pandemic in History.* New York: Penguin Books, 2005.

Bay, Mia. "Love, Sex, Slavery, and Sally Hemings." *Beyond Slavery: Overcoming Its Religious and Sexual Legacies,* edited by Bernadette J. Brooten, 191–212. New York: Palgrave Macmillan, 2010.

Bolton, Charles C. "Farmers Without Land: The Plight of White Tenant Farmers and Sharecroppers." *Mississippi History Now.* Mississippi Historical Society, March 2004. https://www.mshistorynow.mdah.ms.gov/issue/farmers-without-land-the-plight-of -white-tenant-farmers-and-sharecroppers.

Brown, Elsa Barkley. "'What Has Happened Here': The Politics of Difference in Women's History and Feminist Politics." *Feminist Studies* 18, no. 2 (1992): 295–312.

Brown, Vincent. "Social Death and Political Life in the Study of Slavery." *American Historical Review* 114, no. 5 (Dec 2009): 1231–49.

Brown, William Wells. *Clotel; or The President's Daughter: A Narrative of Slave Life in the United States.* London: Partridge & Oakley, 1853.

Carmichael, Jacqueline Miller. "Jubilee." *New Georgia Encyclopedia,* 2004. https://www .georgiaencyclopedia.org/articles/arts-culture/jubilee.

Carson, Clayborne, Emma J. Lapsansky-Werner, and Gary B. Nash. *The Struggle for Freedom: A History of African Americans.* New York: Pearson, 2007.

"Chapman Family Tree." Ancestry.com.

Chesnutt, Charles. *The Conjure Woman.* Boston: Houghton Mifflin, 1899.

———. *The Marrow of Tradition.* Boston: Houghton Mifflin, 1901.

———. "The Wife of His Youth." In *The Wife of His Youth and Other Stories of the Color Line.* (1899). Ann Arbor: University of Michigan Press, 2002.

Coates, Ta-Nehisi. *Between the World and Me.* New York: Spiegel and Grau, 2015.

Crawford, Amy. "A Massive New Database Will Connect Billions of Historic Records to Tell the Full Story of American Slavery." *Smithsonian Magazine,* January/February 2020. https://www.smithsonianmag.com/history/massive-new-database-connect-bil lions-historic-records-tell-full-story-american-slavery-180973721/.

Crummell, Alexander. "The Attitude toward the Negro Intellect." In *Destiny and Race: Selected Writings, 1840–1898,* edited by Wilson Jeremiah Moses, 289–300. Amherst: University of Massachusetts Press, 1992.

de la Fuente, Alejandro. *Havana and the Atlantic in the Sixteenth Century.* Chapel Hill: University of North Carolina Press, 2008.

Deyle, Steven. *Carry Me Back: The Domestic Slave Trade in American Life.* New York: Oxford University Press, 2005.

Dobbins, H. P., C. B. Andrew, and Warren Grice. *First Hundred and Ten Years of Houston County, Georgia (1822–1932).* Warner Robins, GA: Central Georgia Genealogical Society, 1983.

Douglass, Frederick. *Narrative of the Life of Frederick Douglass, An American Slave,* edited by Houston Baker. NY: Penguin Books, 1986.

Dovich, Mark, Jeff A. Chamer, and Hazel Tang. "Black Farmers Accuse the USDA of Racism." *USA Today,* 27 September 2021.

Fauset, Jessie. *Plum Bun* (1928). Boston: Beacon Press, 1990.

Faust, Albert B. *List of Swiss Emigrants in the Eighteenth Century to the American.* Vol. 1. Washington DC: National Genealogical Society, 1920. https://archive.org/details/list swissemigrant01fausrich/page/n15/mode/2up.

Felipe, Fonte. "Southeast Africa." *Tracing African Roots: Exploring the Ethnic Origins of the Afro-Diaspora.* https://tracingafricanroots.wordpress.com/maps/southeast-africa/.

Fishel, Leslie H., and Benjamin Quarles. *The Black American: A Documentary History.* Glenview, IL: Scott Foreman, 1970.

Franklin, John Hope. *From Slavery to Freedom: A History of African Americans.* 7th ed. New York: McGraw-Hill, 1994.

Ganster, Mary. "Fact, Fiction, and the Industry of Violence: Newspapers and Advertisements in *Clotel.*" *African American Review* 48, no. 4 (2015): 431–44.

Gaines, Kevin K. *Uplifting the Race: Black Leadership, Politics, and Culture in the Twentieth Century.* Chapel Hill: University of North Carolina Press, 1996.

Gates, Henry Louis, Jr. *The Signifying Monkey: A Theory of African-American Literary Criticism.* New York: Oxford University Press, 1988.

Gomez, Michael. *Exchanging Our Country Marks.* Chapel Hill: University of North Carolina Press, 1998.

———. *Reversing Sail: A History of the African Diaspora.* Cambridge: Cambridge University Press, 2004.

Greenspan, Ezra, "Ezra Greenspan on William Wells Brown: The Most Rivetingly Inventive, Entertaining Black Writer of His Era." Interview by Library of America, 7 March 2014. https://www.loa.org/news-and-views/687-ezra-greenspan-on-william -wells-brown-the-most-rivetingly-inventive-entertaining-black-writer-of-his-era.

Halbert, H. S. "Treaty of Dancing Rabbit Creek." In *Biennial Reports of the Departments and Benevolent and Educational Institutions of the State of Mississippi, For the Year 1894-'95,* 542–45. Jackson: Clarion Ledger, 1896.

Hale, Chelsea, and Meghan Matt. "The Intersection of Rape and Race Viewed through the Prism of a Modern Day Emmitt Till." *ABA Human Rights Magazine.* December 2019.

Haley, Alex. *Roots: The Saga of an American Family.* New York: Doubleday, 1976.

Hansen, Bradley A. "The Farmers' Loan and Trust Company and the Evolution of Corporate Finance." In *Institutions, Entrepreneurs, and American Economic History: How the Farmers' Loan and Trust Company Shaped the Laws of Business from 1822–1929,* 69–93. New York: Palgrave Macmillan, 2009.

Harris, Jessica B. *High on the Hog: A Culinary Journey from Africa to America.* New York: Bloomsbury, 2011.

Hartman, Saidiya. "A Note on Method." In *Wayward Lives, Beautiful Experiments: Intimate Histories of Social Upheaval.* New York: W. W. Norton, 2020.

——. "Venus in Two Acts." *Small Axe* 12, no. 2 (2008): 1–14. https://muse.jhu.edu/article/241115.

Harvey, Paul. *Through the Storm, Through the Night: A History of African American Christianity.* New York: Roman & Littlefield, 2011.

Higginbotham, Evelyn Brooks. *Righteous Discontent: The Women's Movement in the Black Baptist Church, 1880–1920.* Cambridge, MA: Harvard University Press, 1993.

Hill, Patricia Liggins and Bernard W. Bell, eds. *Call and Response: The Riverside Anthology of the African American Literary Tradition.* New York: Houghton Mifflin, 1998.

Holloway, Joseph. *Africanisms in American Culture.* Bloomington: Indiana University Press, 1991.

Hooks, Bell. "Representations of Whiteness in the Black Imagination." *Black Looks: Race and Representation.* Boston: South End Press, 1992.

Hopkins, Pauline. *Hagar's Daughter: A Story of Southern Caste Prejudice.* Edited by John Cullen Gruesser and Alisha R. Knight. Peterborough, Ontario: Broadview Press, 2020.

Howells, William Dean. "Mr. Charles W. Chesnutt's Stories." *Atlantic Monthly* 82, no. 511 (1900): 699–701.

——. "A Psychological Counter-Current in Recent Fiction." *North American Review* 173, no. 541 (1901): 872–888.

Hurston, Zora Neale. *Jonah's Gourdvine* (1934). New York: Harper Collins, 1990.

Jackson, Lawrence. *My Father's Name: A Black Virginia Family after the Civil War.* Chicago: University of Chicago Press, 2012.

Jacobs, Harriet. *Incidents in the Life of a Slave Girl, Written by Herself.* Edited by Jean Fagan Yellin. Cambridge, MA: Harvard University Press, 1987.

Jefferson, Thomas. "The Hopefulness and Hopelessness of 1619." *Atlantic,* 20 August 2019. https://www.theatlantic.com/ideas/archive/2019/08/historical-significance-1619/596365/.

Jefferson, Thomas. "Query 14." *Notes on the State of Virginia,* 138–59. Philadelphia: Prichard & Hall, 1788.

Jones, Claudia. "An End to the Neglect of the Problems of the Negro Woman!" Reprinted from *Political Affairs,* 1–20. New York: National Women's Commission, C.P.U.S.A, 1949. https://palmm.digital.flvc.org/islandora/object/ucf%3A4865.

Jones-Rogers, Stephanie E. *They Were Her Property: White Women as Slave Owners in the American South.* New Haven, CT: Yale University Press, 2019.

Kendi, Ibram X. "The Hopefulness and Hopelessness of 1619." *Atlantic,* 20 August 2019. https://www.theatlantic.com/ideas/archive/2019/08/historical-significance-1619 /596365/.

———. *Stamped from the Beginning.* New York: Nation Books, 2016.

Kirwan, Albert D. *Revolt of the Rednecks: Mississippi Politics, 1876–1925.* Lexington: University of Kentucky Press, 2014.

Kolchin, Peter. *American Slavery: 1619–1877.* New York: Hill and Wang, 1993.

Laymon, Kiese. *Heavy: An American Memoir.* New York: Scribner, 2018.

Lefvendahl, Georgie A. *Oliver-Sistrunk Families: Orangeburg Area, South Carolina.* Self-published, 1964.

Lewis, Davis Levering. *When Harlem Was in Vogue.* New York: Oxford University Press. 1979.

Lewis, J. D. *Commons House of Assembly Election Districts Map #10 - 1761–1768.* Map. The Royal Colony of South Carolina. https://www.carolana.com/SC/Royal_Colony/royal _assemblies_election_districts_map_10.html.

Library of Congress. "Establishing the Georgia Colony, 1732–1750," *U.S. History Primary Source Timeline.* https://www.loc.gov/classroom-materials/united-states-history -primary-source-timeline/colonial-settlement-1600–1763/georgia-colony-1732–1750/.

Lindsay, Lisa A. and John Wood Sweet, eds. *Biography and the Black Atlantic.* Philadelphia: University of Pennsylvania Press, 2014.

Lindsay, Lisa A., and John Wood Sweet, eds. *Plagiarama: William Wells Brown and the Aesthetics of Attraction.* New York: Columbia University Press, 2016.

Litwack, Leon F. *Trouble in Mind: Black Southerners in the Age of Jim Crow.* New York: Vintage, 1998.

Mann, Nicola, and Victoria Pass. "Introduction: The Cultural Visualization of Hurricane Katrina." *Invisible Culture,* no. 16 (Spring 2011): 1–9.

Mannix, Daniel P. *Black Cargoes: History of the Atlantic Slave Trade 1518–1865.* New York: Viking, 1962.

McKittrick, Katherine. "Diachronic loops/deadweight tonnage/bad made measure." *Cultural Geographies* 23, no. 1 (2016): 3–18.

Miles, Tiya. *All That She Carried: The Journey of Ashley's Sack, a Black Family Keepsake.* New York: Random House, 2021.

Miller, Joseph C. "A Historical Appreciation of the Biographical Turn." In *Biography and the Black Atlantic,* edited by Lisa A. Lindsay and John Wood Sweet, 19–47. Philadelphia: University of Pennsylvania Press, 2014.

Millward, Jessica. *Finding Charity's Folk: Enslaved and Free Black Women in Maryland.* Athens: University of Georgia Press, 2015.

Mitchell, Dennis J. *A New History of Mississippi.* Jackson: University Press of Mississippi, 2014.

Morrison, Toni. *God Bless the Child.* New York: Alfred A. Knopf, 2015.

Moynihan, Daniel Patrick. "The Negro Family: The Case for National Action." Report for the US Department of Labor, Washington, DC, 1965.

Mullen, Lincoln. "These Maps Reveal How Slavery Expanded Across the United States." *Smithsonian Magazine,* 15 May 2014. http://www.smithsonianmag.com/history/maps -reveal-slavery-expanded-across-united-states-180951452/.

"Nathan Holcomb Family Tree." https://www.ancestry.com/.

"A New Encounter: Black Slaves in Georgia." Georgia Historical Society. https://georgia history.com/education-outreach/online-exhibits/online-exhibits/encounter-and -exchange/a-new-encounter-black-slaves-in-georgia/pre-revolutionary-slavery.

"Nicholas Family Tree." https://www.ancestry.com/.

Orangeburgh German-Swiss Genealogical Society. "History." https://ogsgs.org.

Pavletich, JoAnn. "'. . . we are going to take that right': Power and Plagiarism in Pauline Hopkins's 'Winona'." *CLA Journal* 59, no. 2 (2015): 115–30. https://www.jstor.org/stable /44325567.

Pettus, Gary. "Asylum Hill Project: 'What a Great Story This Is'" *University of Mississippi Medical Center News Stories.* March 19, 2018. https://www.umc.edu/news/News _Articles/2018/03/asylum-hill-project--what-a-great-story-this-is.html.

Prince, Nan. "Artifacts: First African American Masons in State," *A Sense of Place* (blog), Mississippi Department of Archives and History, 4 September 2013, https://www .mdah.ms.gov/senseofplace/2013/09/04/artifacts-first-african-american-masons-in -state/.

Proctor, Victoria. *South Carolina Colonial Anglican Parishes Map.* 2000. Map. Marion County, SC, Genealogy & History. http://sciway3.net/proctor/marion/maps/sc_parishes _colonial.html.

Puckett, Newbell N. "American Negro Names." *Journal of Negro History* 23, no. 1 (1938): 35–48.

Raboteau, Albert. *Slave Religion: The "Invisible Institution" in the Antebellum South.* New York: Oxford University Press, 1978.

Rousseau, Peter L. "Jacksonian Monetary Policy, Specie Flows, and the Panic of 1837." *Journal of Economic History* 62, no. 2 (2002): 457–88. http://www.jstor.org/stable /2698187.

Sanborn, Geoffrey. "'People Will Pay to Hear the Drama': Plagiarism in 'Clotel.'" *African American Review* 45, no. 1/2 (2012): 65–82. www.jstor.org/stable/23783437.

Sanborn, Geoffrey. *Plagiarama: William Wells Brown and the Aesthetics of Attraction.* New York: Columbia University Press, 2016.

Scheiding, Oliver, and Martin Seidl. *Worlding America: A Transnational Anthology of Short Narratives before 1800.* Stanford, CA: Stanford University Press, 2015.

Schneider, Elena A. *The Occupation of Havana: War, Trade, and Slavery in the Atlantic World.* Chapel Hill: University of North Carolina Press, 2018.

Scott, Carole E. "The Troubled World of Antebellum Banking in Georgia." *Antebellum Georgia Banks.* 2016. https://www.westga.edu/~bquest/2000/antebellumGAbanks.pdf.

Shalby, Colleen. "What's the Difference Between 'Looting' and 'Finding'? 12 Years After Katrina Harvey Sparks a Debate." *Los Angeles Times.* 29 August 2017.

Sharpe, Christina. *In the Wake: On Blackness and Being.* Durham, NC: Duke University Press, 2016.

"Shirley Whatley Family Tree." FamilySearch.org.

Sisoko, Fa-Digi. *The Epic of Son-Jara: A West African Tradition.* Translated by John William Johnson. Bloomington: Indiana University Press, 1992.

Sistrunk, Thomas. *A Walk Through Caney: The Sistrunk Family.* Self-published, Amazon KDP Publishing, 2018.

Sistrunk, Thomas O., Walter E. Sistrunk, and Jerry E. Sistrunk. *The Sistrunk Families.* Sarasota, FL: Angel Works, 1997.

Stuckey, Sterling. *Slave Culture: Nationalist Theory and the Foundations of Black America.* New York: Oxford University Press, 1987.

Taylor, Astra, dir. *Examined Life.* New York: Zeitgeist Films, 2009.

Trethewey, Natasha. *Native Guard.* Boston: Houghton Mifflin, 2007.

Turner, Richard Brent. "African Muslim Slaves and Islam in Antebellum America." In *The Cambridge Companion to American Islam,* ed. Juliane Hammer and Omar Safi, 28–44. Cambridge: Cambridge University Press, 2013.

Walker, Margaret. *Jubilee.* Boston: Houghton Mifflin, 1966.

"War of Jenkins Ear." Warfare History Network. Sovereign Media, 2021. https://warfare historynetwork.com/daily/military-history/the-war-of-jenkins-ear/.

Watson, Dawn. *Slave Importation Affidavit Registers for Nine Georgia Counties, 1818–1847.* Clayton, GA: Bone Diggers Press, 2012.

"Welcome to Asylum Hill Project." *Asylum Hill Project.* asylumhillproject.org.

Wells, Ida B. *The Red Record: Tabulated Statistics and Alleged Causes of Lynching in the United States.* Chicago: Donohue and Henneberry, 1895.

West, Elizabeth. "Memory, Ancestors, and Activism/Resistance in Charles Chesnutt's Uncle Julius." *Studies in the Literary Imagination* 43, no. 2 (Fall 2010): 31–45.

——. "Community and Naming: Lived Narratives of Early African American Women's Spirituality." *Religions* 11(8), 426 (August 2020). https://doi.org/10.3390/rel11080426.

West, Emily, and Erin Shearer. "Fertility Control, Shared Nurturing, and Dual Exploitation: The Lives of Enslaved Mothers in the Antebellum United States." *Women's History Review* 27, no. 6 (2018): 1006–20. https://doi.org/10.1080/09612025.2017.1336849.

Whatley, Julian Monk. *Whatley Family Reunion: Descendants of James Henry Whatley.* Salt Lake City, UT: Family Search International, 1990. https://www.familysearch.org /library/books/records/item/250931-redirection.

White, Deborah Gray. *Ar'n't I a Woman?: Female Slaves in the Plantation South.* New York: W. W. Norton, 1985.

Wilkerson, Isabel. *The Warmth of Other Suns: The Epic Story of America's Great Migration.* New York: Vintage Books, 2010.

Williams, Brian. "Articulating Agrarian Racism: Statistics and Plantationist Empirics." *Southeastern Geographer* 57, no. 1 (2017): 12–29. https://www.jstor.org/stable/26367640.

Wilson, Harriet E. *Our Nig, or, Sketches from the Life of a Free Black.* Boston: Geo. C. Rand & Avery, 1859.

Wood, Betty. "Slavery in Colonial Georgia." *New Georgia Encyclopedia.* 29 September 2020. https://www.georgiaencyclopedia.org/articles/history-archaeology/slavery-colonial -georgia#print.

Wood, Peter H. *Black Majority: Negroes in Colonial South Carolina from1670 Through the Stono Rebellion.* New York: W. W. Norton, 1974.

Yarborough, Richard, "Introduction." *American Literary History* 30, no 4 (2018): e4-e8. https://muse.jhu.edu/article/710664.

Young, Jeffrey Robert. "Slavery in Antebellum Georgia." *New Georgia Encyclopedia,* 17 October 2016. https://www.georgiaencyclopedia.org/articles/history-archaeology/slavery -antebellum-georgia.

Index

African American culture: family structures, 17, 68–70; folktales, 147–48, 173n18; foodways, 65–67, 71–72; homegoing and burial traditions, 77–81; kinship ties, 10, 15, 20, 34–36, 46, 56–57, 84, 106, 152; naming traditions, 6, 48–50; oral traditions, 138–39, 140, 142, 143–44, 150–51; spirituality and religion, 77–79, 89–90, 100, 103. *See also* Black culture

African Americans: enforced migration, 24, 28, 104, 116, 150; intraracial tension, 68–69

African diaspora, 33, 144

African languages, 18

African Methodist Church, Cedar Creek, 111

African traditions, 17–18, 33

Agricultural Census 1850, 66

Alabama: Dowdell family, 30, 47–48, 51; and transportation of enslaved persons, 24, 26, 27

Alford, T. C., 129–30, 131

All That She Carried (Miles), 5–6

Ames, Adelbert, 81

Anderson, R. L., 132–34

"An End to the Neglect of the Problems of the Negro Woman" (Jones), 17–18

Asylum Hill/Asylum Hill Project, 130–32, 171n46

Attucks, Crispus, 137

Between the World and Me (Coates), 73–74

Biography and the Black Atlantic (Lindsey & Sweet), 19

biohistoriography, 5, 18–20, 31, 146, 151

Black church, 78(ph), 79(ph), 89–90, 100, 101(ph), 102(ph), 103(ph). *See also* Christianity, Anglo-Christian conventions

Black culture: Black family formations, 15, 16–18, 32–33, 35; Black populism, 90; and collective economics, 98; and matriarchy, 17, 33–34; men's roles, 34–35; survival in anti-Black spaces, 150–51; women's roles, 4–5, 14–15, 74, 89. *See also* African American culture

"Black gaze," 63

Black single mothers, 14–15, 16–18, 32–35, 57, 68–70, 74, 152

bootlegging, 108–9, 121

Bottom area, Noxubee County, 81, 84, 85, 91

Bridges, James, 82

Brown, Elsa Barkley, 137

Brown, Hopea (Cistrunk), 84, 93–94

Brown, William Wells, 141, 143, 146, 149, 151, 172n13

Brushfork Baptist Church, 79–80, 88–89, 100, 101(ph), 102(ph), 113

Census, Agricultural (1850), 66

Census, methodology of, 145

Census (1830), 53

Census (1840), 16, 32, 35, 38(ch), 53

Census (1850), 37, 51

Census (1860), 37, 59

Census (1870), 29, 49–50, 67, 83, 86, 87(ch), 88

Census (1880), 1–2, 17, 26, 29, 30, 83, 86, 93, 94, 98, 107, 117

Census (1890), 93

Census (1900), 30, 98, 107, 117

Census (1910), 30, 88, 107, 116, 135

Census (1920), 30, 41, 107, 109

Census (1930), 135

Census (1940), 26, 27

Chesnutt, Charles, 147–49

Choctaw people, 104; Treaty of Dancing Rabbit Creek, 105(ph), 106(ph)

Christianity, Anglo-Christian conventions, 32, 77

church bells, 100–101, 101(ph), 103(ph). *See also* Black church

Cistrunk, Anna Denson, 1, 3, 9

Cistrunk, Annie (Holmes) (1870–1897), 83, 93, 94, 107–8

Cistrunk, Annie J., Dr. (1929–2005), 1, 6, 7, 10, 11. *See also* genealogical charts

Cistrunk, Arah (McDonald), 9, 103

Cistrunk, Bessie, 116

Cistrunk, Bunnie, 9, 11, 41, 58, 79, 88–89, 99, 101, 114, 116

Cistrunk, Carl: in Dr. Annie Cistrunk's genealogical sketch, 7; Cistrunk/Anna Denson lineage, 1; first meeting with author, 3–4; and Freemasonry, 101, 103; genealogical chart, 154(ch); kinship ties, 36, 41, 114, 116; marriage to Anna Denson, 9; personal history, early years, 3, 8–9, 22, 110, 113–14, 115(ph)

Cistrunk, Caroline, 67, 83

Cistrunk, Chany, 67, 83, 88, 93, 94, 107–8

Cistrunk, Charity, 83

Cistrunk, Dossie (Dorsey), 41–42, 92, 94, 107, 118, 124–25, 129, 132–33

Cistrunk, Edgar, 113

Cistrunk, Elisha (Elias), 41–42, 92, 94, 107, 108–9, 118, 121, 124–25, 129, 135

Cistrunk, Evelyn, 116

Cistrunk, Harriet Harden, 84, 98, 117, 124–25

Cistrunk, Helen (Harrington), 11, 14

Cistrunk, Hillman: arrest of, 123; death of, 107, 130–32; debt, 124–25; Emancipation Proclamation, 67–68; employment prospects later years, 129; financial challenges, 95–97, 98, 117–18; land ownership, 88, 91, 95, 97–99, 104, 109; literacy, 88, 100; marriage to Harriet Harden, 84; marriage to Patsy Cutts, 125–26; paternity of, 30, 41, 42, 51, 60; writ of lunacy, 129–32

Cistrunk, Hopea Brown, 84, 93–94

Cistrunk, John: death of, 107; descendants/household, 83, 94, 107–9; farming postwar, 81; financial challenges, 95–97, 99; literacy, 100; marriage and children, 67–68, 70, 86, 93; paternity of, 30, 37, 41, 54–55; personal history, early years, 56, 59; poll taxes, 92

Cistrunk, Lorenzo, 116

Cistrunk, Lucretia (Dobbins, McDaniel/McDonald): children of, 93, 94; death of, 134; household of, 88, 97, 99, 107, 118, 125; land ownership, 88, 117; lawsuit over Hillman's estate, 131–35; literacy, 88, 100; marriage to Alfred Dobbins, 84; marriage to Hyram McDaniel, 107; paternity of, 30, 51, 54; personal history, 56, 59, 60, 67

Cistrunk, Luella Hunt (Lynch) (1883–1989), 7, 8, 10, 11, 14–15, 22, 36, 111, 114, 116

Cistrunk, Lula (born 1902), 8, 110, 116

Cistrunk, Lula Hudson (1882–1903), 8, 11, 110, 111, 116

Cistrunk, Maria (Grimmett), 93, 94, 110, 116, 134

Cistrunk, Nancy, 37

Cistrunk, Noah (1880–1937): Brushfork Baptist Church, 79, 88–89, 101; death and burial, 80; descendants' reunion, 1, 6, 8(ph), 9–10, 9(ph), 10(ph), 11–14, 12(ph), 13(ph), 89–90; employment in industry, 116–17; as family patriarch, 1, 4, 7–8, 14–15, 22, 94, 151–52; farming and land ownership, 99, 110–11, 116–17, 134; financial challenges, 99, 111–12;

genealogical chart, 154(ch); health and aging, 112–13; Lula's death, 111; marriage to Luella Hunt, 111; marriage to Lula Hudson, 110; paternity of, 41; poll taxes, 92
Cistrunk, Noah (grandson of Noah), 14, 69
Cistrunk, Patsy Cutts, 125–26, 129–33
Cistrunk, Samuel, 37, 56
Cistrunk, Shadrick: Brushfork Baptist Church, 79, 80, 101; and community cooperation, 98; death of, 107, 117; DNA testing, 42; as family patriarch, 4, 6, 7, 14, 83, 84; farming and land ownership, 81, 85, 91; financial challenges, 88, 95–98; household/descendants, 109–10; kinship care and bloodlines, 36; land auction and debt, 111–12; land ownership, 91, 97–98, 99, 109; literacy, 88, 100; marriage and children, 1–2, 93, 94; naming of, 49, 50–51; paternity of, 30, 41–43, 47–48, 54, 55, 68; personal history, early years, 56, 60, 67–68; possible charge of theft, 72–73; spelling of surname, 83
Cistrunk, Sophia/Sophie "Francis" (Grimmett/Nichols/Marsh), 7, 8(ph), 10, 14, 15, 94, 110, 112, 114, 134
Cistrunk, Susan Landrum: Brushfork Baptist Church, 79, 101; Dr. Annie Cistrunk's genealogical chart, 6–7; land auction and debt, 111–12; land ownership, 99; marriage and children, 1, 36, 84, 93, 94, 107, 110; move to Tallahatchie County, 116
Cistrunk, Willis, 51, 56, 84, 86, 93–94
Cistrunk family: Dr. Annie Cistrunk's genealogical chart, 1, 6–7, 7(ch), 11; family Bible, 14; farming and land ownership, 81, 94–95; financial challenges, 94–96, 107; genealogical charts, 154(ch), 155(ch), 157(ch); migrations of, 116, 118, 134; reunion of Noah Cistrunk descendants, 1, 6, 8(ph), 9–10, 9(ph), 10(ph), 11–14, 12(ph), 13(ph), 89–90; spelling of name, 21, 64, 83, 152, 159n1

Civil War migrations, 60–68
Clark, Sam, 121
Clotel (Brown), 141–46, 149, 172n13
Coates, Ta-Nehisi, 73–74
Coleman, Leboo, 98
colorism, 41–42, 68–69
Compromise of 1877, 85, 91
conjure tales, 147–48
The Conjure Tales (Chesnutt), 148
Connor, Cy, 119–21
Connor, Elizabeth, 119–21
Contending Forces (Hopkins), 149
contract system, Freedmen's Bureau, 71–72
Cotton, Allen, 125
cotton production, 39, 45, 96
COVID-19 pandemic, 22
Cromwell, Oliver, 90
Crummell, Alexander, 76
Cutts, Patsy (Cistrunk), 125–26, 128–33
Cutts, William, 125

Dash, Julie, 23
Daughters of the Dust (Dash), 23
Davis, A. K., 81
Denson, Anna (Cistrunk), 1, 3, 9
Denson family matriarch, "Grandma Louise," 6
DNA databases and testing, 42, 55, 140–41, 162n71, 162n72
Dobbins, Alfred, 84, 93, 94, 98, 99, 107
Dobbins, Bertha, 134
Dobbins, Emma (Fleming), 93, 94, 107, 135
Dobbins, Lucretia. *See* Cistrunk, Lucretia (Dobbins, McDaniel/McDonald)
Dobbins, Mary Grimmett, 110
Dobbins, Warren, 93, 94, 107, 110
Douglass, Frederick, 32, 71–72
Dowdell, James, 30, 43, 45, 46–47, 51
Dowdell, Lewis Jefferson, 45
Dowdell, Louisa, 47
Dowdell, Lucinda, 47
Dowdell, Shadrack (Shadrick) I, 43, 46–48
Dowdell, Shadrack (Shadrick) II, 47–49, 55, 60, 68
Dowdell, Susan (Lipscomb), 47

Eastern Star (affiliate of Prince Hall Masons), 103
education and literacy, 76–77, 88, 100
Emancipation Proclamation, 63, 65, 67
Emerson, Ralph W., 31
enslavement. *See* slavery
The Epic of Son-Jara, 144
Examined Life (film), 136
extratextual sources, 144–45, 146

family, nuclear, myths of, 15, 17, 33–34, 68, 69. *See also* kinship collectives and models
Fleming, Emma Dobbins, 93, 94, 107, 135
flu epidemic (1918), 22, 127
Freedmen's Bureau, 70–72; and education postwar, 77
freemasonry, 101, 103–4

Ganster, Mary, 143, 145, 146
Gates, Henry Louis, Jr., 142, 150
gendered paradigms, 16–17, 68–70. *See also* men's roles; patriarchy, white male; women's roles
genealogical charts: Dr. Annie Cistrunk's, 1, 6, 7(ch), 10, 11, 14; Sistrunk family, 154(ch), 155(ch), 157(ch); Whatley family, 156(ch)
Georgia: antebellum slave population, 24–25; Cistrunk family migrations, 21, 26, 28–31, 37, 39, 56; Harris County map, 46(m); history of slavery, 25, 43, 47, 52, 55. *See also* Marion County, Georgia
Great Migration, 5, 11, 114, 126–27, 129
Greenspan, Ezra, 143–44
Grimmett, Eveline, 110
Grimmett, Isaac, 110, 116, 134
Grimmett, Lillie, 110
Grimmett, Maria Cistrunk, 93, 94, 110, 116, 134
Grimmett, Mary (Dobbins), 110
Grimmett, Mike, 110
Grimmett, Sophia/Sophie "Francis" Cistrunk (Nichols/Marsh), 7, 8(ph), 10, 14, 15, 94, 110, 112, 114, 134

Grimmett, Will (brother of Isaac Grimmett), 110, 113–14, 115(ph)
Grimmett, Will (son of Isaac and Maria Grimmett), 110, 113–14, 115(ph)
griots, 144

Hagar's Daughter (Hopkins), 149
Haggard, R. A., 126, 129–30
Haggard, Robert Arthur, 126
Halbert, H. S., 104
Haley, Alex, 139
Harden, Harriet (Cistrunk), 84, 98, 117, 124–25
Harper, Frances, 32, 149
Harrington, Helen Cistrunk, 11, 14
Harris, Jeptha, 26–27, 28
Harris, Joel Chandler, 147–48
Hartman, Saidiya, 5–6, 138–39
Haywood, Rufus, 26
Heavy (Laymon), 74
Hemings, Sally, 36, 141–42, 151
Higginbotham, Evelyn, 89
history: as academic discipline, 136–37; archives and sources, 11, 139–41; historiography, expansion of, 137–40; historiography and biography, 5, 18–20, 31, 146, 151; online databases, 139; oral sources, 139–40; reified history, 145–46, 147–48; sampling as methodology, 141–49; speculative historiography, 31, 150; white-centered traditions, 18–19, 152
Holmes, Alabama, 108
Holmes, Annie Cistrunk, 83, 93, 94, 107–8
Holmes, Bonie, 94, 107–8
Holmes, Renee, 94, 107–8
Hopkins, Pauline, 149
Howells, William Dean, 149
Hudson, Cresy, 110
Hudson, Lula (Cistrunk) (1882–1903), 8, 11, 110, 111, 116
Hudson, Nathan, 110
Hunt, Luella (Cistrunk). *See* Cistrunk, Luella Hunt (Lynch) (1883–1989)
Hunt family (Noah Cistrunk's in-laws), 88
Hurricane Katrina, 73

Hurston, Zora Neale, 49
hush harbors, 77, 89

indentured servitude, 70, 82
insanity, writ of for Hillman Cistrunk, 129–32
Iola Leroy (Harper), 149

Jackson, Lawrence, 5
Jacobs, Harriet, 28, 32, 36, 48
Jefferson, President Thomas, 28, 141–42, 143, 151
Jernigan, J. A., 104
Johnson, James Weldon, 127
Jonah's Gourdvine (Hurston), 49
Jones, Claudia, 17–18
Jubilee (Walker), 140

Kendi, Ibram X., 20
kinship collectives and models, 10, 15, 20, 34–46, 56–57, 84, 106, 152. *See also* family, nuclear, myths of
Ku Klux Klan, 75, 128

labor contracts, Freedmen's Bureau, 71–72
landownership and loss, 88, 90, 91, 99, 109, 116, 133–34
Landrum, Aggie, 94
Landrum, Susan (Cistrunk). *See* Cistrunk, Susan Landrum
languages, African, 18
Laymon, Kiese, 74
Lee, Joe, 109
legal system, Black experiences of, 72–74
Lindsey, Lisa, 19
Lipscomb, Andrew, 47
Lipscomb, Susan Dowdell, 47
literacy and education, 76–77, 88, 100
Lloyd, Hester, 98
Lloyd, Joe, 98
Lloyd, Martha, 98, 117, 124
Louise, Grandma (Denson family matriarch), 6
Lynch, Luella Hunt Cistrunk. *See* Cistrunk, Luella Hunt (Lynch) (1883–1989)
lynchings, 109–10, 121, 127

Macon, Mississippi, 100; racial violence, 128–29
Macon Beacon, 92, 106, 110
Marion County, Georgia: courthouse fire, 38; enslaved people, 38; Francis Sistrunk, 36, 54; Hillman Cistrunk, 42; Jacob Sistrunk Jr., 36, 37–38, 50; Jacob Sistrunk Sr., 51; John Sistrunk, 50, Thornton family, 29; Whatley family, 52, 53, 54
The Marrow of Tradition (Chesnutt), 148–49
Marsh, Sophia/Sophie "Francis" Cistrunk (Grimmett/Nichols), 7, 8(ph), 10, 14, 15, 94, 110, 112, 114, 134
Mashulaville, Mississippi, 129
Mashulaville Tiger (Elisha Cistrunk), 108, 121
matriarchy, 14–15, 16–18, 32–35, 57, 68–70, 74, 152
McDaniel, Hyram, 107
McDaniel, Lucretia. *See* Cistrunk, Lucretia (Dobbins, McDaniel/McDonald)
McDonald, Arah Cistrunk, 9, 103
McDonald, Lucretia. *See* Cistrunk, Lucretia (Dobbins, McDaniel/McDonald)
McKittrick, Katherine, 141
men's roles, 34–35
migrations: during Civil War, 60–68; enforced migration and enslaved people, 24, 28, 104, 116, 150; Great Migration, 5, 11, 114, 126–27, 129
Miles, Tiya, 5–6
Mississippi: antebellum slave population, 59; during Civil War, 63, 68; enforced migration and enslaved people, 29, 56; Mashulaville, 129; Neshoba County, 58–60; poll taxes, 92–93; Reconstruction era, 74–75, 81, 92–93; Shuqualak District, 126, 133; Sistrunk family migrations, 30, 40, 56; Tallahatchie County, 88, 112. *See also* Macon, Mississippi; Noxubee County, Mississippi; Winston County, Mississippi
Mississippi State Insane Hospital, 130
Mississipppi Enumeration of Educable Children, 117

Mosley, Ethel, 88–89
Moynihan, Daniel Patrick, 33–34
"mulatto" designation, 60
Murray, Margaret (Washington), 100
My Father's Name (Jackson), 5

names: naming practices and family
    history, 6, 54–55; Sistrunk/Cistrunk
    spelling, 21, 64, 83, 152; surnames, as
    sign of family unity, 83
Native Guard (Trethewey), 137
*The Negro Family: The Case For National
    Action* (Moynihan), 33
Neshoba County, Mississippi, 58–60
Nichols, Lem, 112, 114
Nichols, Mariah, 112, 114
Nichols, Sophia/Sophie "Francis"
    Cistrunk (Grimmett/Marsh), 7, 8(ph),
    10, 14, 15, 94, 110, 112, 114, 134
Noah Cistrunk Family National Organi-
    zation (NCFNO), 11, 14
Noah Cistrunk family reunion, 1, 6, 8 (ph),
    9–10, 9(ph), 10(ph), 11–14, 12(ph),
    13(ph), 89–90
Noxubee County, Mississippi, 74–75, 85,
    86; churches, 77–80; Cistrunk land
    ownership, 109; education and literacy
    postwar, 76–77; farming and land
    ownership postwar, 82; jail, 119–21;
    lynchings, 109–10; Macon, 100; map,
    97(m); Noxubee County Library
    (former jail), 122(ph); political land-
    scape, 81; poll taxes, 92–93; race riot,
    75–76; racial violence, 128–29
nuclear family, myth and paradigm, 15, 17,
    33–34, 68, 69. *See also* kinship collec-
    tives and models
Nunn, E. F., 124–25, 133

Of One Blood (Hopkins), 149
Oliver, Samuel, 40

Parchment Prison, 121, 123
Parks, Jeanette, 89
Parsons, Dr. M. G., 127
patriarchy, white male, 33–34, 69

*Plagiarama: William Wells Brown and
    the Aesthetics of Attraction* (Sanborn),
    144–45
plagiarism accusations, *Clotel* (Brown),
    141–45, 172n13
plantation narratives, 146–47
poll taxes, 91–92, 110–11, 116. *See also*
    voting rights
post-emancipation era. *See* Reconstruc-
    tion Era
poverty, 32, 33–34, 99, 108–9
Prince Hall Masons, 101, 103–4
prison system, 121, 123
Prohibition era, 108–9. *See also*
    bootlegging

racism: in Deep South, post-Civil War,
    75; post-emancipation era, 85; racial
    discrimination, 34; racial violence,
    127–29. *See also* lynchings
railroad land, 91
Reconstruction Era, 75, 81–82, 86, 90, 98
Red Hot Summer, 128–29
The Red Record (Wells), 109
reunion, Noah Cistrunk descendants, 1, 6,
    8(ph), 9–10, 9(ph), 10(ph), 11–14, 12(ph),
    13(ph), 89–90
reuse principles and plagiarism accusa-
    tions, 141–45. *See also* sampling
Robinson, Jane B., 25
Roots (Haley), 139–40

sampling: author's methodology for
    Francis Cistrunk story, 21, 24, 141–52;
    in literature, 149, 173n18; musical
    technique, 20, 142, 146, 172n14, 173n18
Sanborn, Jeffrey, 144, 172n13
Second Baptist M.B. Church, 79(ph), 100,
    103(ph)
"Self-Reliance" (Emerson), 31
sexual exploitation, 27–28, 32, 35, 36–37,
    48, 49–50, 54, 55–56
sharecropping system, 4, 72, 86, 90, 95,
    99, 126
Sharpe, Christina, 23, 141
Shuqualak District, Mississippi, 126, 133

signifying (language play), 142, 147, 150, 152

The Signifying Monkey (Gates), 150

single mothers as heads of households, 14–15, 16–18, 32–35, 57, 68–70, 74, 152

Sistrunk, Elizabeth, 50

Sistrunk, Francis: absence of in documentation, 14; author's first introduction to, 1–2; birth of, speculation concerning, 23, 29–31; death of, 106; enslavement, 16–17, 40–41; as family matriarch, 21, 56–57, 70, 83, 106–7; as freed person during Civil War, 65, 67; genealogical chart, 157(ch); life during Civil War, 63–68; possible purchase by Jacob Sistrunk Jr., 24–25, 26–27; postwar marriage prospects, 68–70; self-empowerment, 48; value of, for Jacob Sistrunk Jr.'s estate, 43, 56, 59; work contracts postwar, 71

Sistrunk, Heinrich (Süsstrunk), 15–16, 24, 39, 55, 56

Sistrunk, Jacob, Jr.: Civil War activities, 50, 63–64; efforts to conceal identity, 50, 64; in 1840 census, 16, 32; in 1870 census, 86; farming endeavors, 45; financial worth and enslaved persons, 43, 56, 59; genealogical chart, 155(ch); migrations, Georgia and Mississippi, 28–29, 40, 42, 53, 56; in Neshoba County, 59; possession of Francis, 24–25, 32; possessions after father's death, 38–39; relationships with former slaves, post-emancipation, 65, 67; residence in Harris County, 37; social status and power, 45, 48–49

Sistrunk, Jacob, Sr., 16, 24, 37, 38–39, 39–40, 51

Sistrunk, Jennie, 64

Sistrunk, John (Jacob Sr.'s brother), 50

Sistrunk, John (Jacob Jr. assumed identity), 50, 64

Sistrunk, Lemuel, 37

Sistrunk, Martha, 24, 50, 86

Sistrunk, Robert (1861–1870s), 22, 60, 84, 86

Sistrunk, Robert (1881–1952), 93–94

Sistrunk, Samuel (Jacob Jr.'s brother), 37, 45, 56

Sistrunk, Samuel H. J. (Jacob Jr.'s cousin), 40

Sistrunk, Thomas, 59

Sistrunk, Viola, 94

Sistrunk, William, 63, 64, 86

Sistrunk, Willis, 21–22, 51, 54–56, 59, 60, 67, 84, 86, 93–94

The Sistrunk Families, 39, 45, 49–50, 59

skin tone. *See* colorism

Slave Importation Affidavit Registers for Nine Georgia Counties (Watson), 25, 55

slave narratives, 19–20, 146

slavery: "Black gaze" and race relations, 63; effects on Black family structure, 15, 18; family separation and forced migration, 29–30, 34–35, 49; hunger and theft, 71–72; influences on post-Civil War Black culture, 65–68, 69, 136–38; and kinship networks, 46, 56–57; leasing out of slaves, 59–60; and sexual exploitation, 27–28, 32, 35, 36–37, 48, 49–50, 54, 55–56; slave traders, 24

Slave Schedule (1850), 26, 27, 34, 43, 45(ch), 53

Slave Schedule (1860), 26, 27, 32, 35, 53, 59, 60, 61(ch), 62(ch)

South Carolina: Charleston and slave trade, 24; and migration to Georgia, 25

Spanish flu pandemic (1918), 22, 127

speculative historiography, 31, 150

Spur, Alexander, 26

storytelling traditions, 144

St. Paul Methodist Church, 78(ph)

Süsstrunk, Heinrich (Sistrunk), 15–16, 24, 39, 55, 56; genealogical chart, 155(ch)

Sweet, John, 19

Tallahatchie County, Mississippi, 88, 112

Tax Digests for Lincoln County, 37

theft, history of, during slavery and post-emancipation, 71–73

Thornton, Dozier, 26, 27, 31, 55

Thornton, Dozier, Jr., 28–29
Thornton, N. M., 26, 27
Thornton family migrations, Georgia,
    28–29
Treaty of Dancing Rabbit Creek (1830),
    104, 105(ph), 106(ph)
Trethewey, Natasha, 137
trust deeds, 95–96, 98–99, 112
Tubman, Harriet, 32

Uncle Remus: His Songs and His Sayings
    (Harris), 147

voting rights, 91–93. *See also* poll taxes

Walker, Margaret, 140
The Warmth of Other Suns (Wilkerson), 5
Washington, Booker T., 100
Washington, Margaret Murray, 100
waterways and fishing, 66–67
Watson, Dawn, 25
Wayward Lives, Beautiful Experiments
    (Hartman), 5–6, 138
Wells, Ida B., 109
West, Cornel, 136
Whatley, Daniel, Jr., 51–52
Whatley, Daniel, Sr., 52–53, 54–55
Whatley, Frances, 55
Whatley, John, 52–53, 55

Whatley, Michael, Jr., 52, 53, 55
Whatley, Michael, Sr., 52–53
Whatley, Seaborn (S. J.), 43, 45, 51, 52,
    53–54
Whatley, Shirley, 52, 54
Whatley, William, 55
Whatley, Willis, 51–52, 55
Whatley family genealogical chart, 156(ch)
White, Deborah Gray, 17
White Line of Mississippi, 75
white supremacy, 75–76, 90, 99, 127. *See
    also* lynchings; racism
Whitfield (Mississippi State Insane Hos-
    pital), 130
Wilkerson, Isabel, 5
Wilson, Harriet, 32
Winona (Hopkins), 149
Winston County, Mississippi: Carl
    Cistrunk, 9; Dossie (Dorsey) Cistrunk,
    41; during Civil War, 64, 67–68; Hill-
    man Cistrunk, 67–68, 131; Hillman
    Cistrunk family, 129; Jacob Sistrunk Jr.,
    64; John Cistrunk, 67–68; Noah Cis-
    trunk, 22, 41, 79, 88, 89, 101; Noah
    Cistrunk burial site, 131; Shadrick
    Cistrunk, 67–68
women's roles, 16–17, 34–35; women
    as heads of household, 14–15, 16–18,
    32–35, 57, 68–70, 74, 152